BEGINNINGS IN RITUAL STUDIES

Ronald L. Grimes

UNIVERSITY
PRESS OF
AMERICA

LANHAM • NEW YORK • LONDON

Copyright © 1982 by

University Press of America,™ Inc.

4720 Boston Way
Lanham, MD 20706

3 Henrietta Street
London WC2E 8LU England

Library of Congress Cataloging in Publication Data

Grimes, Ronald L., 1943–
   Beginnings in ritual studies.

   Bibliography: p.
   1. Ritual–Addresses, essays, lectures. I. Title.
BL600.G74   291.3'8   81–40521
ISBN 0–8191–2210–6   AACR2
ISBN 0–8191–2211–4 (pbk.)

All University Press of America books are produced on acid-free
paper which exceeds the minimum standards set by the National
Historical Publications and Records Commission.

to Thomas Rogers

who set me on the way

&

in memory of

the late Ken Feit

friend and Fool

who reached Forty

ACKNOWLEDGMENTS

Chapter 3 is a revision of "Modes of Ritual Necessity," first published in WORSHIP 53/2(1979):126-141. Chapter 4 was originally written for THE JOURNAL OF THE AMERICAN ACADEMY OF RELIGION, and Chapter 5 was published in the same journal, 43/3(1975):508-516. Chapter 8 is a revision of "Symbolic Processes in Illness and Healing," which appeared in VOICES 16/3(1980):21-29. Chapter 9 is reprinted by permission from THE RELIGIOUS STUDIES REVIEW 2/4(1976):13-25. Portions of Chapter 12 were published as "The Actor's Lab: The Ritual Roots of Human Action" in THE CANADIAN THEATRE REVIEW 22(1979):9-19. Other portions of the same chapter are adapted from "The Rituals of Walking and Flying: Public Participatory Events at Actor's Lab," THE DRAMA REVIEW 22/4(1978):77-82; Chapter 11 was originally written for the same journal. Chapter 13 was published as "The Lifeblood of Public Ritual" in A WORLD OF ART AND RITUAL, edited by Victor Turner (Smithsonian Institution Press, 1982).

For grants to support portions of this work, I thank The Social Sciences and Humanities Research Council of Canada, The National Endowment for the Humanities, and the Research Office of Wilfrid Laurier University.

I am especially grateful to my editor, S.L. Scott, whose literacy and persistence are responsible for untying the knots in my writing.

Thanks to Hart Bezner, Carl Langford, and the staff of Wilfrid Laurier University Computer Centre for generous assistance in designing the format of this book. Thanks also to Linda Glenn for helping type part of the manuscript.

CONTENTS

PREFACE

Ritual is as old as humanity. Perhaps it is even older, since ethologists have now clearly demonstrated the presence of ritualization behavior among animals. But the systematic or comparative study of ritual is not so ancient. In many cultures, especially preliterate ones, ritual knowledge is transmitted from one generation to the next by imitation and osmosis. No apparent necessity exists for the formal study or teaching of ritual. Ritual specialists, such as priests and shamans, pass on their knowledge to successors by way of apprenticeship. As ritual traditions become literate, ritual manuals are written. Their aim is not so much to study ritual as to aid its enactment. Ritual manuals record what is to be done and said. Seldom do they interpret the actions and words of a rite. So even literate religious traditions are not always interested in the critical study of ritual.

When such a tradition, for instance, Christianity, does begin to study ritual, it concentrates on its own rites, often for the purpose of liturgical revision, preaching, or theological debate. The study of ritual from inside a tradition for the benefit of people in it is, in the broad sense of the term, "liturgics." This way of studying rituals, now generally found in practical divisions of theological seminaries, began in medieval universities, which, like modern Bible colleges, were under the tutelage of the church.

The twentieth century has witnessed the formation of departments of anthropology and religious studies, both of which conduct research on ritual without the supervision of a specific religious institution. Anthropologists were the first to study rituals in this way, and they intended their research to be an accurate, impartial documenting of events actually observed by fieldworkers and then analyzed according to a specified theory to reveal their social functions. In this manner ritual came to be regarded as the purview of social science.

Meanwhile, religious studies, usually regarded by universities as a humanity or art rather than a social science, was rapidly differentiating itself from the scholarship done in seminaries and Bible colleges. This process, which was burgeoning in the 1960's, continues today. Until now, the study of ritual in religion departments has been conducted sporadically by a few comparativists and historians of religion. Mircea Eliade is the best known example.

Recently, a small number of psychologists and sociologists of religion have begun to be interested in ritual. So far, however, research on ritual by religionists has been unsystematic.

"Ritual studies" is a term initially used, as far as I know, in 1977, when the first Ritual Studies Consultation was held during the American Academy of Religion's annual meeting. So ritual studies, or "ritology," is a new field, not because doing ritual or thinking about it is new, but because the effort to consolidate methods from the humanities and social sciences for the study of ritual in a context that is free to be cross-cultural and comparative is new. It is new as a distinct sub-discipline of the academic study of religion. The bulk of written material on ritual is not great if we compare it with mythology or theology. And most of the writings on it are liturgically or anthropologically oriented. So there is an immense need for annotated bibliographies, fieldstudies of specific rituals, typologies and taxonomies, and more fully developed theories. In addition, there is a need for studying the connections between ritual and therapy, theater, theology, political science, kinesics, and psychosomatic medicine. The time for beginning ritual studies is ripe.

The essays which follow are forays into various disciplines in search of a methodology and properly defined field of ritual studies. They do not so much reflect the state of an already existing field as they constitute tentative proposals for the consolidation of one. Already, the hard boundaries between performance theory, symbolic anthropology, kinesics, liturgics, ethology, psychosomatic medicine, and proxemics are becoming permeable, and the time for fuller comparison, more comprehensive theories, and clearer ritual criticism is upon us.

This collection of fifteen essays, written in a variety of styles for a wide range of audiences, does not constitute a coherent theory or system. Rather, each essay is like the spoke of a wheel—a new beginning from a common center, the academic study of ritual. The essays are strongly influenced by symbolic anthropology, hermeneutics, and dramatistic sociology, but they invite criticism and amplification from other perspectives. I make no attempt to survey all that is written on ritual or to do justice to every major strategy regarding it. Rather, I have explored what I consider some of the most interesting possibilities, hoping to stimulate enough interest among other students of ritual that more systematic research will follow.

At this juncture there are only students of ritual. Presently, they are isolated from one another in various fields: liturgics, religious studies, anthropology, drama, psychology, sociology, and folklore, with a few in literature, philosophy, classics, political science, kinesiology, ethology, and speech. They are separated by their methodologies and academic traditions, but have in common an interest in performative phenomena such as play, rituals, games, storytelling, dance, civil ceremonies, and sports—in short, people and animals as they enact and embody meanings. Ritual studies asserts the priority of persons-in-action and interprets words and cultural objects in the light of this acting. Aesthetics distinguishes plastic and performative art; kinesics distinguishes verbal and non-verbal communication. Ritual studies pays its fullest attention to the performative, non-verbal elements of action.

Ritual studies is a field, not a single, prescribed methodology. In this respect it is like religious studies as a whole. There is no "ritual studies viewpoint," but rather a field upon which are focused multiple viewpoints. Hence, what is needed presently is what literary critics call an "anatomy," religionists a "phenomenology," and anthropologists a "taxonomy" of performative actions. We must sketch the shape of the field. To do so is a pre-methodological task, though not an "objective" one without presuppositions. Such an undertaking requires what in Zen is called "beginner's mind" (shoshin) and in phenomenology "bracketing" (epoché). Theology is always being rewritten by each generation, and philosophy, as Husserl reminded us, is always returning to its roots to begin again. So to write a book of "beginnings" in ritual studies has nothing to do with condescending to a primary vocabulary for the sake of students. Instead, it is to acknowledge fully the student one is.

Behind these chapters lie several specific contexts which influence their style, method, and content: a year's field study of public ritual and drama in Santa Fe, New Mexico; several months spent as a guest scholar at the University of Chicago's Committee on Social Thought, working with Victor Turner on comparative symbology; a year and a half studying ritual dimensions of theater in Actor's Laboratory of Toronto, Ontario; a fieldstudy of selected examples of North American Zen practice; field work in Poland with Jerzy Grotowski's Tree of People Project and his Theater of Sources Project; a fieldstudy of "Tempest on Snake Island" with Welfare State International of England; and regular teaching of university courses in ritual, ceremony, and celebration.

In our present stage of degeneration
it is through the skin
that metaphysics must be made to re-enter our minds.

—Antonin Artaud (1958:99)

PART I

THE RITUAL FIELD

INTRODUCTION

The roots of ritual are various—our bodies, the environment, cultural traditions, social processes. There is no one place an interpreter of ritual must begin to study it. Ideally, the study of ritual begins by informed participation in, and observation of, it, but we live in a time so ritually poverty stricken that students of ritual often find themselves bewildered. The bewilderment arises, not just from the complexity of the ritual being interpreted, but from lack of a sense of ritual. Ritual itself has become foreign to us.

Hermeneutics is the science of interpretation, especially the interpretation of ancient or foreign documents. A broader view of hermeneutics does not restrict itself to ancient texts, but includes consideration of contemporary actions as well. Part I is about the hermeneutics of ritual action. In the first part I show how difficult interpreting ritual is. Then I formulate some fundamental questions and categories to aid in the interpretation of it. Each chapter is an attempt to orient students toward the basic assumptions and methods of ritual studies. Chapter 1 is an autobiographical narrative about the search for a style of studying ritual. Chapter 2 is an outline of the field of ritual and a set of questions designed to call attention to various aspects of it. The third chapter categorizes several modes which are present in most rituals. And in the final chapter of this part I define "ritualizing," the process whereby rituals originate.

CHAPTER 1

INTERPRETING RITUAL IN THE FIELD

The word "field" evokes two images: a playing field and a swirling pattern generated among metal filings in the presence of a magnetic force. A field is a physical-social place where one goes to do a study, as well as a pattern of interconnecting forces. The ritual field is both the locus of ritual practice and the totality of a ritual's structures and processes. Ritual studies stresses the idea of a fieldstudy for two reasons: (1) because ritual is the hardest religious phenomenon to capture in texts or comprehend by thinking, so we need to encounter it concretely, in the field, or our study of religion suffers; and (2) because our predecessors in the study of ritual, liturgists and anthropologists, have emphasized first-hand participation and participant-observation, respectively.

Religious studies has yet to develop a style of fieldstudy. It is only beginning to consider fieldwork an important task. The fact that one looks in vain for a description and interpretation of a single Roman Catholic Mass illustrates the chasm between liturgics and symbolic anthropology. Only the Mass, which is to say, the prescriptive text of the Mass, is studied. We do not lack ritual manuals or ethnographies of rituals. Rather, we lack an integrated field of ritual studies. We are left asking how to make sense of ritual if we are not in the service of a church or synagogue nor trained as social scientists. How does a student of religion go about understanding ritual? For the moment, I do not plan to answer this question, but to elaborate it and illustrate its urgency.

Ritual studies best begins with a consideration of style, rather than method, theory, or technique, on the one hand, and belief, faith, or canonical texts, on the other. Making the styles of fieldworkers a central consideration means that as many cues must be taken from aesthetics, drama criticism, and theater as from symbolic anthropology, social psychology, and kinesics. Style, understood in this way, is to ritologists (people who study ritual) what ethos, as Geertz (1966) uses the term, is to ritualists (people who enact ritual) and other symbol-users. Style is the total outcome of conscious and unconscious, intellectual and emotional, bodily and attitudinal aspects of a participant-observer.

Style is the product of personal stance and cultural form. The cultural form involved is that of scholarly theory and interpretation. Ritual studies cannot dispense with either the confessional voice, which it inherited from liturgics, or the analytic eye, bequeathed it by anthropology. Therefore, I will at first speak personally about the search for a style of doing ritual studies and hope my reflections are not merely idiosyncratic, but rather indicative of a more widely shared struggle with ritual.

Employing an autobiographical style while engaging in methodological considerations may seem strange, since methodology is usually our most abstract, impersonal mode of reflection. But for this very reason it is usually the best hiding place for private and ethnocentric hermeneutics. So I find it best not to allow the interpreter-observer to go uninterpreted or unobserved.

GESTURE AND POSTURE IN BLAKE'S ETCHINGS

My training in religion, philosophy, and the arts was primarily textual and verbal in orientation. The methods I learned were literary-critical, linguistic, philosophical, systematic, and dialogical in style, even when the subject matter was performative. Drama was studied as a form of literature containing implicit theological questions, and ritual was presented in the form of prescriptive ritual manuals to be interpreted in the context of the history of liturgy and systematic theology. Embodiment, action, and exteriority were factors about which we barely read, thought, and talked. We seldom observed actual performance in the process of studying ritual texts.

My first hint of hermeneutical dilemma occurred when, in writing a doctoral dissertation on the visionary poetry of William Blake, I found I could make no sense of the bodily postures of the characters in his engravings. At first I was incapable of thinking they had meaning. Meaning, I assumed, is a property of words, not of actions—a very un-Blakean conclusion. In Blake's engravings, I thought, one sees the semblance of action, not action itself—a second poor conclusion, I later realized.

A few years after my doctoral dissertation was defended and published, I found that other Blake scholars were articulating, and even solving, the problem which I had only vaguely felt, and which few of my verbally preoccupied readers had detected. The story is told that a student was trying to interpret the posture of some contorted Blake figure, when a prominent Blake scholar said to him, "Put yourself in that posture; maybe you will learn more about its meaning." This quippish advice, which may even be apocryphal, precipitated a crisis for me. I had no hermeneutics of symbolic action and had failed to comprehend the non-verbal elements of Blakean vision. The study of language and the study of action had been deeply divided for me, and I had no idea how to overcome the split.

MYTH AND RITUAL WORKSHOP

Not long after I began teaching university courses, I was asked to advise a student-designed course in myth and ritual. Students wanted to know in some experiential way how to create their own personal myths and rituals. I entered the course convinced that symbolic forms such as mythic stories and ritual enactments could not be created; nor were they personal. One might create a form of aesthetic value, but never of religious value, I argued. Nevertheless, I agreed to advise the course as an experiment.

We began by putting ourselves figuratively in the postures of mythmakers and ritualists. By trying to believe the stories we told, by pretending so earnestly to be involved in the rituals we performed, we discovered that we could not religiously appropriate what we so self-consciously constructed. Even our "true" stories, not to mention our fantasies and mythlike creations, began to sound hollow in the telling and performing. The pedagogy, I decided, was good, but only because it provided us with clear, negative results.

The myth section of the course worked reasonably well, but the ritual section utterly failed, except insofar as it drove me deeply into a search for method, theory, and experience in ritual studies. On myth we found provocative, thorough literature at both an elementary and advanced level. We learned much despite our failure to create anything that we could accept as myth. In the case of ritual, we could hardly find a clue that would clarify our failures. I could find no satisfactory introductions to ritual. The anthropologists gave us long, but still not full, descriptions of rites; they produced theories about the social co-variants of symbolic actions, but conveyed little sense of ritual itself. And my seminary-acquired liturgics blocked me by having taught me that ritual should proceed from theological conception to symbolic act; and that the normative dimensions of ritual must grow out of the history of liturgy, theology, and the ecclesiastical community, but never out of the actual norms of my own culture and body.

The result of pursuing liturgical assumptions, we found, was a "ritual heteronomy," in which a theological insight was "applied" to ritual action.   This fallacy is the religious person's equivalent of an actor's theatricalism. One pretends to sacred gesture but never actually achieves it. What the act is supposed to mean is confused with what it actually does mean.

So, because of the lack of connection between the anthropology of ritual and liturgics, we found ourselves lost in a yawning chasm. We were neither outsiders nor insiders. Subsequently, I formulated a critique of classical liturgics:

(1) Classical Christian liturgics is a normative discipline responsive to a specific set of institutions and texts. One major problem with it has been its repeated failure to recognize that effective prescription must follow, not precede, sensitive observation and description. We cannot say what people ought to be doing and expect to be genuinely (that is, somatically) heard until we know what they are, in fact, doing. Liturgists sometimes think the meaning of a ritual consists of the thoughts theologians and pastors thought as they designed them. But ritual meaning consists just as surely of the random thoughts and gestures that occur during a ritual. In practical terms this means that more serious attention must be given in seminaries to the anthropology of ritual and to comparative liturgics if we are to find the skills and methods for performing such tasks.

(2) A second problem with classical liturgics is its failure to recognize that normative practices need diagnosis, not just updating. As a result, liturgists have too little skill in detecting ritual pathology. They may have vague feelings that "mysticism" and "groupiness" are liturgically sick, but they seldom can diagnose the specific disease liabilities of their own liturgical traditions. They understand heresy, which is theological illness, far better than they do pathological ritualizing or gestural lying. I do not mean that we must follow Freud in treating every ritual as a repetition–compulsion, but we should know how rituals fail gesturally, posturally, and "actionally," just as we do when they fail theologically or ethically.

(3) Classical liturgics has typically operated from the top down—from synod to worshipper, from intellect to soul or body, from human or divine to animal. In the first instance (church bureaucracy down to grass roots religious people) some changes seem to be imminent. In the other instances, however, I see considerable difficulty. Our rituals are still gnostically disembodied, and our gestures continue to contradict most of our theological proclamations of the incarnation. Furthermore, for fear of idolatry, we do not

acknowledge seriously our roots in the ecosystem, or cosmos, to use a more religious term. Most liturgists have yet seriously to ritualize their own animality (except in the negative sense of "cruelty" or "bestiality") or acknowledge their own kinship to plants and the earth. Most of our rituals seriously ignore, if not bodily contradict, our "lower" (a poor term), biological nature. In such contexts sermons on ecology are useless.

(4) As a consequence, Christian ritual tends to idolize the so-called "higher" senses, namely, speech, and secondarily, vision. Words overwhelm most of our ritual silences and obscure most of the tactile, gustatory, and kinesthetic aspects of liturgy.

(5) And perhaps a repercussion of this particular sensorium organization is that purposive, and often pragmatic or ethical, activities are ritualized to the exclusion of less goal-oriented actions such as play and its religious counterpart, meditation. Ritologically speaking, I think we have divinized action and activity and ignored passion and passivity, Jesus' passion notwithstanding.

(6) Another problem with a long history is the failure of most liturgists to perceive and develop the dramatic qualities of their own rituals. In their insistence that they are serious, not just playfully pretending, liturgists themselves have pretended that their callings are not also roles they play. Insofar as histrionics and liturgics remain divorced, insofar as imagination is construed as the antagonist of revelation, the church and theater alike suffer, the former from pretentiousness (a sublimated form of pretending?) and the latter from frivolousness.

(7) Finally, liturgics has often confused Christian uniqueness, which, ritologically considered, is Christian "style," with exclusivism. Do we need to defend practices whereby ultimate gestures belong only to the ordained, only to this or that denomination, or even only to Christians? What would happen if we defended the faith ritologically instead of theologically?--if we said, for instance, "My Christian brother is whoever breaks bread with me," instead of, "My Christian brother is one who ought to assent to this creed and when he does, he may eat with me"? What would be gained and lost if we valued symbolic actions more than symbolic words, and thus defined "Christian" descriptively and gesturally, rather than confessionally and theologically?

FIELD STUDY IN SANTA FE

After the course concluded, I took a leave of absence to do the research for writing an introduction to ritual. Meanwhile, Victor Turner and I began to exchange ideas on the links between the language of literature and the actions of ritual. I was surprised to find an

anthropologist working on Blake's vision of the city. Turner
convinced me that I could not write the book without first breaking
the hold which textualism had on my understanding of ritual; so I
formulated a fieldwork project for Santa Fe, New Mexico, to observe
and interpret the public ritual and drama of its annual fiesta. A
dominant motive was to work in a modern, urban field rather than a
tribal one, because most anthropological study of ritual had used
examples from preliterate societies, and I was unsure how to transpose
the conclusions to my own society. Some anthropologists considered my
choice of Santa Fe a suspect one. A city of 46,000 people, overrun
with twice as many tourists at fiesta time, was no place for
interviews and other anthropologically informed techniques, they said.
I should either pursue a more sociologically, hence more urban and
industrially, oriented method, or I should, as one anthropologist put
it, "Go study the Pueblos and avoid the 'Disneyland of the
Southwest.'" The Pueblos are studying the Pueblos, I replied. And so
I went to Santa Fe to see what I could of living ritual performance.
After twelve years, I was also returning to the state in which I had
been reared.

     In Santa Fe I took notes, photographed, taped, interviewed,
watched, listened. I did not go to participate—or so I thought.
Part way through the study several events of hermeneutical
significance occurred: (1) I realized that I had no way of organizing
or selecting data; so I was becoming exhausted by trying to take note
of everything. The first two chapters of SYMBOL AND CONQUEST (1976),
my published Santa Fe study, began to sag, because they lacked the
coherence that a more rigorously applied theory would have given them.
Such a theory does not begin to emerge until the end of the book. (2)
One day Pedro Ribera-Ortega, my most knowledgeable informant, jokingly
called me a Tejano ("Texan") and pointed out that my boots were not
the only evidence of my participation in the rituals of the racial
triangle I was studying. In our discussions I began to see how
entangled were methodology and one's style of fieldstudy with
autobiography and cultural background.   (3) I discovered that
modifications were occurring in both ritual and dramatic performances
as a result of my asking what various fiesta symbols meant. (4) I
began to wonder why I was concentrating my interviews on resident,
male, Hispano Catholics, when tourists constituted the bulk of fiesta
attendance. I began to reflect: Who is native to a fiesta? Who is
native to a public celebration? How useful is the distinction,
insider/outsider, in ritual contexts where the outsiders are caught up
in the fiesta spirit, and organizers often have the critical spirit
associated with the act of observing from outside? (5) I repeatedly
encountered artists who incorporated the symbols I was studying and
accounted for their actions by appealing to Eliade and Jung.
Consequently, I could no longer regard either scholar as merely a
theorist. I had to consider both of them as part of the data itself.

So I faced a crisis of theory. I had gone into the field loaded with the writings of Turner, along with those of Eliade, Jung, Ricoeur, Geertz, and Bellah, but I still was unsure what one was supposed to do with them when studying ritual. I did not know in what sense these men had provided me with methods; all I had was a piecemeal vocabulary. Before I had begun collecting data, I tried to force myself to choose one theory, one method. But which was appropriate to the data? I did not know. So I decided to collect data and then re-raise the method-question, but by then the method-question could only be treated as an inquiry about literary style and organization. Why should I now pick a method which merely fit what I had already discovered independently, any more than I should have selected only data which fit some scholarly apparatus which I carried in my head? This was the problem of methodological heteronomy in another form. I was in danger of doing to other people's rituals what I had accused liturgists of doing to their own. The problem is not a new one, but it is especially acute when a religionist tries to study ritual in self-conscious, educated societies. The differences between theoretical and indigenous vocabulary for discussing rituals are not as clear as when one does a fieldstudy of village rites in exotic cultures. To interpret practiced, as opposed to textual or theological, religiosity in one's own culture requires an attitude quite different from that of liturgics or anthropology, because one is not in the tradition as a liturgist or out of it as an anthropologist.

I decided the only way not to violate either theorists like Turner or residents of Santa Fe was to become as invisible as possible. So my Santa Fe study was written, though not conducted in the field, in a style of self-denial. I tried rigorously to be invisible, to watch without disturbing, to question without influencing, to write without value judgment. In short, I disappeared from my own book. By doing so, I began to develop a keen sense that my study was not disinterested, despite my intentions. The best one could achieve, I decided, was a "sympathetic re-enactment in imagination," a phrase Paul Ricoeur (1967) uses to describe the hermeneutical attitude toward ancient myths. But I had imagined away the imaginer. A chapter on ethnic stereotypes, in which I, the observer, began to appear, was edited out of the book. Later I noticed that anthropologists often spoke about rituals in a manner strikingly different from the way they wrote about them. The written accounts typically omitted their own participation, feelings, and value judgments—all of which I thought were as important as the ethnographies and analyses for enabling one to grasp the meaning of a studied ritual. Much later, I found Myerhoff's exceptional book, NUMBER OUR DAYS (1978), a good example of the integration of personal and theoretical concerns in the anthropological study of ritual.

I went to Santa Fe to observe ritual celebrations and dramatic performances. I left convinced of the dramatic and ritualistic character of scholarship itself. I learned that my style as a scholar was sub-drama, or occasionally even counter-drama, in the field situation. By trying to deny my participation in the field, I discovered the vast extent of it. Whether I wished it or not, I, like the missionary, was an agent of change.

I recognized that method involves far more than having a technique to apply, a theory to validate, or a vocabulary to mobilize. It extends to a treatment of style, tone of voice, way of watching, intended audience for writing, and imagined monograph. These are the hidden, thus most efficacious, factors, because they are the points at which methods are the most ethno- and religio-centric; they are the nodes at which the most significant cross-cultural, cross-religious, and cross-generational learning occurs.

Besides relativizing my sense of participant and observer, the Santa Fe project forced the collapse of a neat separation between theory and data. I thought my theorists provided me with something to "apply" or "test" in the field, but when I ran into Jungian Pueblo Indians and Eliadian Catholics, I felt the microbe was studying the eye through the microscope. My scholarly world slipped; I underwent what Kuhn (1962) calls a "paradigm shift." Whereas I had thought theorists might be able to explain ritual and drama in Santa Fe, I was becoming sure that the very notion of explanation was subtly ethnocentric; so the problem became how to study ritual critically without becoming intellectually imperialistic.

What I accomplished in my study was the rendering of historically oriented, indigenous views of fiesta participants in synchronic, systematic form. From observed ritual processes, I formulated the symbol system, and thereby made visible the gaps and contradictions implied by the performances. This "translation" produced the critical, culture-contact edge of my study. My contribution (also my criticism) occurred at those points where I was able to infer unintended or unrecognized meanings. By a charting operation, I turned informant-information into a system, thereby calling attention to "meaning blanks," which I then filled by further observation, more listening, and imaginative inference. Afterwards, I invited and incorporated indigenous responses to my inferences.

JUNK AS FETISH

After Santa Fe I returned to the university and began teaching a lecture and seminar course in ritual studies, though I had not produced my intended introduction for it. Each time I taught the course, whether to undergraduates or graduates, I came to the same conclusion: we lacked a sense of ritual. The monographs we read were boring, though we suspected the rituals themselves were not. The theories were interesting, but the study of them easily became self-serving, a substitute for the study of specific rituals. Inevitably, the class was forced to reflect on its lack of ritual experience and on ritual pathology and failure. We seemed unable to understand ritual; we could only gather information about it. Something fundamental was wrong, because even the rituals of our own culture and faiths felt foreign to us.

In the seminar I presented a series of lectures and slides on festivity, folk drama, and Hispanic Catholicism in Santa Fe. One day, I made a long digression into Protestantism in the form of "cowboy Christianity," intending to discuss its conflicts with Hispanic Catholicism and Pueblo religion. I found myself dwelling on a dozen or so old keepsakes, including a toy gun, a rosary, and some stones called "Apache's tears." Around them a story, a kind of ritualized autobiography, gelled.

Eventually, I formulated a critique of initiation rites that do not occur, marriage rites that do not bond, and symbols that are mere dead objects. The course took a fundamental turn as a result. It began to swing between theological and anthropological concerns, between confessional and analytical stances. We did not try to design our own rituals, as my classes had done before Santa Fe, but to articulate critiques of our ritual heritage, as well as our methods for studying them. I worked with theology students and graduate archeology students to uncover presuppositions and bedrock feelings about ritual. We produced some "fictive archeology," imaginative ritual accounts based on actual ancient Near Eastern shards and artifacts; and we imagined other stories to account for the origins of familiar rites such as baptism, marriage, and funerals. If we had been unable to create rituals in workshops or have a feeling for them in lectures and discussion, we did succeed in imagining significant rituals. By imagining, I felt for the first time that I was on the right track.

RITUAL AT ACTOR'S LAB

The next stage in my inquiry into the style of ritual studies began in October of 1976 at Actor's Lab, presently located in Toronto, Ontario. The Lab aspires to achieve a universal theater; it wants to find archetypal themes, gestures, settings, and rhythms. Its ethos is overtly ritualistic, and many of its performances are laden with myths and symbols.

At the Lab I had to re-open the question whether it is possible to create ritual, because the Lab, unlike my class in 1971, was able to create ritual processes during actor training. In the view of Lab members, genuinely symbolic forms are discovered not made; yet one discovers them in the midst of an active process of creative search (which is more fully described in Chapter 12). One need not merely wait to receive a handed-down tradition from some mainline religious body, they maintain. In view of such a claim, and, I think, such a fact, I had seriously to confront the usual assumption of religious studies that one cannot create myth and ritual.

The first hermeneutical problem I encountered at Actor's Lab was definitional. As in the case of the Santa Fe Fiesta, I was studying ritual performance, and in both cases the performances were on the borderline between religion and drama. The Santa Fe Fiesta and Actor's Lab's research (which I will compare fully in Chapter 13) were neither drama in the usual stage sense nor religion in a traditional Christian sense; yet both were ritualistic according to most of the usual scholarly criteria. For Lab members "the work" was ritualistic, though they seldom used this word.

The very necessity of saying what kind of action I was interpreting led me to see only selected aspects of it. The very fact that the Lab did "performances" almost led me to conclude that their productions were not rituals, since, by some definitions, a ritual is a traditional, anonymously originated form. But the Lab did, I repeat, "create" rituals.

The second problem was that the Lab fostered some very private, fragile work at which no mere observers were allowed; so I agreed to participate, as a condition of observation and study. I became a scholarly apprentice. I was quite ready to do so, since I had decided to explore a style quite different from my Santa Fe one. When I entered the Lab, I considered the study of ritual itself as a rite of passage, the liminal stage of which generates a new social category: insider/outsider, participant-observer, in short, a ritologist. A ritologist, at the hands of the ritualists, dismembers the ritual process and reassembles it in new sets and combinations. I was a "virtual" (Langer) initiate acting in the "subjunctive mode" (Turner).

In Santa Fe I had become aware of the influence on a field exerted by my preconscious postures and gestures. At the Lab I decided to take an active part in identifying and responding to named roles which I found thrust at me, for example, "Bear," "Carlos" (juxtaposed with the director's "Don Juan"), and "the prof." I became for Lab people a one-man audience-in-training; I was part of their data. I did research on them and they, on me. Sometimes I was asked to reflect back what I saw. I was alternately an authority and a raw neophyte needing to be led by the hand and shown everything. I at once knew too much and too little. At first, I resisted making value judgments. Later, I made them openly. The refusal to judge, I began to see, was experienced by them as a refusal to take seriously. My objectivist refusal to share my interpretations, discoveries, and judgments was sometimes taken to be a hoarding of intellectual wealth. The "natives" of the Lab were not content with glass-bead gifts to buy information; they wanted me to expose my mind and risk my body. So I had to give up the privilege of posing as an invisible "I," though I was determined not to "go native." The problem I faced was how to avoid both scholarly voyeurism and intellectual whoring. This is the basic problem of hermeneutical style. It was one which involved not only my actual behavior at the Lab but also my academic way of thinking and speaking. Style consists of not only how one interacts with others to obtain data or how one communicates with colleagues but also how one thinks about, and analyzes, those data.

A style of participation and fieldstudy is the product not only of scholarly methods but also one's body and values. My body does not always follow the tracks laid by my theories, and since the study of performative modes such as ritual and drama involves bodily presence, I could not merely ignore my own physical responses. Style includes body; therefore, methodology ought not ignore it. By exercising with the Lab—they to prepare for performances, I, for observing them—I found that my bodily state astonishingly modified how I saw and what I wrote. I did not always become more sympathetic by participation. Often I became more critical, and what I thought or wrote seemed more grounded, rather than less objective, as I had anticipated.

One of the most sadly neglected roots of scholarly method is bodily attitude. Hermeneutics speaks of the interpreter's "viewpoint," but does so only metaphorically. Yet I found that where I sat and how I focused my eyes radically affected what I saw and understood. I found that I could predictably and effectively modify a performance by the way I watched it. To see is to effect. Most scholarly observers know this, but their habitual antidote is to defend themselves further by hiding the fact of their watching.

In opposition to this methodological voyeurism, which I increasingly began to suspect on both ethical and methodological grounds, I began to practice and teach a series of exercises that I called "active seeing," or "audience training."

A group of active watchers is much more akin to a ritual congregation, even if its intention is ultimately scholarly or critical. Thinking and writing as scholarly activities should be responses to the studied group, as well as to professionals and colleagues. Scholarship should be a gift, not a theft.

One day, while doing a study, a Lab performer found himself consistently blocked. He was struggling to find an appropriate gesture for killing his rival in a performance of "Blood Wedding." Only the director and I were watching. My presence, my pen, and my notebook were among the sources of his problem. I wrote the following in my field notes:

He is feeling vulnerable before my eyes. He knows that I may see the unseemly signs of birth still in process. At the moment my position is one of power. Like a fortress I am unexposed, while he is struggling and confused, still unconsolidated. Head drooping, he is now pacing. Nervously, angrily, and self-consciously, he has been striding around the room for several minutes.

I shift to the floor from the folded blanket on which I sit. Still too intrusive, I lie on the floor and turn my gaze to the ceiling. Pen and paper are at my side. I decide not to write, but quickly revoke the decision as I remember that I have a role which, for the moment, must be played out despite him. Both of us must perform as if the other were not present. I take my pen and paper and begin to write, "Question: To what extent is a god a symbol of the ultimate audience? How do ritual and drama differ in their employment of 'audiential' principles?" I see him seeing me from the corner of his eye.

Later, as we talk, he confesses that he thought I was only pretending to write so as not to embarass him by direct watching. Gesturally, we were second-guessing one another. I admitted that my pen was not yet an extension of my whole presence; it was a conspicuous eyesore, an advertisement. How could I have made the weight of my eyes light and the stroke of my pen choreographic in response to the fragile study which had unfolded before me?

Pen and paper are power objects, fetishes; theorizing and observing are ritual gestures laden with ideology. And our valuing them only as tools to use, and not also gifts to give or trade, eventuates in a ritually destructive style. With this actor-ritualist-friend I found myself on what one might call "the way of the liminar." I sought for the threshold between him and me. Finding it demanded mythologizing the movement of my pen as dance. For a while, we even considered doing an actual movement-study with my pad and pen, but this became unnecessary. As soon as he and I began to take the motion of my scholar's pen as a dance, both his performing and my writing changed. The greater change was probably in my writing.

This occurrence was the first time I was able to do anything about my discovery that the style a viewer embodies is itself a symbolic act. The missionaries at least were aware that they were importing a counter-ritual. The anthropologists who followed them sometimes were not. Their rituals were often invisible to themselves, but even if they recognized or articulated their own presence as observers, they typically did so in ways that left their memoirs unintegrated with the analytical material they published. They, or their editors, excised the most interesting portions, as my editor and I had in SYMBOL AND CONQUEST. In most writings about ritual, one searches in vain for the horizon of intersubjectivity, where informant- and observer-values clash and dance.

At Actor's Lab I watched and re-watched a performance of Garcia Lorca's "Blood Wedding." When I first saw it, I was moved by much of it, but just as thoroughly disturbed by other portions of it. As I began to write, I at first lapsed into the voyeur's strategy of neutralizing my feelings with a set of "phenomenological" brackets, so I started over. This time my eyes were written into the account of the performance. I maximized interaction with what I saw.

After several more viewings, I found the dialogue in my head quieting; most of it was now on paper. But I began having physiological responses to the play. My body was still interpreting. It was trying to run. What did my legs know that I did not? What meaning had the twitches, muffled groans, posture shifts, and head tilts that characters and actions were evoking? After tracking my own responses for quite some time, I found myself imagining a scenario which was a re-make of the part I had so consistently disliked. I then began actively and deliberately to imagine myself playing the part. Only as I imaginatively re-directed and performed the whole play, did I begin to see what the performance itself was about and discover the grounds for criticizing its presuppositions. As long as I denied my projections, they had me. I could not even locate them. But as soon as I began to honor and embody my projections, I began to find the boundary between my values and those of the performance. As Blake says, "If a fool will persist in his folly, he will become wise."

Lab people used a phrase which became significant for me. "Going with" is an aikido-like entry into the vector of another person's movement. One does not imitate, which would be the ritual equivalent of selling oneself as a scholarly whore to whatever one observes; nor does one violate by voyeuristic staring. Without designated form, two people try to find a way of moving together in which the one does not merely ape nor overpower the other. A third form is generated out of the patterns enacted by the two participants. The interaction is sometimes identifiable as, say, play or competition; sometimes it is not nameable at all. "Going with," by avoiding both voyeurism and whoring, is the first task of students of ritual. Our second is to find our way from this subjunctive deed to a language which is marked by the smell of the process by which conclusions were attained.

After more than a year's fieldstudy of, and with, Actor's Lab, I summarized its implications for the study of living ritual processes in post-modern industrial cultures:

(1) Ritological style is a mode of ritual research which articulates as part of the data the gestural and symbolic dimensions of the researchers themselves. These data include one's own bodily and imaginative activities in the face of a ritual enactment.

(2) It calls for bodily training as part of scholarly preparation and bodily risk as part of scholarly participation and observation. It rejects the "gnosticizing," or disembodying, of scholarship. Furthermore, all the senses, not just seeing, must be developed for studying ritual.

(4) Since the study of ritual is a virtual initiation rite in a subjunctive mode, the intersubjective process, not merely the conclusions, should be treated in scholarly monographs. Every writer should be required as part of fieldstudy to write a how-I-am-changing-my-mind essay.

(5) Criticism should take the form of imagining and embodying actions "forward" toward their own implicit telos.

(6) The heteronomous application of theories to performance (voyeurism) or becoming a convert and rejecting theory (whoring) are at best temporary tactics for tricking out meaning and should not become determinative of scholarly style.

(7) The goal of fieldstudy is to maximize the process of interaction, not to arrive at "conclusions" (stoppages? blockages?) or make predictions. Ritological style is a mode of gift-giving and "going with."

(8) All descriptions of symbolic actions should lead to descriptions of insider/outsider, performer/audience, value conflicts.

(9) A scholar in the field should pursue a specific set of bodily, imaginative, and intellectual exercises for unlearning, for achieving the no-mind of a student, for not-doing. We learn by contrast; the would-be knower must practice ignorance and blindness if he or she would continue observing other people's actions.

TEACHING RITUAL STUDIES

Eight years after advising a student-initiated workshop on myth and ritual, I decided to try again. Instead of my usual seminar in ritual studies, I offered a "laboratory" course in ritual and drama.

After studying Actor's Lab, I had a clearer sense of how symbols were gestated; I also had developed an eye for the abuses and dangers that surround ritual experiments. I thought I knew where the myth and ritual course had gone wrong: it had tried to create rituals by thinking about them, writing them, and then doing them script-in-hand. We had wrongly taken "Hamlet" and THE BOOK OF COMMON PRAYER as our models. The error lay in beginning rationalistically—from the top down, from idea to action. We had not learned to wait receptively for actions to arise. Instead, we had willfully coerced them—with stillborn consequences.

My goal now was to help arts and seminary students to develop skills in construction of ritual events: birthdays, weddings, regular worship, ordinations, and the like. I was not transmitting any particular religious tradition, but was teaching skills, as a professor of music or painting might. So students read cross-cultural accounts of rituals, as well as anthropological, dramatic, and theological materials. The emphasis in the course was on learning to follow and respond to sounds, objects, gestures, and spaces. The aim was neither liturgics nor actor training. We aspired neither to holiness, convincing portrayals, nor therapeutic self-revelation. Instead, we set out to learn the basic skills for ritual construction.

Talking was minimal during the sessions; the course lasted for twenty-six weeks. Note taking was not allowed, but each session had to be described and interpreted in journals. I kept "field notes," which were shared with the students.

In the first session students who chose to stay ceremonially signed a large scroll.   Then we discussed stylization and the placement of our signatures. We considered the rite of signing one's name, as well as invisible, everyday ritual practices. In the second session students brought some object of their own choice to begin the ritual explorations. Below is an illustrative excerpt from my notes:

They have brought objects to this room, in which they sit, without shoes, on the floor. I say, "In your own time and way, place your object in the middle of the floor." One person moves as if this were a directive instead of an invitation. Another holds back as if it were a trap. Soon the center is a clutter: a set of chain links for mountain climbing, a lady's gold ring, a ceramic cream pitcher, a guitar, a wooden figure standing by a pile of rocks on an airletter, a red plastic bear full of soap bubble solution, a long staff, a small piece of wood.

"Imagine how they are connected to one another. Guess their relation to their owner," I say. They do so. Some smile. A few chuckle.

After several minutes of silence and fantasy, I give them permission: "If, without violating anything in the center, you wish to do something with one of the objects, do so."

Action occurs more quickly than it has in previous classes. The chunk of wood is moved to one end; it is placed by the climbing chain. The pitcher is set upright after a tentative gesture which imitates the action of pouring. The ring is laid atop the wood. The rocks are stacked, and the wooden man put on top. A person shudders. The staff is made an upright, the guitar a transverse. Someone is building a cross.

One student pushes the staff so it no longer forms the axis of such a transparent symbol. The person who shuddered moves her rocks, man, and letter onto the guitar top. Another reaches to save a rock from scratching the instrument. Competition begins over the placing of two objects. One puts it here, another there.

Then the chess-match pace dies down, and for several minutes people forget about thinking, planning moves, and trying to communicate obvious meanings. Quite rapidly, first one, then another, shifts the position, and hence, meaning, of a thing. We laugh repeatedly. Once we are dumbfounded. People are alert. One person weeps. The moves continue.

Suddenly, the wave recedes, and the action is clearly at an end. Eye checks eye. I double check. Our medicine bundle, collage, treasure cache, junk pile is finished.

No one says what we have resolved or accomplished. I note the stages of our actions: random, nervous, or experimental shifting of objects; planned moves to create a traditional, recognizable symbol; iconoclastic moves to break the traditional symmetry; moves to express categories of relations (of subordination and superordination) among the objects; spontaneously generated moves which eventuate in a sense of completeness.

We say nothing about our feelings. But
something significant has occurred. People marvel
that this is only our second time together.

A basic premise of the course is that some of the same processes
underlie the enactment of traditional rites, the fieldstudy of ritual,
and the rehearsal and actor training process of certain types of
theater. These processes include: discovering life in inert objects,
orienting abstract spaces into founded places, responding to another's
movement, repeating actions without loss of meaning, finding evocative
sounds, observing without falsely objectifying, criticizing without
judgmentalism, absorbing meanings below the threshold of language and
reflection, listening to one's environment, allowing symbols to rise
and recede rhythmically, anticipating consequences of symbolic acts,
and knowing how the context of a gesture or position of a symbol
alters its meaning.

The course, which I have taught now a number of times, has
finally found its proper beginning. My previous attempts to teach
ritual studies had largely failed. It is too early to predict the
outcome for ritual studies as a field if it proceeds on the basis of
experimental premises. Religionists teaching ritual studies are in
the position of someone who teaches musical theory in a culture where
music is seldom heard. Religious studies has a tradition of insisting
that cognitive learning be accompanied by affective learning and
values criticism. So the style of ritual studies is one which calls
for, rather than suspends, these dimensions. Studying ritual will be
fruitful if we recognize that we can only articulate its meaning after
we have been grasped by its sense.

CHAPTER 2

MAPPING THE FIELD OF RITUAL

The style of an interpretive task is not identical with its method or theory. Rough, but useful, distinctions can be made among the three dimensions. Method consists of the "map" of formal categories and questions one carries into a field. Style is the way one handles a method. It is how our presuppositions, unconscious attitudes, deepest values, and bodily presence appropriate method and respond to a given field situation. Theory is how we account for, and sometimes predict, regular patterns of co-variance and provide for criticism of methods. The distance between the reflection on style in Chapter One and the examination of method in Chapter Two is considerable. Both kinds of tasks—the intersubjective and the analytical—are necessary for understanding ritual. The first calls for self-knowledge and recognition of our feelings. The second demands suspension of self-interest and requires concentration on actions and values that are not our own.

Some interpreters contend that the idea of a map for use with rituals is questionable. Using an interpretive framework, it might be argued, violates a ritual by imposing foreign categories on it. Tom Driver (1978) calls for less method, not more, in studying ritual. I agree that we must work to minimize bias in the study of anything, especially ritual. Also, we must work to reach the felt experience of ritualists. But a map, I suggest, can either inhibit or facilitate these interpretive goals. The result depends as much on the user as on the instrument.

All interpretive efforts are surrounded by implicit questions. This is an elementary axiom of hermeneutics. To make some of these questions explicit insures that we have sufficient grounds for comparative discussion and criticism. We can judge the value of such a framework on the basis of its ability to: (1) enable ritual to speak most fully for itself, (2) aid interpreters in discerning the continuities and discontinuities between their symbols and those of participants in a ritual, (3) generate helpful theories of ritual, and (4) precipitate a sense of the living quality of ritual in written accounts of them.

If we are to understand a ritual adequately, the first prerequisite is as full a description as possible in the form of a monograph or film. Whatever the medium, full descriptions of rituals are both hard to produce and difficult to interpret. Some rituals are long, complex, and lacking in commentary from participants. But if we are to treat rituals as seriously as we have ethics and theologies, we must work with full, evocative descriptions, not mere summaries of the values and beliefs implicit in them. Any description should make explicit whether its source is an actually performed ritual, a ritual account produced by an observer, a ritual exegesis produced by a participant, or a ritual manual that prescribes what ought to happen in the ritual.

Below, I provide a set of categories and accompanying questions which I and students have used in the field. To make them more usable, references to supporting illustrations and theories are included in parentheses. Also, I have included short illustrations from my field study of public ritual and drama in Santa Fe, New Mexico—a situation combining fiestas, processions, Masses, pageants, parades, contests, and a host of other activities which employ ethnic, ecclesiastical, civic, artistic, and political symbols.

Using these questions mechanically as a short-answer quiz is the worst use of them I can imagine. They are neither magical nor sacred, and they demand constant modification as one asks them of a specific ritual. If asking them of a ritual does not sometimes force their reformulation, they are probably being misused. Some questions will be more pertinent than others, and some will elicit "not applicable" responses. These responses, by revealing a ritual's omissions, often provoke the most fruitful insights, if one wrestles with reformulating the questions until the right way of putting them is found. Charles Winquist, following Hans-Georg Gadamer, identifies hermeneutical consciousness with our capacity to see what is questionable. Questioning, says Winquist, is a way of "thinking darkly":

Foundational questions yoke the actuality of immediate experience with concepts and images of possible connections that surround the experience and define its place in the material and imaginal worlds. Questioning loosens experience by asking how experience looks against a different background, under an expanded horizon or when integrated through different formal patterns. The display of formal possibilities alters consciousness by generating contrasts between immediate experience and what could have been or what can be. Questions can lead to new juxtapositions of images reversing and even eliminating temporal sequence. The resultant non-temporal condensations are images that speak new meanings (1981:32).

RITUAL SPACE

Where does the ritual occur—indoors, outdoors, in a randomly chosen place, in a special place? If the place is constructed, what resources were expended to find or build it? Who designed it? What traditions or guidelines, both practical and symbolic, were followed in building it? What styles of architecture does the building follow or reject?

If the space is a natural one, is it high or low, secluded or accessible? How rigidly are its boundaries defined? Do they seem clear or amorphous? What objects, such as trees or rocks, have special status, and which function merely as background?

Is the ritual place permanently or temporarily set aside? What rites were performed to consecrate or deconsecrate it? What rites mark the transitions in and out of it? Is the space portable or stationary? If portable, what determines where, say, the tent will next be raised? Are the roads and ways leading to the site considered sacred? Are journeys to and from the place ritualized?

How are areas outside the ritual space regarded? Are they profane, neutral, potentially sacred (see Eliade, 1961)? Is the space duplicated or extended, for example, are there shrines at home which replicate motifs from a central altar (see Christian, 1972:ch.2)? What things are viewed as detachable or merely decorative, for example, statues; and what things are treated as part of the edifice itself, for instance, a baptistry?

What is the history of the use of the place? Was it once part of another ritual system? What do its strata or renovations and deteriorations reveal? If relocation were to occur, where might the next site be—in a wealthier area, a more secluded one, a re-designed one?

What shape is the space? What size is it? Do participants regard its shape as symbolic? Is the place a replica or analogue (see Bachelard, 1969:ch.2) of anything else? For instance, the Hindu lingam and yoni are shaped like male and female genitals. What are the functions of color and light in the place? What actions do they activate, discourage? Does sight, sound, or some other sense seem best provided for? What role do paintings and tapestries, for instance, play in the ritual?

How is the place oriented? What direction does it face? What directional symbolism is designed into it? Do up and down, left and right, back and front have values associated with them? Where are behind-the-scenes spaces (see Goffman, 1959:112), and who has access to them? What is the relation of informal and adjacent areas to the formal ritual center, for example, a social hall to a sanctuary, a drummer's shed to a dancing ground (see Heilman, 1976:ch.2). What spots within the bounded precinct are most consistently used?

Are participants territorial or possessive of the space (see Hall, 1973:ch.10)? To what extent is their identity bound up with the geography of the place? Do they, for example, feel that "when a man lives somewhere for a long time, his name is in the ground. . . " (Schieffelin, 1976:41-45)? Is ownership invested in individuals, the group, or some divine being? How are boundaries and thresholds marked—by stones, walls, gestures, or strips of no-man's-land (see Van Gennep, 1960:15-25)?

What hierarchies does the space facilitate?   For example, is there a men's side and a women's side (see Bourdieu, 1973)? From what spot does one have the best view, the worst? What is the most common visual perspective on the place? What spots are ignored or avoided? What sort of sightlines and blocking does the place have? Where are the most private spots, the most public ones (see Sommer, 1969:39-57)?

Are there fictional, dramatic, or mythic spaces within the physical space, as when the chancel became the sepulchre in medieval Quem quaeritis tropes, or when a balcony becomes heaven in a Christmas pageant (see Hardison, 1965:ch.5-6)?

Spatial considerations during the Santa Fe Fiesta are exceedingly complex. Many people regard the city itself as "the soul of the Southwest" and outlying areas as removed from the cultural and religious heart of the region. The entire city becomes a dramatic set in one moment, a sacred precinct in another. Although the Cathedral of Santa Fe, for example, is permanently sacred, the city streets become temporarily so if a procession moves through them, say, to the Cross of the Martyrs, located on a nearby hill, or to Rosario Chapel and its adjacent cemetery at the edge of town. In addition, a pageant set is erected which becomes the scene of a re-enactment of Don Diego de Vargas' "bloodless reconquest" of the city in 1692. The set is a rough reproduction of Santa Fe's central plaza, the primary site of civic and artistic activities during fiesta time.

During the performance of the Entrada Pageant, the set is at once on a literal section of property in the city of Santa Fe, a symbolic representation of the plaza in the seventeenth century, and a sacred-dramatic zone in which actors playing priests and conquistadors extract a ritual of submission to God and king from actors playing Tano Indians.

All fiesta sites except the plaza physically elevate personages who occupy places at the apex of some hierarchy, for instance, priests, Marian statues, the governor of the state, or the mayor of the city. The plaza as a ceremonial arena is generally more level and egalitarian, and the bandstand's elevation is more practical than symbolic of hierarchy. No group can quite lay claim to either the plaza or bandstand in the way the Catholic Church can claim ownership of the cathedral and chapel or the Caballeros de Vargas, the pageant set.

Although the altar of the cathedral is usually its most sacred spot, at fiesta the north transcept becomes the dominant center of religious fervor, pilgrimage, and devotion on account of the enshrinement in it of La Conquistadora, De Vargas' conquering virgin. When she is carried in procession, a wake of sacred space is generated, particularly toward the rear of the procession, the place of most honor. Since she is typically carried through the plaza on the way from the cathedral to the chapel, the effect is to sacralize civic space momentarily.

RITUAL OBJECTS

What, and how many, objects are associated with the ritual? What are their physical dimensions, shape, weight, and color (see Turner, 1967:ch.3)? Of what materials are they made? Are the making and disposition of the objects ritualized? What is done with the object? What happens to it before and after the ritual? In whose custody is it? Where is it kept? What uses would profane it? Must it be in some special position? What does it symbolize (see Ferro-Luzzi, 1977)?

How did the object become special? What stories are told about it? What would occur if it were missing? Is power said to be resident in it, or does its power come and go, depending on its use? Is its power animate or personified (see Reik, 1976:226-245)? Has the object a significant name? Does its efficacy require the presence of other objects? Is it valued more for what it means or for what it does? Is it ever considered dangerous?

What skills were involved in its making? How did the object get from its maker to its owner, if they are different? Is the object owned? What status accrues to its owner or keeper (see Firth, 1973:ch.10)? Can it be inherited or given away? Do outsiders desire it or find it valuable, useful? Can it be replaced? Is it considered a work of art? Could the object be sold, given away? Is it deteriorating? Is it viewed as an extension of a ritual edifice or ritual officiant (see Evans-Pritchard, 1956:231-247)? How detachable from the ritual place is it? Has it a "home" spot? Is it ever worn?

La Conquistadora is a wooden statue twenty-eight inches tall. She is a santo, a sacred object. The craftsmanship of it is not particularly outstanding; yet when it was stolen in 1973, the State of New Mexico mobilized its forces, along with those of the church, to search for her. Devotees usually refer to "her," seldom "it." In Santa Fe the public outrage was so great that the crime was often labelled "kidnapping" rather than "theft." Santa Feans called her the "patron saint of New Mexico" and eventually thwarted the demand for $150,000 ransom.

As a symbol of the Virgin Mary, her power lies in her purity. Our Lady of the Conquest is not usually associated with miracles, as is the case with some other New Mexico bultos ("statues"), but with civically and ethnically infused devotion. She is considered above petty city politics or squabbles about genealogy; yet she is treated as a mother by those most involved in these concerns.

Members of her confraternity clean her, make her clothing, dress her, and sing her canticos. Ordinarily, she sits high on an altar in the Cathedral of Santa Fe to receive prayers; but periodically she makes visits, riding in a catafalque carried by the Caballeros de Vargas, her honor guard.

She is credited with inspiring the actions of De Vargas by providing him with the courage to enter Santa Fe without armor and weapons, which, in turn, is said to have inspired the Tanos to surrender the city without bloodshed. The story of this action is the charter which warrants her special standing, as recognized by the Vatican and residents of the Santa Fe area.

RITUAL TIME

At what time of day does the ritual occur—night, dawn, dusk, midday? What other concurrent activities happen that might supplement or compete with it (see Myerhoff, 1978:ch.6)? On what date does the ritual occur? At what season? Does it always happen at this time? Is it a one-time affair or a recurring one? When will it next occur?

To what extent are watches and calendars used; to what extent are they ignored or prohibited? Do the people organize time in terms of more than one calendar, say a liturgical one and a civil one, a fiscal one and an academic one (see Ortiz, 1969:84,98,104)? Has the ritual displaced an earlier one which was held at this time?

Are solar, lunar, or other natural cycles significant for the timing of the ritual (see Evans-Pritchard, 1973:75-81)? Are divination rites done to find the proper time? What lifecycle rhythms, e.g., menstruation or maturation, are significant for the rituals?

How does ritual time coincide or conflict with ordinary, social times, for instance, milking time or dinner time? How do people modify the rhythms of their schedules during the ritual? Do they go to sleep later, get up earlier, shift meal times? What units of time are used—shifts, watches, days?

Does the ritual commemorate historical eras or recall paradigmatic events, for example, the year of the great flood? Is it essential to remember things, events, or persons of the past? Does the ritual anticipate a particular future? Is divining or envisioning the future part of the ritual? In what tense do participants describe and do their rituals? Are they past-oriented? Are some centuries or eras more valued than others?

What is the duration of the ritual? Does it have phases, interludes, or breaks? How long is necessary to prepare for it? How long does it have impact after its conclusion? Are its phases of equal importance, of equal length? What elements are repeated within the duration of the ritual? Does the ritual taper off or end abruptly?

Are ancestors felt to be present during the rite? Was there a past or mythical time which is a model for the present enactment? How far back do memories of the ritual go? What role does age play in the content and officiating of the ritual? Do participants think of it as changing, evolving, or devolving? Does the event emphasize beginnings or endings? In the ritualists' view, how is time divided or counted?

Daily devotions, fiestas, novenas (series of special Masses), and processions are the main rituals involving Our Lady of the Conquest. Her rites occupy a number of time systems.

Before the birth of Jesus, Mary lived as an ordinary woman in eschatologically conceived, historical time. Between the Middle Ages and the nineteenth century, her devotees began to ascribe to her an existence in a timeless, eternal zone as well. Presently, as concretized in the statue enshrined in the Santa Fe Cathedral, she inhabits the cycle of the church year and in early summer goes on procession. In addition, as "first Lady of Santa Fe," she enters the civic calendar by her presence at the Labor Day fiesta.

Besides symbolizing Mary, she also is a guardian of the genealogies of descendants of Spanish conquerors. So her ethos is steeped in conserving the past. Stories are recorded about the statue's being saved from a fire set by attacking native people. This, and the artistic style of the statue, suggest that the bulto was probably made in the seventeenth century, though the use of conquering Virgins goes back to pre-Columbian Spain.

Fiesta scheduling, another aspect of ritual time in Santa Fe, has been controversial. Those who wish to cultivate tourist trade want the fiesta held before the summer ends, specifically during Labor Day. The more religiously oriented have tried to set it later. Fiesta timing is largely a matter of conventional, hourly scheduling. Religious events open and close the four primary days. A solemn Mass and candlelight procession enclose the Entrada Pageant on a Sunday, as if to emphasize its sacredness.

Fiesta rhetoric envisions a future of tri-ethnic harmony, occasionally even delcaring that it is already present during fiesta time, as it was during the "bloodless re-conquest" of 1692. The pageant looks backwards and declares that De Vargas set Santa Fe on the way of peace. A moment of the past is offered as a model for emulation in the present and future.

The fiesta includes Masses which, of course, have their own way of symbolizing temporality. A Mass is a commemorative meal which re-presents Jesus' last supper with his disciples and anticipates an eschatological banquet inclusive of all the faithful. Ritually, the fiesta links this sense of liturgical time to the historic sense of time and the civic need for scheduling that determine fiesta rhythms. The tourists who attend are usually on holiday "with time on their hands," while Santa Feans, particularly during the day, are on work time. Nighttime sees revelry at its height, so Our Lady remains indoors as her children roam the streets "making time" and "keeping time" to Hispanic musical rhythms.

RITUAL SOUND AND LANGUAGE

Does the ritual employ non-linguistic sounds such as animal sounds, shouting, or moaning? How does one learn them? Who interprets these sounds? Are words ever used causally or magically (see Tambiah, 1968)? Is language thought only to describe reality or actually to effect it (see Finnegan, 1969; Ray, 1973:17)? How are instrumental and vocal sounds related—chorally, in unison, antiphonally? What musical sounds and instruments predominate? How would you characterize their style? Are there discernible connections between rhythmic or musical patterns and social circumstances (see Jackson, 1968)? Are any elements of the vocal or instrumental sounds

archaic or imitative? What moods do the sounds most often evoke?
What moods are avoided? Is there a distinction between sacred and
secular music?   What is the role of silence in the ritual?   Are
musicians sacred personages or only assistants?

Does the ritual presuppose literacy? Does it depend more on
written texts or oral lore? If both, what are the relations between
texts and lore? Do the people consider it important to talk about the
ritual, to talk during the ritual? Are there parts of it for which
they do not have verbalizable meanings? What forms do words about the
ritual take—narrative, expository, anecdotal?   Does the ritual
tradition have theologians or teachers who talk about the rites? How
are the rites explained to children? What questions do participants
ask about their own rites? Are anti-ritualistic sentiments to be
found?

How important is language to the performance of the rite (see
Lawson, 1976)? What styles of language appear in it—incantation,
poetry, narrative, rhetoric, creeds, invective, dialogue? In what
tones of voice do people speak? What metaphors, metonyms, and other
figures of speech are central (see Bauman, 1975)? Do participants
sing or chant things they would never say? At what points do words
and actions seem in tension with one another, in harmony?

Do people use books during the ritual? Are books or scrolls
venerated? Are they illustrated, elaborated, annotated, or otherwise
paid special attention?   Are notions like "word," "name," or
"language" used as metaphors for other parts of the ritualists'
reality? To what extent is the language formulaic or repetitious (see
Gray, 1972)?   How is the language of the rite connected to the
ordinary language of participants (see Grainger, 1974:12)? How much
of the language is spontaneous, how much, planned? What stories are
told either verbally or gesturally in the ritual?

New Mexico is officially bi-lingual. During the Santa Fe Fiesta
one hears English, Spanish, and occasionally one of the Pueblo
dialects. A few Latin phrases mark solemn Masses, some of which are
in Spanish. Canticos, which are devotional hymns, are in Spanish.
Since English is more likely to be known by all three ethnic groups,
it is used more often. Even the pageant is in English, though it is
sprinkled by viva's (rallying cries) in Spanish and contains the "Te
Deum" in Latin.

Ecclesiastical rites held during the fiesta are printed in both
ornate and inexpensive, popular versions; whereas, ethnic and civil
ceremonies are usually only typewritten for those who lead formal
introductions, salutes, honorary presentations, and the like. Scripts
for the pageant and fiesta melodrama are usually typed and circulated
privately.

Newspapers typically carry fiesta advertising and commentary. Events are more often described than critically reviewed. Language is more often celebratory or complaining than analytical. Both oral and written commentary are, for instance, more able to interpret the De Vargas figures than the Fiesta Queen. And historical recitation is by far the most common style of exegesis of these symbols. Occasionally, sociological criticism about various forms of ethnocentrism or racism is offered in private conversations and public letters to the newspaper.

Within the fiesta, pleasant banter and civic declaration are normative. A great deal of public idealization and self-congratulation supplement adjurations to have a good time and to cultivate harmony. People yawn during the introductions and speeches, but would feel that something was amiss without them, just as they would miss "Good morning" if it were omitted. Public proclamations, like public prayers, are of necessity vague, generalized, and hortatory in order to avoid offending some group.

The musical idiom is Hispanic, though a few events offer native drumming, folk song, ballroom dance, or popular rock music. Even some Masses change their auditory idiom to <u>mariachi</u> style.

As on most festive occasions, what is done takes precedence over what is said. Fiesta language is significant for what it avoids saying, namely, that one ethnic group or one denomination is better than another. One must avoid anything pointed or controversial in order to "familize" the city. Of course, the effort not to offend sometimes fails despite people's intentions. The pageant is offensive to some native people despite Hispanic intentions. Since public rhetoric must be innocuous to avoid being inflammatory, the most crucial symbols are objects and gestures--eating food, slapping on the back, dancing together, walking in processions, and watching Zozobra ("Old Man Gloom") burn, for example.

RITUAL IDENTITY

What ritual roles and offices are operative--teacher, master, elder, priest, shaman, diviner, healer, musician (see Mol, 1976)? How does the ritual transform ordinary appearances and role definitions (see Goffman, 1971:ch.6)? Which roles extend beyond the ritual arena, and which are confined to it? Who participates most fully, most marginally? Do participants have ritually conferred names, such as Christian names or <u>dharma</u> names? Do they have special names only when they are in the ritual precinct or functioning in their ritual roles? To what extent can they put on and take off their roles? On what occasions do people slip out of character (see Goffman, 1959:ch.5)? Do participants undergo a transformation of consciousness such that they are regarded as divine beings or sacred vessels? How are ritual roles determined—heredity, personal choice, divine calling? What kinship metaphors are important in the rite—brother, mother, grandfather?

What groups receive ritual recognition—clergy, laity, family, clan, moiety, men, women, children, adults, rich, poor? Who initiates, plans, and sustains the ritual? Who can criticize it? Who is excluded by the ritual? Who is marginal to it? Who is the audience, and how does it participate? What political, economic, or family interests does the ritual serve, threaten? Does the ritual cross ethnic, national, or regional boundaries? If so, how adapted is it to the present locality?

What feelings do people have while they are performing the rite, after the rite? At what moments are mystical religious experiences heightened? Is one expected to have such feelings or experiences? How are individual and collective elements of experience connected, disconnected? For example, in the Sioux vision quest, an individual is left alone, but returns to share his vision with the elders. Does the ritual include meditation, possession, psychotropics, or other consciousness-altering elements? Can participants be more than one identity at the same time, for example, a medicine man and a snake, a woman and a buffalo? Which is most emphasized—action, feeling, thought, or intention? What room is there for eccentricity, deviance, innovation, and personal experiment?

Are masks, costumes, or face paint used as ways of precipitating a transformation of identity (see Polhemus, 1978:ch.5,6)? How prescribed or individualized are these exterior manifestations of identity? What rules mark identity transformation? Where are pretending, playing, or other fictive moods allowed, denied?

A good example of a problem with ritual identity is the role of "Indian" during the fiesta. In addition to native people, particularly Pueblos who sell crafts at Governors' Palace or perform dancing exhibitions, there are "Indian figures" who are part of De Vargas' staff. They appear not only in the pageant but also at parades, formal audiences, and social occasions. Earlier in fiesta history actual native people played these roles. Presently, only the queen's court has native participants. The problem for De Vargas' staff was so acute during the pageant of 1973 that Hispano children played the Tano Indians who were holding the city. The result was an unintentional, but deep, insult.

The first question most often asked the Chamber of Commerce by tourists is where to find "real" Indians. Because of Western novels and movies, most Anglo tourist attention is focused on native, rather than Hispanic, culture. But during fiesta, Hispanic culture is on display, though supplemented by smaller contributions from the other two ethnic groups. Indian figures in the fiesta are sometimes regarded as fake, rather than fictional; whereas, the De Vargas figure and the Franciscan figures are treated as authentic. The dramatic nature of their roles is accepted. No one seems to object that these roles are dramatic, because they represent normative, Hispanic history. They carry social and ethnic weight.

In the pageant, Naranjo and Popé, two leaders of the native revolt, darken their skins and wear costumes of questionable authenticity. They appear in the play as "ghosts from the past." Meanwhile, the conquistadors are more authentically costumed and appear as characters, not ghosts of characters. They are live characters, while the rebel leaders are symbolically dead. Since these roles are set within a dramatic frame, criticizing them is difficult. One can always dismiss the pageant as "only a play." But the fact that, before it is performed, De Vargas is ritually knighted and the Fiesta Queen crowned to confirm their roles, while the Indian figures undergo no such ceremony, means that the former are more convincing. The ritual preceding the drama reinforces cultural conquest while rejecting military conquest.

Several Anglo roles play into this situation, three of the most important being "cowboy," "tourist," and "heavy." Anglo identity during fiesta is mediated largely by economic transactions and audience participation. Anglo values clearly determine most of the economic and linguistic currency of the fiesta. Nevertheless, the fiesta creates a minor, Anglo identity crisis. Anglos are in some sense outsiders and latecomers, even if they live in Santa Fe and serve on the Fiesta Council. Anglo culture has weight, but this very fact means that Anglos sometimes feel they have too much of it, in all the wrong places. Anglos have land and money, but Hispanos and Indians have the symbolic resources. Entertainment or civic rites, such as rides, dances, or fashion shows, are less likely than liturgical or dramatic ones to precipitate identity quandries.

RITUAL ACTION

What kinds of actions are performed as part of the ritual—sitting, bowing, dancing, lighting fires, touching, avoiding, gazing, walking? In what order do they occur? Does one kind seem more emphasized than another? What are the central gestures, the actions that facilitate them? What actions are not ascribed meaning? What actions are symbolic? What meanings, causes, or goals do participants attribute to their actions (see Burke, 1969)? What actions are inherently valued and need no justification? Which seem ordinary, spontaneous, stylized? Which actions occur in contexts beyond their ritual ones? Are there discernible pairs or sets of actions?

What actions seem incongruent with other actions, with the context, with the words that accompany them (see Birdwhistell, 1970)? Which actions are repeated? What gestures mark transitions? What are the recurrent postures? What qualities of action persist—quickness, slowness, verticality, hesitancy, mobility, linearity, exuberance, restraint? What sort of bearing characterizes the demeanor of ritual officiants? Are parts of the ritual framed theatrically (see Goffman, 1974:ch.5)? If so, does the drama have efficacy or merely entertain (see Schechner, 1976:207)?

What parts of the body are emphasized by participants' kinesthetic style? What senses are most often used? Are certain senses avoided? How would you characterize their sensorium organization (see Ong, 1967)? How does the physical context influence the actions? What actions are done with objects?

Is activity or passivity most pronounced? What actions are inner-directed, outer-directed? What actions are regarded as work, as play? What would happen if the actions were left undone? What actions are optional, required? What cues would be regarded as symptomatic of illness (see Siirala, 1981:ch.3), moral error, inspiration?

The fiesta is a celebrative event: one is supposed to have fun. Things are to be done because they are enjoyable, not because they are obligatory. But the motivation of the celebration is commemorative—to remember 1692 in order to foster religiously based inter-ethnic harmony. The fiesta's functions are many—generating income, raising civic pride, creating jobs, displaying resources, making new acquaintainces, for example.

The most widespread actions are spectating, purchasing, and consuming. They are done partly out of necessity but mostly for the sake of participation. The more devout perform other gestures--cleaning up graves in Rosario Cemetery, recalling genealogies, visiting La Conquistadora, attending Mass, performing, singing, and dancing.

Exuberance is expected on the more festive occasions, solemn restraint on the more liturgical ones. A certain stylized complaining about noise, prices, tourists, and the heat is also conventional.

The fiesta is perambulatory. One walks from booth to booth, joins processions, goes on strolls just to see other fiesta-goers. Actions are usually more intense at night than during the day, and in the evening, more likely to become overtly erotic or aggressive. Male swagger and other competitive or courting gestures intensify during the fiesta. Among officiants, assuming a bearing of tranquil dignity is expected when on public display, and one of jovial informality when involved in face-to-face interactions.

Lack of spirited participation can elicit criticism, but is not likely to be taken as a sign of illness or breach of a moral code. Gestures are most valued if they are expansive, outer-directed, and corporate. The places for inner-directed actions are in small side-chapels, domestic shrines, or at home.

INTERPRETING RITUALS

This set of questions is nothing more than a device to elicit full descriptions and call attention to the constituents of a specific rite. Responding to it provides at best a description, not an interpretation, of a ritual. Most of the questions are aimed at formulating indigenous responses and uncovering emic categories (those belonging to ritualists themselves. Interpreting requires, in addition, that etic (participant-observer) categories come more fully into play. Admittedly, even my set of questions is etic and therefore implicitly interpretive. In Santa Fe considering the fiesta as a synchronic system of symbolic actions, rather than a diachronic, or historical, outcome of the events of 1692, was considered interpretive to a radical degree. Interpretation requires that an interpreter take a point of view, and thus a risk, by going beyond observing and reporting. Otherwise, one can be lost in a maze of tiny bits of disconnected data. Along with sympathetic participant-observation and systematic description, a number of theoretical options are open. Among them are:

(1) Describing the ritual's phenomenology—its themes, processes, and types (Eliade, Van Gennep).

(2) Identifying its underlying structures as a symbol system (Geertz), gestural grammar (Birdwhistell), metalanguage (Bateson), performative utterance (Austin), logic (Cassirer, Langer), or deep structure (Lévi-Strauss, Leach).

(3) Considering its social functions (Durkheim), co-variants (Douglas), processes (Turner), and roles (Goffman, Schechner).

(4) Considering how it is related to individual and group psychology and thus regarding the ritual as a set of archetypes (Jung, Neumann), mazeways (Wallace), compulsions (Freud), developmental stages (Erikson), or games (Huizinga, Neale, Caillois).

(5) Explaining it as an ecological (Rappaport) or biogenetic (d'Aquili) operation.

(6) Tracing historically and theologically its precedents and consequences (Bouyer, Jungmann).

(7) Entering into imaginative, sympathetic participation with it and concentrating on its style of constructing life-worlds (Ricoeur, Gadamer, Palmer) or ultimate realities (Tillich, Berger).

Some of these interpretive strategies overlap, for instance, treating a ritual as part of a symbol system requires in some theories that co-varying elements be identified. But some of the strategies are fundamentally different. Tracing precedents and consequences is a diachronic method which accounts for processes in chronological time, while thematic or typological considerations treat a ritual synchronically, as if it were timeless or as if all parts of it were operative simultaneously.

Religious studies has generally avoided theorizing about ritual in favor of the classification or history of it (see Lawson, 1976), because it fears explaining ritual away. Whereas social and psychological reductionism has been avoided by many religionists, formalist and structuralist methods are presently attracting much of their attention.

So far, ritual studies has no theory unique to itself. It is growing up in the midst of a number of alternatives, and the temptation is to treat them as phases in a single method rather than mutually exclusive alternatives chosen on the basis of academic specialization. However, time and space preclude the utilization of every theory, just as they prevent answering every question one can invent about a ritual. So I suggest that ritual studies' cohesion as a field will depend more on style than theory. The hermeneutical option takes account of style, but, as far as I know, has yet to deal directly with rituals because of its preoccupation with texts. Ritual studies cannot afford to hide behind the skirts of hermeneutics or phenomenology in order to avoid commitment to theory. If it takes seriously the hermeneutical mandate for "an interpenetration of horizons," it must be open, on the one hand, to the reductions of theory and, on the other, to the commitments of theology. This mediating position of ritual studies is itself liminal and distinctive.

CHAPTER 3

MODES OF RITUAL SENSIBILITY

Ritual studies is differentiated from liturgics insofar as it conceives liturgy, or sacred ritual, as one among several kinds of ritual. If "ritual" is used as a synonym for "religious rite," or "vain repetition" (cf. Mitchell, 1977:ix-xii), we are unlikely to attend to the ritual dimensions of ordinary life. If "liturgy" is used as a synonym for "Christian rite," or even more narrowly, "Christian Eucharist," we probably will look down on the word "ritual," regarding it as a pejorative term for other people's practices in the same way popular usage treats "magic" and "myth."

I suggest that ritual pervades more of our life than just an isolated realm designated "religious." It suffuses our biogenetic, psychosocial, political, economic, and artistic lives as well. I also suggest that liturgy is not just Christian, but characterizes other traditions as well. There is pressing need in ritual studies for a set of distinctions among types of ritual sensibility. The usual distinctions, sacred/profane or rites of passage/seasonal rites, are insufficient. As a beginning, I propose to distinguish six modes of ritual sensibility: ritualization, decorum, ceremony, liturgy, magic, and celebration. I regard these, not so much as types of ritual, as sensibilities, or embodied attitudes, that may arise in the course of a ritual. If one of them dominates, then, of course, I would speak of a "ritual of decorum," for example.

RITUALIZATION

Often we begin to speak of ritual in far too lofty a way by referring to ultimacy, sacredness, awe, sacrifice, or eternality, or in too specific and normative a way by confessing our faith regarding specific personages or religious traditions.   As a result, we sometimes unwittingly disincarnate ourselves from our own bodies, our own present, and our own ordinariness.   This beginning leads to pretentious ritual studies and gnostic liturgics.

Ritual begins with ritualization.   "Ritualization" is the term used by ethologists (e.g., Huxley, 1966) to designate the stylized, repeated gesturing and posturing of animals.   Ritualization is most obvious in the mating and aggressive behavior of many species, and typically, it consists of a sequence of actions having no obvious adaptive or pragmatic functions such as getting food or fleeing an attacker.

An example of ritualization is the so-called "inciting ceremony" of ducks.   When the common European shellduck threatens, she extends and lowers her neck and then runs straight toward her enemy.   Then she returns to her mate with head raised.   If she stops in front of her mate and threatens the enemy again, she cranes her neck over her back.   Her behavior is appropriate to the physiology of the duck and to the pragmatics of the situation.

On the other hand, if we watch a mallard duck threaten, something else happens.   The mallard <u>always</u> incites with her head craned over her shoulder; the more excited she gets, the sharper the angle of her neck and body.   Her movement becomes stylized and ritually fixed.   As Konrad Lorenz notes, she seems to be saying gesturally, "I want to threaten that odious, strange drake but my head is being pulled in another direction" (Lorenz, 1966:50).   Her gesture is analogous to symbolic ones that arise in the history of every religion.   When meaning, communication, or performance become more important than function and pragmatic end, ritualization has begun to occur.

I see no reason why we should not view ourselves as ritualizing animals.   The time is past when, with romantic existentialists and anti-Darwinians, we need to insist that humans are utterly different from "lower" nature, from animals.   We are somewhat different, not wholly different, and if we forget our kinship with beasts and plants, we are likely to become in a perverse way what we deny.   We are animals—sometimes rational ones, sometimes divine ones, sometimes social ones—but still animals.   And our most sacred rituals still concern our "animal" functions—eating, drinking, moving about, reproducing, dying, mating, fighting.

The grounds of ritualization as a human necessity are ecological, biogenetic, and psychosomatic.   We cannot escape ritualization without escaping our own bodies and psyches, the rhythms and structures of which arise on their own. They flow with or without our conscious assent; they are uttered—exclamations of nature and our bodies. Among the modes of ritual action, ritualization leaves us the least choice. Whether we are involved in ritualization is not ours to decide. We can only choose whether to be attentive or repressive in the face of actions that compel us.

Anthropologists sometimes speak of us as "programmed" or "enculturated." Our heads are filled with "mazeways" and our bodies with "bio-rhythms," of which we are only diffusely aware. Psychologists refer to our "repetition-compulsions" and "obsessive neuroses." These terms are ways of calling attention to what is given, preconscious, or determined about the patternings so characteristic of us animals.

Not every pattern constitutes ritualization, but every instance of ritualization presupposes a process, a dancelike quality (see Capra, 1975), of interaction between the ecosystem and persons. The rituals which embody ritualization processes most fully are seasonal, agricultural, fertility, divinatory, funerary, and healing ones, because they make explicit the interdependence of people with their physical environments and bodies. Therefore, ritual studies must pay attention to the systemic connections between unintentional symptoms and mannerisms, since they are latent ritual gestures.

Because of its ecological and psychosomatic roots, ritual has survival implications (see Rappaport, 1971). Ritualization can contain both survival values and disease liabilities; so it is not mere decoration because of its dependence on exteriority and physicality. Ritual can become decadent, in which case it becomes an actional illness, a dis-ease of body and environment.

Ritualization is presupposed in all the other ritual modes: decorum, ceremony, liturgy, magic, and celebration. Yet a process can be presupposed as much by being denied as by being affirmed. Ritualization has been rejected or repressed by some practitioners of Western, so-called "historical" religions; ritualization is treated as belonging to "nature," fertility, or pagan religion. But even the most spiritualized monistic and dualistic religions depend on physical and biological processes in their meditative rituals, even if to deny, chastize, or mutilate the body. And even the most thoroughly historical religions embed their re-presentings and rememberings in repeated liturgical seasons and rhythmic incantations. Moreover, even ritual-denying Protestant groups depend heavily on psychosomatically informed processes like "being moved," "feeling the spirit," or "having a full heart." As far as I can see, there is no escaping ritualization—the stylized cultivation or suppression of biogenetic and psychosomatic rhythms and repetitions. The history of the renewal of ritual action is the story of the eternal return to what are commonly called "nature" and "the body."

Ritualization is not just a symbolic way of pursuing survival, but is a quest for a specific style of being in our bodies and world (see Booth, 1979). Ritualization is how we stylize our genetic heritage. We have no choice: anatomy is destiny, though what we do with a given anatomy—say, reduce it to gender—is modifiable.

Coming together and pushing apart—intimacy and aggression, symbiosis and isolation—are the most basic rhythms of which ritualization is constructed; hence, they are quite susceptible to habituation (see Kane, 1978). No ritual should fail to deal with the systole and diastole of human action. Habituation is the bane of ritualization. It is imposed in the form of ought-filled, unmindful heteronomy, and then the secret of this imposition is glossed over. So authentic (ecological, holistic) ritualization should not be dismissed by our linking it to habituated personalities who impose actions on themselves.

Ritualization includes the patterned and the random (the repeated and the idiosyncratic, the routine and the non-pragmatic, the habitual and useless) elements of action and interaction. Of course, a single action may have both characteristics, for example, cigarette smoking can be at once useless and habitual, but also communicative.

On closer consideration we often find that useless or random activities are not so meaningless as one might initially think. A duck's inciting gesture, which is useless as a means of attack, may in some species communicate an invitation to pair. The gesture is combatively dysfunctional—it is an "actional remnant"—but still functions as a communication of intention, even though its meaning is indirect and symbolic. Likewise, a smoked pipe is relatively useless for me, but among Sioux it symbolizes the totality of the cosmos, which is brought to witness and ratify the sacred, peaceful intention of the acts which follow the smoking. Noting this, I reconsider my pipe smoking and find that I usually do it when I am drifty and relaxed or else anxiety-ridden. The action encodes at least two different messages.

Ritualization among animals sometimes takes the form of scuffling and mock fighting. Even though the combat is theatrical, and therefore in a special frame, it helps socialize the animal, perhaps even prepare it for self-defence by keeping it from confusing genuine aggression with mere testing and display. So a useless element of our behavior often has unconscious, hidden, or slow-to-surface meanings visible only to the intuitive or trained eye.

Repetitious actions bother us almost as much as useless ones. The latter offend our pragmatic sensibilities, the former, our craving for excitement and things different. We know that repetition is inevitable, but we create diversions so we do not have to be directly aware of the fact of repetition. We turn on the radio to distract ourselves from washing dishes. We learn a good habit so well that we can afford to forget it. "It" will do itself without my having to waste time thinking about, or deciding upon, it.   Practically considered, habits free us to pursue other, more exciting or important things such as holidays, recreation, leisure, religion—that is, "useless" or ultimate things. So we see that the repeated and the useless exist in symbiotic relation to one another.

The roots of ritual are inescapably biological and natural. Since religious ritual is a rhythmic response to the patternings and events which precede and define us, we only understand the fruits of ritual by considering the change of seasons, the fluctuations of mood, the periodicity of history, and the flowing curvature of rivers and trees.   Ritualization is rooted in the rhythms which we are—the combined repetitiousness, indirection, and playfulness characteristic of us as biological animals.

DECORUM

A second mode of ritual is decorum, which springs from our civic and social life, just as ritualization springs from our organic and biological nature.   Ritualization is the issue of "genetic culture"; so it has an instinctual, inescapable quality about it.   Decorum, on the other hand, occurs at the moment a society or group, reflecting on the ritualizations it cannot help, decides to use gestures and postures for the purpose of regulating face-to-face interaction. When our patterning, indirection, and repetition become part of a system of expectations to which we are supposed to conform, we have passed from ritualization to decorum. The rules of etiquette are only the tip of a social iceberg laden with implicit rules for regularizing everyday behavior.   Erving Goffman (1959;1967), who has written many provocative works on this subject, calls this "interaction ritual." Such ritual is almost invisible to its practitioners until it ceases, or they find themselves in a foreign culture (see Hall, 1976).

We social animals say "Good morning" when it is not, "Come again" when we mean only "Good bye." We brush our teeth twice a day, get off at five every afternoon, and, without thinking, kiss our children at every departure and arrival (see La Fontaine, 1972:1-71). Our speech is full of stock phrases, and our gestures repeat themselves endlessly without significant variation.   With little conscious intention, we sit and dress in such a manner as to display our national origin, economic status, psychological state, and occupation.

By virtue of my co-operation and shared patterns, I am considered a reliable employee, a trustworthy friend, a consistent thinker, and a psychologicially healthy human being. Without decorum I fail to communicate with my fellows and traumatize my children with my inconstancy.

What is distinctive about ritual decorum is its courteous formalization and stylization. No longer elicited primarily by natural rhythms of the biological, genetic, and seasonal kind, decorous action marks the rhythm of social occasions. "Occasions" are moments in socal interaction, which, because they are moments of crossing a social boundary, demand a ritual bridge. Occasions such as greeting, leave-taking, and socializing are marked, facilitated, and complicated by the use of formulaic language and stereotypical gestures. "Good morning" and "How are you?" along with handshaking, kissing, and making eye contact are formalities about which we often complain, but which we continue to practice because they are expected of us.

Some decorous gestures, for example, leg-crossing for women, are grafted upon biological factors such as sexuality or age; no absolute distinction between ritualization and decorum is possible. Whether the stereotypical male swagger is rooted in biology or sociology is hard to determine except in a cross-cultural perspective.

Decorum is conventionalized behavior. Convention is a mutual, socially reinforced agreement about the form, though not necessarily the meaning, of an action. We shake hands or kiss after a quarrel. We have formalized our conclusion of the matter. Yet the convention may serve as much to mask residual ill feeling as to declare our intention to let go of it.

The social conservatism implicit in many rituals derives from the decorous layer of symbolic interaction. Even though decorum, like its etymological cousin, "decoration," is inessential, because it is a feature added on to the biological substratum of action, it is usually taken to be symbolic of my social identity. One who violates the decorum of an occasion, say, by wearing a sweatsuit instead of a robe when saying Mass, will be heard by a congregation as saying ritually that he or she does not participate in the solemnity of the occasion.

Decorum ordinarily carries a lightweight cultural "ought" with it. One "ought to behave," that is, act decorously, and the sanctions for breaking rules of decorum are usually light. The result of a violation is that I am ignored, snubbed, gossiped about, or frowned at. I am not imprisoned or excommunicated, nor do I so quickly get ill, as is the case when I ignore biological rhythms. Decorum is enforced socially, not religiously, legally, or psychobiologically. The voice of decorum is not assertive but interrogative. Its actions have the quality of "How are you?"

Decorum is rhythmic and responsive, as is ritualization. Walking decorously down a crowded street requires many stylizations of which we are only half aware, such as stepping to the right, not following too closely, averting one's gaze, not touching from behind, and so on. Pedestrian traffic is as predictable as rigorously choreographed dance or heavily rubricated liturgy. Yet we are seldom instructed on how to walk down a sidewalk.

Decorum is a way of displaying our roles, statuses, and interpersonal intentions. It is also a way of affirming sociability itself. Although I may be able, on a given occasion, to ignore or violate some aspect of decorum without heavy censure, repeated or full violation may have psychosomatic or legal implications. I may, for example, become legally stigmatized as "insane" if I never change my sweatsuit, wearing it not only to Mass, but to bed, to town shopping, in the shower, and finally to the psychiatrist's office. Decorum is adiophora (ritually optional) only if I continue to observe its rules.

Much of our decorum, such as our patterning of social space, is invisible to us, so the apparent optional character of it can fade almost completely; it becomes a "social unconsciousness." At this point it is virtually inescapable for a given member of society and thus resembles the psychosomatic necessity of ritualization.

The Japanese tea ceremony is as rich and complex an example of decorous ritual that I know. E.F. Bleiler calls it a "social sacrament" (in Okakura, 1964:xvi). In some forms, well over a hundred customary rules inform the participation of host and guests. At times in Japanese history, collecting and admiring tea ware was an elaborate social display of wealth and power. Tea became the setting for great political intrigues, such as the conflict between Hideyoshi and Rikyu, the founder of cha-no-yu, the tea ceremony (see Castile, 1971). Yet, the way of tea is also one of simplicity, especially as sometimes practiced in Zen monasteries, where one "just drinks tea, nothing else"; this turns the interaction into a potential vehicle of enlightenment. So the sanctification of interaction can become as thorough as the reverence for bodily and environmental rhythms is when ritualization processes develop into healing rites.

CEREMONY

Thus far I have identified ritual modes which seem biologically inescapable or socially obligatory. When we turn to the next mode, ceremony, we are considering rituals which seem less ordinary and more intentional. Ceremoniousness is of legal, tribal, or racial import; it includes gestures such as standing for a national anthem, wearing a tribal lip disc, or bearing a clan's coat of arms into battle. The distinction between decorum and ceremony hinges largely on the differences between face-to-face and large-group, political interaction. Labor rallies, political fanfares, coronations, inaugurations, convocations, Olympic games, and courtroom sessions are all laden with the pomp of ceremony. On a decorous occasion the ritual director is a host, but at a ceremonious event he or she is an officiant.

Ceremony invites the participant to surrender idiosyncracies and independence to some larger cause, for which one is willing to fight, die, or pay homage. This cause is not only considered righteous, it is legally enforced and therefore binding under direct threat. Nevertheless, I am expected to give myself to it not only willingly but even joyously. Whereas decorum is of secondary, or at least of unofficial, importance and is a means of expressing one's character and recognizing other participants in the occasion (Goffman,1967:54), ceremony has imperative force; it symbolizes respect for the offices, histories, and causes that are condensed into its gestures, objects, and actions.

Implicit in ceremony is what symbolic anthropologists call "social drama" (Turner, 1974a:ch.2-3). Ceremony is manifestly competitive, sometimes conflict-laden. This is obvious in demonstrations, revolutionary congresses, and military parades. At times such as thanksgivings, independence days, and states of the nation addresses, an implicit we/they distinction is extolled. Whereas decorous actions are typified by their politeness and exaggerated courtesy, ceremonious protagonists are so certain, and yet defensive, of their ideological territory that they dramatize their own victorious heroism. Gracious understatement gives way to solemnly pious, political overstatement. Ceremony is no longer face-to-face. The "other side" is caricatured, since ceremony both expresses and creates "our" solidarity as opposed to "theirs."

Power is a central consideration in ceremony. Not that it is irrelevant to either ritualization or decorum, but in ceremony the actions often symbolize power itself--either the power to conserve or to make change. Power of whatever kind—political, military, legislative, influential, economic—is always ambiguous; it is both a source of conflict and a means of resolving it. Whenever a ritual symbol masks an ambiguity or covers a social contradiction—and it often does--we have to do with ceremoniousness, even if that symbol appears in an explicitly religious ritual. So it is easy to see how the symbolism of power presented for public veneration and draped in such a way as to expose only its righteous, legitimate qualities, easily becomes the core of a religio-political system. Japanese Shinto, Chinese Confucianism, and Maoism, along with certain rituals of Judaism, Christianity, and Islam are as ceremonious as they are liturgical. They contain elements of "civil religion" (Bellah, 1974) and spawn "rites of rebellion" (Gluckman, 1963). By now it should be obvious that the modes of ritual sensibility fade in varying degrees into one another.

LITURGY

I do not restrict "liturgy" to Christian rites. Rather, I call "liturgical" any ritual action with an ultimate frame of reference and the doing of which is felt to be of cosmic necessity. Work is not extraneous to liturgy, as its etymology, "work of the people," suggests. Power is the capacity to do work, but power is more comprehensively understood in liturgy than in ceremony. And work is understood in a less goal-oriented way than it is in magic. Liturgical power is not mere force, but is a mode of tapping the way (tao) things flow, connecting with the order and reason (logos) things manifest. Liturgy is a way of coming to rest in heart of cosmic change and order.

Liturgy is as far "beyond" us as ritualization is "below" us. We are not animals only, but spirits, soul-searchers, Chosen People, Made People (Ortiz, 1969:17), and so on. We participate as surely in the dances of angels on the heads of pins as we do in the aping of chimpanzees. In liturgical rituals we overstep ourselves, and as a result there is always something inherently clumsy about the liturgical stride. For this we ritually apologize by confessions of sin, cleansings, baptisms, and incensations.

What is unique to liturgy is not that it communicates (decorum communicates), proclaims (ceremony proclaims), or exclaims (ritualization exclaims). Liturgically, one approaches the sacred in a reverent, "interrogative" mood, does necessary ritual work (makes a "sacrifice of praise," for instance), waits "in passive voice," and finally is "declarative" of the way things ultimately are. In liturgy we "actively act" in order to be acted upon. Liturgy is "meet, right, and fitting so to do," while at the same time it is an action done through us. This paradoxical pursuit of and by power runs through liturgical acts as diverse as the Christian Eucharist, Sufi dance, Taoist alchemy, Zen meditation, and shamanic trance. Liturgy occurs in moments when power does not need to be seized and held, as is the case in ceremony, or put to immediate use, as in magic. In liturgy we wait upon power.

Liturgy is a symbolic action in which a deep receptivity, sometimes in the form of meditative rites or contemplative exercises, is cultivated. In it we actively await what gives itself and what is beyond our command. This is what separates liturgy from magic and what lends it an implicitly meditative and mystical character. Since liturgy is a structured waiting upon an influx of whole-making (holy) power, it is inescapably a "spiritual exercise." There is a sense in which a liturgical rite is but a mere preparatory exercise, a way of biding valued time; this is the origin of inevitable liturgical monotony. But there is another sense in which the exercise is the hierophany. Ritual symbols and gestures bear the sacred. Bread does bear the Presence. Dogs do have Buddha nature. If either dogs or bread is incapable of bearing the sacred load, so is everything else, including written and oral Torah, preached words, incarnate lords, warmed hearts, chanted syllables, and visions beheld.

Liturgical action is a vehicle capable of carrying us—but only part way. Then the Christian begins a protest on principle, the Zen Buddhist reminds us that the raft is not the shore, and the Hindu repeatedly utters, "Neti, neti, neti ," ('No, no, no')—the Holy is not that." In the end, liturgy, even though it is not causal work, must always reverse itself as a form of action. It aspires to more than it has power to produce. It must become reception—what we sometimes call "passion" or "deep receptivity."

Every liturgy attempts to answer every question, to declare, "This is the way things are." Of course, it does so in the words of a specific tradition. A liturgy tries to focus all things through a few things. Like speakers who try to say everything, such liturgies must be monotonous, but monotony is appropriate to liturgy. Like any work, a liturgy needs monotony. Only when monotony, a quality we do not know how to appreciate, degenerates into boredom, does the liturgical vehicle break down.   Boredom is what occurs when the excitement-obsessed must abide in the monotonous. Instead of having our defenses lulled, which is one of the many good uses of monotony, we defend ourselves against repetition and sameness. What many students of ritual consistently fail to recognize is that a ritual does not have to be exciting to exercise power.

Liturgy as a form of work does not surprise, though it may keep us open to the serendipitous moment by its very monotony. When I hear the word "monotony," I think of "monochrome" paintings. From the point of view of a Walt Disney cartoon, a Japanese ink painting or a Doré illustration is monotonously monochromatic, but what these lack in color spectrum they more than make up by what they do to our usual perceptual cravings for splashy color.   They teach us to see the colorfulness of black and white.   Liturgy is a full emptiness, a monotony without boredom, a reverent waiting without expectation. If this way of putting it sounds excessively paradoxical, I can only say that I do not know a single religious tradition which does not find itself eventually in a vacuum plenum (full/emptiness) paradox when it tries to speak about the relationship between ritual work and sacred referents.

Liturgies do two things.   They "re-present" events and "event-ualize" structures. An event is literally unrepeatable; by definition this is so. So every event, not just the exodus of the Hebrews, the incarnation of Christ, or the enlightenment of Buddha, is unique. Some unique events (to be redundant), however, become definitive ones. We allow those events to define us, much as we define words. Jesus dies on a cross. Buddha sits under the Bo tree. Moses comes down a mountain. In these events some people find themselves defined, that is, judged, enlightened, and put into fundamental touch. But not one of these events is repeatable on the same level at which it occurred. So we must re-present them in enactments. One of these definitive events and consequent performances may save us, but just as surely, we, by our ritual action, save such events from becoming mere artifacts from the past. Without rituals such events have no presence.

Liturgies not only present events, they event-ualize structures. Certain processes, for example, changing seasons, growing up, growing old, and childbirth, appear to be relatively stable structures. They seem always to be there, just as surely as events seem always to be receding into the past. Yet a structure is but a patterning of events, so no absolute difference obtains between events (of history) and structures (of nature), and consequently, between liturgy and ritualization. The commonly accepted dichotomy between the historicity of Christianity, Judaism, and Islam, and the naturalness of other religions has been grossly overstated. Events threaten to evaporate because of their specificity, and structures, to become commonplace because of their generality. Rituals rescue structures by concentrating them punctually, as it were, into events. Death in general is transformed by a funeral into the event of this man's, John Doe's, dying. His "natural" demise is made for his family and friends an "historical" occurrence.

MAGIC

"Magic," as I use it here, does not refer only to other people's rituals but to ours as well. It is not a pejorative term. The word refers to any element of pragmatic, ritual work. If a ritual not only has meaning but also "works," it is magical. Insofar as it is a deed having transcendent reference and accomplishing some desired empirical result, a rite is magical.

Westerners regularly include curses, divination, and fertility rites in the category of magic. Some also include healing rites, unless they are sanctioned by their own traditions and belief system, in which case they refer to them as miracles and deny that such happenings are rituals at all. For example, a prayer, if one expects it to precipitate specifiable results such as healing or world peace, is magical. If the person praying is simply adjuring us to be peaceful, the prayer is hortatory and ceremonial.

Liturgy speaks in an interrogative voice, then a declarative one: "Can this be?" then "This is the case." Magic depends on the declarative to reach the imperative: "This is how things work;

therefore, let this be the case." Magic has in common with ceremony a propensity for performative utterances, but the frame of reference of the former is political, while that of the latter is transcendent. Magic uses a transcendent frame of reference to effect change in the ordinary reality of social interaction.

Healing rites, whether of the shamanic sort or the modern therapeutic and medical varieties, provide provocative insights into magic. If a doctor gives me a placebo, treates me with "fictive medicine," or even performs a mock operation (Kiev, 1964:x), I may be healed. Our consensus is that the frame of reference is chemical and physiological, but the healer "transcends" it, albeit in a fictive-theatrical direction rather than a supernatural one, as might the case in a theistic worldview.

The force of magic lies in its use of desire as a major contributing factor in causing hoped-for results. The usual mood of magic is anxiety (Neale, 1969:121). Since the dominant mood of ritualization is ambivalence, it is often found in tandem with magic because of the similarity in dominant moods. Whereas ritualization seems to be uncontrolled, magic restores, or takes, control by employing symbols more for their consequences than for their meaning. Of course, they would have no consequences if they had no meaning.

Magical rituals are not automatically manipulative, any more than ceremonies are. Having control is not manipulation; hiding control is. If a sick person calls a medicine man or requests annointing with oil, and healers use their symbols in accord with this desire, the action is not manipulative, even though it may involve trickery. But as soon as magic is put in the service of ceremony, as happened when Hitler wanted to heal Germany by consolidating Aryans against Jews, magic-as-manipulation can begin. Magic can be employed to hide and horde power or to share and control it. But any ritual sensibility, not just magic, has its pathological forms.

Whereas liturgy is likely to evoke interpretation, magic often provokes a search for explanation, especially in the modern world. Explanation is how we account for causes and consequences; interpretation, for meanings and interconnectedness. If a magical ritual leads to other responses, awe or thankfulness, for instance, it is one step nearer liturgy or celebration.

Magical rituals are often associated with trickery. Since trickery can be manipulative or playful, magic can in some circumstances move toward the playfulness of celebration. This is what we mean by speaking of a "magical evening." If magician and audience collude, agreeing to enjoy illusion without expecting empirical results, a festive ethos displaces an anxiety-laden one. Collusion undermines magical "transdendence," by which I mean not only supernatural reference but any frame not immediately shared by the participants. To agree to be deceived, like suspending disbelief while seeing a performance or reading fiction, is a ludic frame of mind; so speaking of celebrations as "magical" is not an entirely incorrect usage. It at least recognizes that wonder in the face of mystery, not just causal explanation when confronted by a problem, can be a response to rituals that work.

Magical acts seldom displace pragmatic or scientific ones (see Malinowski, 1954:85-87), and we have no reason to assume that magic is absent from technological societies, although it is probably adumbrated in them. I suspect magic is minimal in modern agriculture, but modern therapy and modern sexuality are as laden with magical thinking as healing and fertility rites ever were. In addition, advertising is full of it. People deny that they believe in magic, but ingest this pill and use that shampoo expecting "somehow" (the cue for magical transcendence) to become what they desire. A more responsible example of modern magic is Carl Simonton's (1975) use of imagery in therapy for cancer patients. A person treated in his clinic wills and imagines a cancer as soft or dissolvable and surrenders images of it as a rock, army, or steel armor. Considerable success is had in directly using symbols for such concrete ends.

CELEBRATION

I have now sketched all but one of what I take to be fundamental impulses of ritual: ritualization, decorum, ceremony, liturgy, and magic. Each arises from a different concatenation of forces; each has its own kind of weight or necessity. Ritualization is compelled; decorum is expected. Ceremony can be enforced. Liturgy is a cosmic necessity, and magic is desired. The final sensibility for consideration is celebration, but, unlike the other modes of ritual, its root, play, is distinctive, because in an important respect it seems unmotivated, spontaneous. For this reason, the ludic element of ritual is at once the most relevant and most irrelevant to liturgical rites.

In our robes and other drapes of holiness we are always something of a clown. Our shabbiness is comic, but on liturgical occasions it is typically overpowered by finery; so the comedy is seldom evident. But somewhere there is a summersault and a grin—detached from us while playing with us. Imperceptibly, liturgy begins to shift toward celebration.

However serious our stride and tone, however fundamental our rhythms and ultimate meanings, we are pretenders to office; our work is dramatic and therefore fictional. Our robes are always too big; the pleats are a stylized cover-up for our under-size. We are incapable of absolute belief and total sincerity, and holiness does not need our struttings and smoke. So liturgical "work" transcends itself, becomes its own opposite, in moments of play and performance.

Despite the obvious opposition of holy work and holy play, in all liturgy a note (often obscured) of playfulness, fictionality, and drama arises.

When this note is fully sounded I call the ritual a "celebration." A celebration rite is one in which there is no bargaining, no gain, no pursued result, no magic. Celebration is expressive play. Celebration takes a variety of forms: carnivals, birthdays, feasting, pretending, gambolling, gaming, dancing, singing, music-making. Whenever we begin to detach ourselves from ordinary matters requiring pragmatic modes of participation so we may toy with forms themselves, we are beginning to play. Since ritual itself is a mode of formalization, it is inescapably connected to the ludic impulse. Play is at once a root of ritual and a fruit of the same. The imagining we do as-our-bodies, which is what play is, is a culturally creative moment. Celebration rites arise from expressive culture; hence, their link to the arts. They are subjunctive, and their "as if" quality, like that of good fiction, must be at once convincing and specially framed. They evoke feelings, but the feelings are formalized (see Moore, Myerhoff, 1975:27-32). They are at once spontaneous and gamelike. So a celebration, we must say, is "spontaneous." The quotation marks are essential, because a celebration's basic mood is one of formalized feeling. Ritual expressivity is expected, cultivated, self-aware. These traits differentiate celebration from ritualization, which is not so reflexive or socially buttressed.

I need not be embroiled in theological controversies about the righteousness of good works versus the imputed righteousness of grace to know that something is drastically wrong with an understanding of ritual which can only apprehend it in terms of work. If ritual freezes into a structure of liturgical work alone, it becomes not celebration, but magic, that form of ritual preoccupied with results and accomplishments. I do not want to suggest that there is something wrong with magic; rituals do, in fact, sometimes accomplish empirical ends, for example, healing. I do, however, think such ritual "results" are the issue of dramatic and symbolic means, not causal ones. Every religion has both magical (achievement-oriented) and celebrative (expressive or ludic) processes deeply imbedded in its ritual system. Celebration is ritualized play. It is the inverse of magic, ritualized work, as Caillois (1961), Neale (1969), and others have recognized. In celebration we do what we do to achieve no external end. Celebration tends toward pure expressivity and response. While playing a celebration (as we might a game or a drama), we are, for the moment, utterly disinterested and yet fully engaged in the act at hand.

Festive occasions cannot be commemorative without lapsing into ritual work. Festivity revels in the presence and power of what is transpiring and cannot be reduced to the mere fulfillment of theological, ritual, or moral obligation without becoming holy busy work again.

Celebrative rites do not have the monotonous characteristics of liturgy. They are ritually polychromatic. They are events, transitions rather than structures. In liturgy we work to prepare for metamorphosis, for ritual transformation. All liturgy, then, is structurally parallel to rehearsal. Liturgy is ritual practice. It is a necessary but insufficient condition for celebration. When celebration occurs, we are whole and without need of what is conventionally expected. Such ritual play occurs in a moment, in the twinkling of an eye, between two beats of the heart, and it is gone.

Celebration is social and metaphysical fiction. When we are in the midst of it, questions about the reality of its characters (gods, heroes, tutelary spirits, incarnations), along with questions about its continuation, authenticity, and origin are irrelevant. When celebration occurs, theology as a separate, critically reflective discipline, is not needed. When that action which is whole arrives, partial acts are included. Whereas in liturgy I am afraid that I might be duped into confusing a mask or icon with what it symbolizes, in ritual play I celebrate the coincidence of my knowledge that a craftsman carved the thing with my experience of the thing as a power lending me its rhythms, shape, and life. I do not care to protest. I am little interested in what is merely fictional, playful, dramatic, and imaginative, on the one hand, and what is metaphysical, real, and eternal, on the other, because in festivity I know there is no difference in value (though there may be in form) between what is utterly serious and what is playful.

Celebration is not to be identified with Western optimism; it is not mere yes-saying. It is a mode of embracing the present which draws future and past into itself. But that embrace may take many forms—a Christian kiss of peace or Zen swat with the kyosaku stick, for example. Celebration can take the form of a Christian "Yes!" or a Buddhist "Mu!" ("Nothing"). The Christian's politically and theologically critical Yes or the Zen Buddhist's humourously serious No are equally capable of cutting attachments to rewards, goals, the status quo, and even spiritual accomplishments by dramatizing their irrelevance in rites of celebration.

This concludes my sketch of the six modes of ritual sensibility. Below is a chart that summarizes them:

MODES OF RITUAL SENSIBILITY

	FRAME OF REFERENCE	DOMINANT MOOD	'VOICE'	BASIC ACTIVITY	MOTIVATION	EXAMPLES
RITUAL-IZATION	ecological psycho-somatic	ambiva-lence	exclamatory	embodying	compelled	symptoms mannerisms gestures
DECORUM	inter-personal	politeness	inter-rogative	co-operating	expected	greeting departing tea drinking
CEREMONY	political	conten-tiousness	imperative	competing	enforced	inaugu-rations rallies legalities
LITURGY	ultimate	reverence	interrog-ative / declara-tive	being	cosmically necessary	meditation invocation praise
MAGIC	transcen-dent	anxiety	declara-tive / imperative	causing	desired	healing fertility divination
CELEBRATION	expressive	festive	subjunctive	playing	"spon-taneous"	carnivals birthdays feasts

By constructing charts, one usually finds how thoroughly the categories interpenetrate each other. Distinctions presuppose connections, and this chart is no exception. Rituals treated in terms of these categories fade into one another at the seams. When put to use, the various types seem to demand one another; so we find magical ceremonies, decorous liturgies, and ritualized celebrations. Sensibilities are not slots. An object may go in this or that slot, but sensibilities co-exist. If, for example, we considered Greek festivals in honor of Dionysus and wanted to interpret the dramatic competition, we would have to regard it as a ceremonial celebration because it combines ludic and competitive dimensions. Or if we were to consider sacred marriages in the ancient Near East, they would have to be treated as magical ceremonies because of the way they combine political and fertility motives.   In Chapter 7 I will use the framework to interpret Zen ritual, and in Chapter 13 I will employ it again, this time to compare two rituals.

CHAPTER 4

DEFINING NASCENT RITUAL

In 1979 anthropologist Victor Turner reported on his collaboration with director and performance theorist Richard Schechner in designing exploratory workshops on selected Ndembu rites. Turner refers to such experiments as "enthnographic drama" (1979:91); Schechner, as "restored behavior" (1979:21).

In 1980, after collaborating with anthropologist Colin Turnbull, director Peter Brook (1968) presented a repertoire of performances, including "The Conference of the Birds" and "The Ik." In addition, individual members of Brook's Le Centre International de Creations Theatrales performed "A Dybbuk for Two People" and "Interrogations," a piece based on Zen Koans. All these performances were powerfully marked by ritual qualities.

In 1977–1981 Jerzy Grotowski (1973, 1978) of the Polish Theater Laboratory collaborated with an international group, including part of a Voodoo community from Haiti, in the Theater of Sources Project, which involved participants bodily in a search for the sources of ritual.

And in the summer of 1981 John Fox and Welfare State International of England, a group of "civic magicians" who design public celebrations, collaborated with Toronto Island residents in developing a week of celebration rites called "The Tempest on Snake Island."

These events epitomize a kind of action crucial to both the practice and study of religion, particularly ritual studies. I was invited as a participant–observer to the last two and have observed some of the results of the first two. Although important differences mark the experiments, they share a common ethos. They tap the cross-cultural resources of ritual and try to shake theater out of the slumber of aestheticism. They also foster enactments closely akin to those of religious practice. The attitude of these experimenters-with-symbolic-processes is neither pre-modern naïveté nor modern secular irony. Instead, their mood is highly reflexive and seriously ludic, with a strong emphasis on processual motifs such as flight, search, transformation, flow, and pilgrimage. Sustained and, I think, successful attempts to generate post-modern ritual processes and actively incubate religious symbols are occurring outside the domains of sectarian movements or traditional religious institutions.

DEFINING RITUAL

Taxonomies of action are not nearly so developed as generic studies of literary modes (see Gerhart, 1977; Tyson, 1975); so current terminology is makeshift. We use words such as "opus-process" (Grotowski, 1978:11), "paratheatrical event" (Mennen, 1976:1), "restored behavior" (Schechner, 1979:1), "ethnographic drama" (Turner, 1979:91), "liminoid phenomenon" (Turner, 1978:ch.1), and "parashamanism" (see Chapter 15), as well as the many "ritual" derivatives such as "ritual exploration," "meta-ritual," and "ritual exercise." The proliferation of hyphenated terms and coining of neologisms are indications that a nascent genre of action, to which I refer as "ritualizing," is precipitating a new view of ritual itself.

Victor Turner's theories, especially his notions of the liminoid and communitas, continue to be fruitful for interpreting creative, processual elements in ritual. However, the definition of ritual which he uses does not convey the sense of it one finds in either his theories or the collaborative explorations./1/ He defines ritual as "formal behavior prescribed for occasions not given over to technological routine that have reference to beliefs in mystical beings or powers" (1978:243).

This definition is not satisfactory for several reasons which I will summarize but not elaborate: (1) Rituals are sometimes composed of de-formalizing behavior. "High" ritual moments may be more formalized than moments of ordinary action, but "low" ones may be less formalized. De-formalization is an important ritual strategy, not to be excluded or ignored by definition. (2) Magical rites are occasions which refer to mystical powers in a technological manner, so ritual must not be definitionally separated from technology. (3) Not all ritual traditions or religions refer to mystical beings or powers. Zen Buddhism is a prime example. (4) Technological routine itself has a ritual quality which ought not be overlooked simply because it does not refer to divine beings.

Most definitions of ritual are disappointing because they define the word too narrowly or lack fruitful images. Turner's genius is to have amplified a fertile image of ritual, namely, threshold-crossing. His expanding this image to include not only the liminal phase of rites of passage in traditional cultures but also liminoid phenomena in post-modern, industrial cultures implies, I think, the definition of ritualizing I am about to propose.

Defining is an action of boundary-marking; it is a framing which establishes a center/periphery or figure/ground relation. Hence defining, like footnoting (see Lincoln, 1977), is a scholarly ritual in verbal form. Dictionary definitions, like many scholarly ones, express consensus views. Often they are functionally conservative. But not all defining, any more than all ritualizing, is by definition functionally conservative. Definitions may demarcate an established field and thus assert scholarly territoriality. But they may also point to unmapped frontiers in order to turn attention away from overworked areas.

A "hard" definition is an abstractly stated consensus established by a tradition of usage and calling attention to what is in bounds. A "soft" one typically congeals around nascent phenomena and calls attention to the bounding process itself or to the spaces between boundaries. It operates like a naming rite and develops largely on the basis of images. A hard definition of ritual is a "model of" (Geertz, 1966:7) properties of known rituals. A soft one is a "model for" attending to what is yet relatively unknown about them. Hard definitions attempt to establish a clear figure. Soft ones aim at surveying and connecting adjacent fields. I propose to comment on the following "soft" definition for "ritualizing," the process whereby ritual creativity is exercised:

> Ritualizing transpires as animated persons enact formative gestures in the face of receptivity during crucial times in founded places.

RITUALIZING

Like "myth," when it is used as a synonym for "false belief," "ritual" has a bad reputation. In popular usage it connotes "boring, empty routine."

The usual scholarly view is that ritual is: (1) repeated (e.g., every Sabbath); (2) sacred (related to the Holy, of utmost significance); (3) formalized (consisting of prescribed, unchanging movements such as bowing or kneeling); (4) traditional (not being done for the first time, claiming an ancient history or authorized by myth); and (5) intentional (non-random actions, done with awareness of some reason or meaning).

The popular definition of ritual identifies it pejoratively with bad ritual, and the scholarly one, I suggest, too narrowly, with liturgical ritual. I want to speak of "creative" or "nascent" ritual, so I use the name "ritualizing." Ritualizing is, of course, closely related to the ritulization mode discussed in Chapter 3. Ritualizing is an attempt to activate, and become aware of, preconscious ritualization processes.

Ritualizing is a process which occurs continually, and it may or may not result in stable structures that a culture deems "rituals." Ritual includes a variety of types, which I have identified previously. Not all of them are handed down solely by cultural means, nor do they all come from definable or longstanding traditions. Ritualizing emerges periodically in the interface between our cultural and genetic heritage. Some rituals are intentionally chosen, but others arise spontaneously or preconsciously. The danger of defining ritual in terms of more mature or sacred examples such as the Passover celebration or the Mass is that we miss the continuity between habits, symptoms, or mannerisms, on the one hand, and civil ceremonies, formal liturgies, or ludic celebrations, on the other.

Rituals are commonly spoken of as paradigms, models, or structures. They are regarded as ways of classifying the world. But if, in our scholarly taxonomies of these concrete ways of classifying, we do not attend to nascent, as well as more traditional, rites we fall into the conservative fallacy, which holds that rituals originated but cannot presently originate, that rituals do not change. Elements in Jung, Eliade, and Tillich tend toward this direction, but fieldstudies show that rituals do change and are, in fact, being created. Therefore, I speak of "ritualizing" when I want to call attention to their originative moments.

An example of nascent ritualizing is the simple but important discovery in three groups I have observed that people asked to walk in random directions choose a counterclockwise direction more frequently than a clockwise one. Other examples are the flapping, flowing gestures in Brook's "Conference of the Birds," guttural sounds of shadow puppets in Welfare State's "Tempest on Snake Island," and Yoshi Oida's twisting and quivering as he wrestles with Zen koans. Any of these could be read as a mannerism, symptom, or aesthetic device. But I am suggesting that the context and intentions of directors and performers increasingly warrant our reading them also as momentary ritual gestures. When ritualizing instances such as these are recognized and developed, they become rites of passage, seasonal rites, meditative practices, carnival celebrations, and so on. But without an eye for their fragile first presence and a protected place for their incubation, we regularly abort the newest forms of ritual life, regarding them as symptoms of obsession-compulsion and habituation or ignoring them altogether as random and meaningless.

TRANSPIRES

Rituals are events; they have lifespans. Only secondarily do they reside in texts, scenarios, scripts, or rubrics. Thinking of them as unchanging is a half-truth. They are not artifacts. They are not structures in the sense that a building is a structure. They are structurings, as a dance is. They surge and subside, ebb and flow. One can infer the structure of a ritual. But the inference is not the event. A ritual structure, like a ritual text, is a residue. And texts, as Walter Ong (1977:421) reminds us, are monuments. Rituals deteriorate. Entropy is the rule; therefore, they must be raised up constantly from the grave of book, body, memory, and culture. Rituals have lifecycles and lifespans. They occur. They do not merely recur. A ritual is a performance, a "going through form." Schechner coins the provocative word "transformance" (1977:71) to suggest the change-evoking possibilities of ritual.

"Ritual process," currently a much used term, encompasses numerous forms of ritual change: (1) the historical development, or revision, of a ritual, (2) the phases internal to a particular rite, (3) the "processing" of persons by a ritual, (4) the changing relations between rituals and their social context, and (5) the process whereby rituals give birth to other rituals, as when "dharma combat" or Zen dokusan ("formal, master-disciple dialogue") spawns elements in ritualized actor-training workshops by Yoshi Oida.

We can no longer assume that all forms of ritual are static. "Ritual" and "tradition" are not synonyms. Ritual and creativity are not mutually exclusive. In the Theater of Sources project, for example, Saint Soleil, a Haitian group, had two animator-directors, as well as a traditional Voodoo houngan ("priest"). Creativity as well as convention were evident. Rituals are not "givens," because we just as surely create them as we receive them from traditions and revelations. Ritualizing is the action by which we mediate what is given and what is made, what is involuntary and what is chosen.

Rituals transpire (trans, spirare = to breathe across). Like breathing, ritual fluxuates in frequency, force, and volume according to its cultural context. The cultural animators of Welfare State International, for instance, give domestic force to celebration rites when they do child-namings, civic force when they ritually burn Parliament on Guy Fawkes Day, and dramatic force when they do performances in theater festivals. They often design one-time events which are built and then deteriorate or go up in smoke. This breathlike rhythm is constitutive of their sense of ritual.

Breath is containable (we can blow up balloons) and it is controllable (we can blow smoke rings). But breathing always gets away from us. Likewise ritual. We can form it and modulate it, but because it is a response to processes that encompass and exceed us, we cannot contain it for long. It escapes, finds other forms, and spawns new modes.   As for breathing, so for ritualizing: their semi-voluntary, life-sustaining, phasic qualities are central.

Rituals typically have phases but seldom anything like a plot. As a result, they cannot survive well by virtue of their entertainment value, as myths sometimes are able to do because of their narrative force.   Ritualizing requires monotony and meandering; it is not reducible to causal, narrative, or rational sequences.   This driftiness of logic and storyline is undramatic, even though rituals may abound in theatrical elements, such as the greatly elaborated, elegantly proliferated symbols one finds in Hispanic fiesta Masses. For this reason a culture whose sense of symbol is largely narrativistic and climactic, as ours is, sometimes finds rituals boring.   Ritual actions, we might say, curve with indirection or ambivalence; they have high evocative power but low entertainment value.   While ritualizing, we pursue what compels us.

AS ANIMATED PERSONS

Who is the subject, or actor, of ritualizing is a complex question. One ritual actor does not necessarily displace another. Ritual actors are personae, so we begin to suspect ritualizing is occurring whenever a layering or stripping of identities intensifies. Ritualizing tends to co-vary directly with the coalescing of classificatory distinctions ordinarily kept separate, for instance, male/female, divine/demonic, human/animal. In "A Dybbuk for Two People" a deported spirit and an onstage character become so identified in a human actor, yet remain so separate, that they mutually animate one another.

A person engaged in ritualizing is surrounded by brackets (which call attention to the parenthetical quality of what is enclosed in them); the person is in a special "frame" which transforms the relation between interior and exterior. One's exterior mask, or persona, to use the Latin root-idea, begins to resound with presence. I do not mean "mask" only in the ordinary sense of a facial covering but in the broader, etymological one, which suggests that spirit can become fully resonant in exteriority—in the skin, demeanor, and style of action. A persona can be a deceptive display, a façade, but also an external revelation of what is deeply interior or wholly other than one's ordinary self. So by "persons" I mean to connote personae as they concretize and display values by means such as clothing, facial gesture, posture, or even objects. A person is one who invests surfaces with a sense of significance.

A "person" in this sense may or may not be human. Humans do not have exclusive rights to ritualizing, as ethologists studying the mating and aggressive actions of animals have amply demonstrated (Huxley, 1966). Furthermore, ritual experiments in shamanism such as those conducted by Michael Harner at the Center for Shamanic Studies suggest that "dancing one's animal" (1980:66) is a post-modern possiblity. The anima can manifest the persona of a divine animal.

Whether the ritual persona is anthropomorphic, theomorphic, zoomorphic, or otherwise, it is an animated persona, or, at least, it awaits animation. To animate is to "enspirit." However, rituals left unattended atrophy; personae ossify and become mere dead, exterior things. So enlivening is needed. Illusion, sin, loss of potency, and lack of awareness are but a few of the ways of identifying what necessitates the continual re-animation of persons in ritualizing processes.

Ritualizing usually presupposes that animation does not reside permanently in the exterior, which is why exteriority so easily is regarded as an inert shell awaiting a breath of life. So I use the term "animation" because it suggests that the compelling force of ritual exceeds private ownership. Whether we imagine the animating power as a soul, deeper self, god, state, spirit, animal, cosmos, or society, the body in some sense borrows the life breathed into it. In this respect all ritual persons are mask- or puppet-like. This quality of contemporary ritual actors is marvelously illustrated by Bread and Puppet Theater, as the giant puppet head of the washerwoman in "Washerwoman Nativity" seems to animate the tiny human legs and arms of the animator below it.

ENACT

"Act" is the proper root word. "Behavior" is what an observer sees. "Action" is what someone does. An "actor" is both one who does and one who pretends to do. A ritual enactment is not an ordinary action like changing a tire, nor is it an imitation of an action such as pretending to die on a stage. Rather, it is a kind of action which is in a category distinct from either of these. It is action thick with sensory meaning. Ritual action should not be considered "transcendent" in contrast to dramatic action, which is "pretend." Such a view does violence both to theater and to religion. Ritual personages often put-on, and theater people sometimes find acting to be a mode of real contact with "The Wholly Other." The difference between ritual and drama, then, has to do, not with the differences between belief and make-belief or doing and pretending, but with the degree to which the acting in both senses is felt to be in touch with inescapable rhythms (like the Tao), historically definitive transitions (like the Exodus), or deep processes (like the collective unconscious).

The enactment which a ritual actor performs is not necessarily goal-oriented or intentional.   Unintentional, non-goal oriented actions such as playing and gambolling, as well as preconscious habits and mannerisms, must not be excluded by definition from ritual, since they are the seedbeds of ritualizing.   Ritual does not originate solely in, nor is it exhaustively explainable by, conscious actions and theological rationale.   Particularly in Grotowski's forest explorations, participants learn to run, whirl, dance, and walk with a kind of circular, sensory attunement to the environment without the intervention of conscious intentionality.

Ritual actions are not without sense just because those doing them cannot say what the actions mean.   Ecclesiastical liturgies and civil ceremonies may have verbal meanings codified or separable from their actions, but these are specific instances and should not be considered definitive for nascent ritualizing.   Neither rituals nor their symbols necessarily have "meaning," a metaphor borrowed with only partial success from linguistics (Sperber, 1975).   Rituals are deeds; they are not just colorful or oblique ways of "saying" something.

In ritual enactment we attempt to wed the indicative and subjunctive, the literal and symbolic, the real and the dramatic.   In Brook's "Conference of the Birds" we know we are seeing ordinary people moving with colored strips of cloth, yet we also know we have seen the real Hoopoe bird and followed it to the king.   In ritualizing, we act in the interstices between pragmatic acts and imitations of actions.   In doing so, one may build huts or enact roles, but such acts are not definitive of ritualizing.   What is definitive are enactments that momentarily bridge the real/dramatic split by embodying it.

Apart from embodiment no ritual enactment transpires (see Dixon, 1976:419). Even rituals such as meditative ones, calculated to deny or overcome the tangible, use the body in order to effect this denial. And even when the body is decorated or mutilated with tatoos, circumcisions, and subincisions, or is so heavily draped and costumed that it becomes a thing, it remains the central, concrete fact of ritual.   The study of ritual fails, then, if it ignores the tangibility and subjectivity of ritual enactment and only objectifies (see Driver, 1978).

FORMATIVE GESTURES

It is common to regard rituals as enactments of myths, theological ideas, or moral principles. The result of these views has been to reduce ritual to mere illustration or to treat the body as if it were only incidental to enactment. The ritualizing moment, when enactments begin to form, is a non-discursive, bodily way of knowing, not to be disparaged when it lacks narrative or systematic elaboration. In fact, intellectual exegesis, especially in the midst of nascent ritual, can insure its deformation, if not its death. So I am suggesting that "formative gestures" are primary, and narrative, moral, or intellectual formulations secondary, objects of enactment. If, for example, I want to interpret a Haitian dance before Saint Soleil ("Holy Sun"), I should attend to the style and rhythm of the dance's gestures before leaping to stories or expositions associated with it. Ritual studies proceeds best if we attend first to a ritual's least verbalizable qualities, its "choreography" and "musicality," and then to its "meaning" or "function." Done in reverse order, interpreters often find lots of "meaningless" gestures which never receive the dignity of being regarded as symbols.

Ritual actions, such as eating or drinking during the Eucharist, can inform basic gestural values, for instance, those held by a consumer-oriented society. But the reverse is also true: social values can penetrate ritual gestures, as might happen when an agape ("love") feast is revived by a consumer-oriented society. Ritual gestures constitute a class of mediating actions which transform the style and values of everyday action, thereby becoming the very ground of action itself. Ritual gesture, therefore, always concerns the sources of action.

The basic unit of ritual is a symbol, but not every symbol is ritualistic. Only those symbols which are, or evoke, gestures are of ritualistic significance. A symbolic object, for example, a statue of the Boddhisatva Kuan-yin, because it is easier to isolate, can draw our attention away from the actions it evokes. The interpretion of an action is more difficult than the interpretation of an object, but this should not prevent our focusing interpretive efforts on gesture, the heart of ritualizing. The color red, a circular shape, a totem pole, a sacred grove are ritual symbols only by virtue of the symbolic gestures they evoke.

Gesturing and posturing, the fundamental units of ritual enactment, are dialectically related to the baseline of ordinary interaction, even though they may be embedded in it. Enactment consists of not only socially warranted gestures or those based on a scenario or text but also unconsciously animated actions. And gestures so motivated may appear twisted, oblique, or exaggerated to such a degree that they elicit interpretations which are themselves symbolic. In other words, ritualizing tends to set in motion a regressive series of interpretations, the languages (or actions) of which are themselves quasi-ritualistic.

A gesture, in the strict sense of the word, is a dynamic symbolic act which contrasts with posture, a symbolic stilling of action. But in its broader usage "gesture" includes both movements and poses as bearers of evocative power. In this broader sense "gesture" is virtually a synonym for "attitude." An attitude is not simply a state of mind or set of values. It is the total bearing of a body expressing a valued style of living. A ship's attitude is its tilt, which expresses the dynamic interplay among the direction and force of the wind, the weight of the boat, and the size of its sails. To interpret a ritual attitude, one must learn to recognize style, and style is hardly perceivable with one viewing. We only recognize an actor's style by seeing him or her in several roles.

Whether we consider gesture, style, attitude, or symbolic action, avoiding excessive reification is important, so I have added the qualifier "formative." Others might have said "archetypal," "fundamental," or "paradigmatic." However, these ways of putting the matter have a history of becoming entangled with static objectifications. As soon as we utter them, we begin assuming there are models, archetypes, or paradigms lurking somewhere. As soon as we say "forms" instead of "formative," we can easily lose track of the flowlike, verblike qualities of ritual.

A gesture is an evocative rhythm embodied in an enactment (see Delattre, 1978:282-284). What it evokes are the feelings and sensibilities that can be said to be "generative" or "formative" of culture. A good example of formative gesturing in Welfare State's "Tempest" project with the Toronto Islanders was the construction and ritual destruction of cultural monuments, for instance, a model CN Tower ("the world's tallest freestanding structure") and a cardboard reproduction of the Toronto skyline. The group used junk and refuse that had washed ashore, built a momentary symbolic city, and then returned it to junk again. If such a gestural rhythm of construction and destruction were deeply absorbed by participants, I would expect to find new cultural values forming outside the celebration. We might find, for example, a more creative use of discarded materials or less need for architectural displays of technological prowess.

Among performance artists the gesture of recycling is becoming a useful metaphor for the way ritualizing itself occurs. Romantic symbol theorists, such as Thomas Carlisle, William Blake, and Samuel Taylor Coleridge, usually set organic and industrial metaphors in opposition: one "gestates" rather than "constructs" symbols. Re-cycling, not just as an environmental ideology, but as a metaphor for ritual creativity, combines organic and industrial metaphors. The metaphor implies that one must "receive," as well as "create," ritual gestures. Ritualizing is how we actively await formative pulsations. The goal of ritualizing activities is not to be original—this is a modern aesthetic concern—but to locate and attend to originative impulses.

Ritualizing activities, such as Grotowski's experiments with running, whirling, and walking in the Polish "forest womb," are not formalized as, say, the wedding walk is in Protestant ceremonies. The gestures are "formative," which means they are transformatively related to everyday actions. A formative gesture emerges in a way that enables either formalization or deformalization. Both are of ritual value, but the study of ritual has wrongly concentrated all its energies on the positive, formal instances. The negative aspects are most obvious in certain meditation rites, rites of rebellion, and carnival inversion. In these a minus sign is gesturally posted before cultural forms. In Welfare State's ritual clowning and mumming, to cite one example, a minus is placed before the ritual form itself: a Caliban figure baptizes us with polluted water from Lake Ontario.

Formative gestures are physical ways of searching for the sources of creativity, struggling to connect what feels disconnected, trying to discern climactic turns in ongoing processes, and becoming receptive to death or other radical transformations. Ritualizing is a mode of knowing (see Jennings, 1981) in which knower and known conjoin. The outcome can serve either to maintain or undermine psychosocial chasms, but in either case it not only elicits reflection on cultural forms but re-shapes our bodies, and thus our minds, to be congruent with these forms. Ritualizing enactments operate dialectically under circumstances in which polarities are too important to be chosen between. Participants seek some third way on a plane different from that occupied by the first two alternatives. A ritual enactment is an attempt to comment gesturally on a psychosocial double-bind (see Bateson, 1972). But since ritualizing must embody the very rift it would reflect on, the mood of it becomes more ambivalent the closer its gestures come to revealing the vulnerable heart of some psychosocial rift. Ritual enactment at once awakens the reflexivity of consciousness and tranquilizes the anxiety provoked by doing so. Torontonians were delighted to see their city and tower symbolically burned by Welfare State; they were also horrified. Ambivalence is the heart of a ritualizing attitude.

IN THE FACE OF RECEPTIVITY

Ritualizing is enactment in the face of imagined, socially experienced, and mythologically construed receptivity. For ritualizing to occur, the surroundings must expose a vulnerable (vulner = wound) side. Whether the vulnerability stems from a human or divine face does not seem definitive, but that some aspect of the cosmos appear to be responsive is necessary for ritualizing to gestate. The more deeply an enactment is received, the more an audience becomes a congregation and the more a performance becomes ritualized. "Sacred" is the name we give to the deepest forms of receptivity in our experience.

One's "face," as I am using the term, reveals formative attitudes. To "countenance" is to show an attitude of support. The face before which ritualizing is enacted is not reducible to the mere surface, or front part, of something. Rather, the face is that facet upon which some action depends. This is the sense of the word when we speak of "the face of a document" or "losing face." For most of us our face is the exterior area by which presence is mediated to others. It is that tangible surface by which vulnerbility is exposed or withheld.

In Western cultures we regard our faces, or perhaps our gentials, as our most vulnerable physical areas, so actions emanating from them tend to be the most ritualized by gestures of guarding or displaying. When analyzing a specific ritual, we must always ask where a given culture locates its faces and how it stylizes them into countenances.

Because receptivity is essential to ritualizing, gestural enactment always has a communicative, as well as cognitive, dimension, even when it is performed in solitude. A ritual enactment must be received by others, perhaps the Wholly Other, perhaps the ancestors, perhaps the powers that be, perhaps a therapist, perhaps only the tourists and anthroplogists.

The face of receptivity is variously named: "emptiness," "a supportive community," "God." And it is variously located in the unconscious, society, surrounding environment, or attendant spirits. Sometimes the principle of receptivity is in need of energizing by the actions of ritual; at other times it is actively solicitous. In either case, the face of receptivity is not objectifiable, though it is "other." It is as much inside the ritual actor as outside.

In grammar we differentiate the active and passive "voices" of verbs. When interpreting ritual processes, we likewise distinguish action and receptivity. A decline in the importance of ritual is usually signalled by a symptomatic loss of receptivity and a consequent confusion of enactment with sheer willful activity divorced from cultivated passivity. If we consider rites in terms of their active-passive "ratio," magical rites are high on the active side and meditative ones, on the receptive side. It is no accident, then, that the ritually creative projects developed by directors like Grotowski, Brook, and Fox are characterized by a specifically meditative or celebrative ethos.

DURING CRUCIAL TIMES

Crucial times are "cross-tensed" in a variety of ways. Cyclical time is a crossing of present and past; eschatological time, of present and future. We are too prone to regard as timeless all senses of time other than the chronological. But notions like "the eternal now" (Tillich), "eternal return" (Eliade), "dreamtime" (the Arunta alcheringa), as well as the "just now" of Gestalt or Zen, are not identical. The sense of timing in a ritual is as distinctive as it is in a piece of music.

One kind of ritual time is associated with transitions—changes in social status, seasonal transitions, and crisis moments in histories and lifecycles. Ritualizing often precipitates or accompanies a sense of "the time between the times" and so is manifested by gestures which heighten feelings and calm them with monotony in the same moment. Grotowski collects watches and takes participants on unscheduled night prowlings, and Fox schedules "Tempest" to coincide with sunset in order to displace the usual sense of chronologically ordered time.

Ritual is formative of the ways we bide our time. Rituals concentrate, and thereby consecrate, time. The auspicious moment (Booth, 1969), the kairos, is a pulse of opening and closing. It occurs when enactment and receptivity are in synchrony. Such times can occur without warning in illness, disaster, or social breach./2/ Ritualizing processes spontaneously proliferate in these moments. No one has to decide to create them. So, unlike established ceremonies and liturgies, they do not have to be regularly repeated. This sense of transition time is a hotbed of nascent ritual symbols. Times concentrated in this manner feel timeless, quick, of short duration.

Another sense of crucial timing is "anticipated time," or what some, following Mircea Eliade (1959:ch.2), call "circular time." Circular time is not the only form of ritually concentrated time, though this is the view of many who talk about ritual. The return of the Sabbath, the arrival of yet another new year, commencement day for still another class of graduates are times which establish the cycles that constitute our sense of the way things flow. We know they are coming; they do not surprise us. In them time is not "timeless," leaving us feeling as though it hardly exists. Rather it is "timeful." It weighs on us; it reminds us. In this kind of time we ponder the weight of the ages. Unlike "unanticipated transition time," this "anticipated returning time" is not focused at a point and experienced as a breakthrough or breakup. Instead, it feels like an overlap or reversion.

We must not forget, then, that ritually crucial times involve both: once-in-a-life times and here-we-go-again times. The former are more characteristic of artists' experiments with ritualizing processes, the latter, of civil ceremonies and traditional liturgical rites. A rite of passage combines both examples of ritual time.

IN FOUNDED PLACES

Founding may occur literally, for example, when a group of Poles and Haitians construct a "forest womb" or a group of English and Canadians establish "stations" for a procession-celebration on Snake Island. There are many ways to set aside the foundational substructure of ritual. But founding a space may also occur by defining an area with actions, rather than cordoning off an area with rope or erecting huts. Snake Island became a "founded" place by our processions to it and dances on it; the Polish forest, by our standing still among its trees, lying on its floor, and crawling through its underbrush.

"Space," which is empty, uniform, and abstract, is given shape and life so it may become a ritual "place" such as a burial ground, courtroom, or cathedral. All of these are curiously vacant, even haunting, when the actions of ritual are not occurring in them. Ritual place is a matrix of ritual life. It is a generative center, though it may be geographically on the edges. A founded place is sequestered from the hubbub, even when it consists only of a circle formed by Welfare State musicians in an urban shopping center. A founded place is a forcefield eliciting gestures from ritual actors.

Ritualizing may occur without objects or implements but not without founded (fundus = "bottom," "fundamental") places. Ritual traditions differ in their views about the length of time such a place is pregnant with formative power. For some, the founding ends the moment the action ceases. For others, the place is set aside once-for-all by consecration.

Founded space and sacred objects coalesce in the art of the "new ritual artists," many of whom are painters or sculptors who emphasize wrapped, layered, and bundled assemblages large enough to enclose people and elicit formal installations or other ritual actions (Murray, 1980). Founding, essential to all ritual, public and esoteric, occurs with the establishment of perspectival boundaries: inside/outside, hidden/revealed, open/closed, front/back. The distinction participant/observer is most fundamentally displayed by where and how one stands when ritual action is occurring. Not only is space founded to become ritual place, but actors themselves become grounded by acting in it. We hide, display, and boundary-mark ourselves by the way we transform space into place. How we do this determines the extent to which we are an insider or outsider. The ways we cross boundaries of founded places say who we are.

Founding is more than mere, neutral setting aside. It is to sequester, to spirit away; the action, implicitly at least, hides as much as it reveals. Of course there are public rituals; not all rites are esoteric. But even public rituals display, however minimally, some potentially secretive quality. Often the mere establishment of a front and back side of the action is enough to effect this.

NAMING EMERGENT GENRES OF ACTION

> Ritualizing transpires as animated persons enact formative gestures in the face of receptivity during crucial times in founded places.

By naming ritualizing in this fashion, I am arguing for the legitimacy of explorations such as those of Grotowski and the Haitians, Welfare State International and the Toronto Islanders, Brook and Turnbull, Schechner and Turner. Ricoeur says that naming a genre is not a mere nominalistic exercise: "To master a genre is to master a 'competence' which offers practical guidelines for 'performing' an individual work" (1973:135). To engage in ritualizing processes is to conduct research, not just on, but in, ritual. This is a fact of post-modern culture. And it is a phenomenon no longer easily written off as private pathology, idiosyncracy, or irresponsible syncretism. Post-modern ritualizing has indissoluble links to both theater and healing, and my way of defining it, I hope, lays theoretical grounds for developing the connections further.

Directors and therapists establish founded places. Therapists see clients at crucial times. Artists and counselors are attentive to gestural symbols. Actors aspire to animate audiences, and therapists aspire to provide faces of receptivity. And so on. These facts are bound to provoke the question, "How does ritualizing differ from theater and therapy?" In some cases, not at all—especially in traditional shamanic and post-modern, liminoid sub-cultures such as experimental theater circles. If each of the terms of my soft definition is treated as a criterion, current dramatic and healing practices sometimes appear ritual-like, but often crucial factors are missing for ritualizing processes to develop into established ritual structures. A great deal of theoretical and field research is needed before we can specify with any confidence how rituals and ritual systems develop from nascent ritualizing processes. Processual and developmental thinking about rituals is relatively recent /3/, but already it shows us that we have erroneously defined the whole of ritual in terms of its middle phases to the neglect of its emergent and decaying ones. A clear priority for ritual studies is the formulation of precise, developmental typologies which do not preclude our connecting ritualization among animals, personal mannerisms, decorous actions, civil ceremony, liturgy, and celebration events. Therefore, I hope ritual studies goes easy on exclusive, hard defining, since this scholarly strategy of boundary-marking is more useful for the middle-age of a field. Instead, by more softly naming nascent ritualizing, we can recognize and nurture what is still in incubatory phases.

NOTES

/1/ Two provocative, but less well known, definitions of ritual are as follows: Rituals are "The acting out of metaphoric predication upon incohate pronouns which are in need of movement" (Fernandez, 1971:56) and "Those carefully rehearsed symbolic motions and gestures through which we regularly go, in which we articulate the felt shape and rhythm of our own humanity and of reality as we experience it, and by means of which we negotiate the terms or conditions for our presence among and our participation in the plurality of realities through which our humanity makes its passage" (Delattre 1978:282).

/2/ Victor Turner (1974a:ch.2,3) has provided two excellent studies of ritual processes in the midst of social breach. One is on the Mexican Revolution, the other on the clash between Thomas Becket and Henry II.

/3/ Besides the work of Turner, Erik Erikson's "The Development of Ritualization" (1968) is especially important in this regard.

PART II

RITUAL PROCESSES

INTRODUCTION

Whether one wants to study ritual symbols, structures, or processes, an interpreter is confronted with a number of methods. Among them are typological, comparative, and modal strategies. All three are cross-cultural, though the first and third can be used within a single ritual system. "Process" easily degenerates into a catchword these days. It sometimes is used as a polemical opposite to "product" or "structure." I have already suggested that we should specify which ritual process we are considering, since a number of different ones are encompassed by the term. Whether an isolable element is regarded as a structure or process is not always immediately obvious, since the distinction is typically an observer-, not a participant-, category. Because of the imprecision of language, as well as the squabbling of rival schools of thought, an interpreter is often unsure whether disagreements are genuine or merely verbal, since every process presupposes a structure, and vice-versa.

In this part I avoid summarizing or criticizing the discussions about ritual processes in order to illustrate some of the processes themselves. Chapter 5 treats the ritual action of masking and identifies several types of attitudes toward it. Chapter 6 compares sitting and eating, the central gestures of two ritual systems, Soto Zen and Catholicism. The next chapter looks again at Zen but, instead of focusing on the paradigmatic gesture, looks at the ritual system surrounding it.

CHAPTER 5

MASKING

Ritual studies attends to the styles, stories, and experiences of both observer-interpreters and participants. It also attends to theories, typologies, and phenomenologies in order to interpret symbolic actions. In addition to these two basic strategies, it sometimes isolates gestures for description, comparison, or interpretation. Masking is a widely found ritual gesture, and comparing its modes can be as productive as comparing whole rituals.

An interpreter of ritual must pay serious attention to the surfaces of things. Even if one assumes that a ritual performance implies a deep structure, access to that structure leads through an exterior which, as Boehme and Paracelsus suggested, bears the "signature" of an essential interior. But reading the signature of an exterior is no easy matter. Only recently in the field of kinesics has anyone begun systematically to write a grammar of gesture with sufficient precision that we might learn to speak as penetratingly of symbolic actions as of words and sentences. Ritual studies needs to collaborate with anthropology and psychology in producing some rather careful, detailed microkinesic studies of religious body motion along the lines illustrated by Ray Birdwhistell's provocative analyses of diaper changing, smoking, and smiling in his KINESICS AND CONTEXT (1970).

Meanwhile, I would like to offer a broader phenomenological sketch of one kind of ritual gesture, namely, masking. By "masking" I mean to include what we ordinarily think of as masks, but I also intend to encompass any mode of facial stylization, including make-up and the expressions we wear. My concern is not the ethnographic one of describing and classifying kinds of masks, nor is it the historical one of interpreting a set of masks in a specific historical and cultural setting. Rather, I propose to inquire into the possibilities of the act of masking. My question is, "In what ways might we interpret the act of donning a mask, regardless of who wears it and what it looks like?" I will offer here a typology of four moments in the masking process: (1) concretion, (2) concealment, (3) embodiment, and (4) expression.

First, however, I must say a word about the problem of definition. It might seem a simple matter to decide what a mask is, but the variety of phenomena complicates the matter. The Dogon have a "Great Mask" (iminana) which is displayed every sixty years and is nearly thirty feet long. Obviously, no one wears it. Yet it is a mask despite its lack of an animate human figure inside. Masks are sometimes treated as sculpture by art historians and aesthetic anthropologists, but such treatments ignore the illusion of "wearability" which separates mask from sculpture. Even though the Dogon Great Mask is not worn, it is an iconographic semblance of an exteriority which presupposes a human or divine interiority.

Definitional problems are also presented by headdress masks, veils, miniature masks, face paint, and make-up./1/ Some masks are worn on the body. Some are carried. Some are worn on top of the head so they can be seen by the deities above. And some are for practical or protective purposes, e.g., gas masks and surgical masks. Since I am concerned here with the interpretation of masking as a symbolic action, I will eliminate practical masks from consideration and concentrate on those with cultural, religious, or dramatic meanings. But I propose to define the phenomenon of masking broadly enough to include any body-transforming device concerned with the head area. This includes masks worn on the top or back of the head, stylized facial gestures, masks not worn at all, death masks, and masks merely carried or displayed. Masking is the making of a "second face," and the variety of masks derives from the multiplicity of ways in which cultures construe this second face in relation to the primary one.

MASKING AS CONCRETION

When a human exterior is interpreted as the bodying forth or fixing of an external power, I speak of "concretion." I can best illustrate what I mean by referring to two examples of masking, the use of death masks, especially in nineteenth century Europe, and the use of half-masks in Italian commedia dell' arte. Perhaps the most consistent feature of masks is their fixity or rigidity. When masks develop moving parts, as in Japan, they typically do so as part of puppetry, which is a different form of exteriorization (one which I will not discuss here). It is no accident that Lommel (1972:217) regards the death mask, along with the animal mask, as the basic prototype for all masks. Dying, like masking, is a rigidifying process. In the view of many people, personhood, though it remains effective after death, nevertheless is fixed by death. The fixed is not to be confused with the powerless. In fact, a death mask is a means of appropriating the power of deceased personhood. To die is not to become powerless, but to become powerful in a fixed mode. A dead face is static when considered formally, but the observation of such a sight is a moving experience.

The widespread use of death masks in Peru, Central America, Japan, Africa, and Melanesia has either historical or formal relations to head- and scalp-hunting in the Americas. Whether the head is of a friend, ancestor, or enemy, it concretizes the power of its previous owner and can be appropriated by one's carrying or wearing it, or even by wearing masks modeled after the deceased. Dying is lapsing into rigidity, and masking-after-the-dead is testimony to the power of an exterior. As one writer put it, "By masking, one unmasks a supernatural source" (Anon., 1972:18).

Even Europe has known the ritualistic use of death masks, particularly by royalty and among the privileged classes. The making of death masks was part of a complex ritual involving the construction of life-size wax and wicker effigies and mannequins of French and English royalty for use at their funerals. Since the effigies were modeled as if the king were alive, and the actual body was in a closed coffin, the royal personage could, in effect, reign over his own funeral. Even as late as 1793 such an effigy was made of the murdered Jean-Paul Marat and used for revolutionary propaganda. Ernst Benkard argues that only after the French Revolution did the making of death masks become a possibility for non-royalty. Hence, the casting of such masks reached its vogue in the nineteenth century.

Benkard calls the death mask a "boundary mark" which divides two mysteries, life and death, and he argues that the death mask of Gotthold Ephraim Lessing (d. 1781) is the first example of a "death mask taken purely in reverence" (1929:37,40). With this mask, he claims, the custom is freed of superstition, magic, and witchcraft, but not, I might add, from German Christian idealism, for Benkard concludes, ". . . The death mask becomes symbolic of the faith that death, though it parts us, can never dissolve a spiritual bond" (38).

Though the distance is considerable between a mask interpreted as an incarnation of the dead, on the one hand, and a symbol of the dead, on the other, a death mask is nevertheless regarded with awe and reverence because of what it effects. Whether the mask's power is attributed to magical causality or memory, a plaster or wooden mask presents a static dynamis ("power")—at once a living-dead thing and a dead-living being. So both the making and wearing of masks are activities hedged with an array of protective rites. In Africa carving frequently requires fasting, sexual abstention, and sacrifice to prevent the carver's becoming a victim of the power which his mask draws to itself (Herold, 1967:14). Masking is an activity laden with precautions and taboos in most cultures, including industrial, urban ones.

The same rigidity of a mask which lends itself so easily to the fixing of death's power among the living also lends itself to typification in Italian commedia dell' arte. Whereas a masked ritual participant is frequently a concretion of the dead, the masked actor is a type. So, in the history of European popular theater, character-types are closely associated with grotesque characters such as Harlequin and Punch, both of whom evolved from the so-called "comedy of masks." The masks of commedia were supposed to represent stereotypical, or stock, characters from various regions of Italy. Pantalone was the typical Venetian; Brighella, the typical Lombard, and so on. These characterizations were called "masks," not merely because the actors wore half-masks, but because of the stock nature of the characters themselves. The same character appeared in a multitude of plays. A character that was built up across many different plays, rather than within a single play, created the illusion that it was a living being, as Allardyce Nicoll (1963:21) has pointed out. But like any type, such a character is so familiar to the audience that it becomes predictable, frozen as it were, despite the liveliness with which roles are imaginatively played by actors. So strong was the popular masking tradition that we now speak of any list of characters (not actors), stock or not, as the dramatis personae.

A character-type is to drama what a death mask is to ritual, namely, a concretizing of dynamis in a fixed form. What is at once terrifying and comical, if not grotesque, about masked figures is the paradox of form and dynamic. At any moment the mask can come off, revealing that it is a mere lifeless thing and the man underneath a mere mortal. But the lifeless thing also threatens to attain a life of its own, seize the pretender inside, and terrify the gawking spectators outside. A mask is a dead thing impersonating an affective being, and impersonation can be a form of either pretense or incarnation. Masked performers are comic only when they incessantly remind audiences that they are human, mortals as we are. For this reason many commedia masks were half-masks; they allowed actors to spew forth ribald profanities and other exaggerations of comic fallibility.

Typed man and dead man have a certain singularity and one-dimensionality which have immense possibilities for terrifying. As Fletcher (1964:55-68) has noted with regard to allegorical characters, their singlemindedness and one-dimensionality—their obsession with the archetypal goal—are frequently associated with the diabolically possessed or with a robot, a machine-as-a-man.

Masking-as-concretion is a reduction to one dimension, namely, to empowered exteriority. In the moment of concretion a mask is a fixation of what is normally a process, and this one-dimensionalizing is so radical that exteriority seems to develop a life of its own, a life which is quite different from the multi-dimensional, normal state which is marked by a dialectic of interior and exterior. In this moment a "second face" appears as solidified <u>dynamis</u>. The fixed face is exterior just as the dead, the demonic, and the divine are exterior to the human self. Far from being impotent because of their exteriority, they are powerful energizers of human reality because of it. Both the mask of the dead and the mask of types embody what is considered essential, if not eternal.

MASKING AS CONCEALMENT

Masking is not only an act of forming and fixing power. It can also be an act of concealing identity. To don a mask is to don otherness and doff selfhood. But if the act is incomplete—if there is a disjunction of interior and exterior, rather than a seizure of interior by exterior—dissimulation is the result. In such a case pretending does not lead to possession but to pretense. So there are really two kinds of fear involved in masking: one, more dominant in tribal and pre-industrial societies, that exterior powers will take over and run wild; and the other, found primarily in industrial, urban societies, that a mask will only partially take hold of the wearer, thus allowing a person to become merely a manager of images. Both concretion and concealment have their dangers. When masking becomes manipulation, the wearer threatens the viewers, as well as the very notion of cultural roles. From a hidden position one can scoff at the very exteriority which evokes fear in the beholder. A masker can use roles instead of playing them or becoming subject to them.

Hence, along with the playful, dramatic use of masks to create types and the ritualistic use of masks to embody the powers of the dead or nonhuman living, is the use of masks for social control. Of course, all three functions may co-exist in a single ritual, culture, or unit of symbolic action. The use of masks among Hopi and Yaqui Indians, like the performances of painted Pueblo ceremonial clowns, combines all three functions at various times in the respective ritual cycles. If one understands the structural congruence of role and mask, it is easy to comprehend the specifically cultural, not just the supernatural, danger of putting on and taking off masks. Masks are frequently the mark of secret societies and are usually the prerogative of males. Many such societies are agents of social control. Putting on masks is a form of control that requires a degree of self-consciousness about the fabric of culturally defined roles.

As long as strong ritual sanctions bear on the wearers, their manipulative power remains under control. But an individual or group of maskers may escape their fear of being possessed by what they wear. Such cases open the possibility of playing the bogeyman who punishes all _other_ violators of cultural role-propriety. In processes of concretion otherness resides in the mask; in concealing phases otherness is generated and used by the masker. In short, the wearer of masks may stand outside roles and use them to control those who observe. Masking, then, is no longer a solidification of exterior powers, but is a deception for socially acceptable ends.

Masking-as-concealment appears in the role-inversions of Mardi Gras, Halloween, and other revelrous occasions such as masquerades and some forms of the courtly masque. On these occasions whole cities or groups indulge in licensed dissimulation. Covering the face, and thereby symbolically denying or inverting roles and normally constituted facial communication, becomes more important than bodying forth a deity or a type. Who one is not becomes more important than who one is. Wearing a mask becomes a role-denial. The concretizing motive de-emphasizes the reality of a wearer and emphasizes the absolute reality of a mask-as-other, whereas the concealing motive makes sport of the reality of mask-as-role and suggests that reality is hidden deep behind the eye holes of the mask. The concealing masker exaggerates exteriority in order to break the absolute hold of roles over personal interiorities or social in-groups.

Only a fraction of an inch separates the authorization of ritual clowns to exercise social control or the licensing of ritualized revelry from the concealing practices of banditry. License is socially sanctioned role-ridicule, but the highwayman, with eyemask or bandanna, has no license. The bandit does not use anonymity for revelry, celebration, and sexual adventure, or for activities which relieve the pressure of too conscientious an observance of roles and laws. Rather, bandits use masks on the highway—on the way where travel obscures corporately defined roles. A masked highwayman does not use masks for social control but to gain power over such control. The concealer is a master of dualism.

That masks should, on the one hand, be instruments of law enforcement, and on the other, law-breaking, should not surprise those familiar with the Lone Ranger, Batman, the masked blind lady of justice, and the Ku Klux Klan. Personhood and personality are important for social interaction, but impersonality and anonymity are requisites for social enforcement or social violation. A masked hangman is like a masked highwayman. Both are outside the law, though the former is "above" it, while the latter is "below" it. No human has a right to do what either the hangman or bandit does, and since what is human is defined by cultural roles, the concealing masks symbolically suspend role and personality and puts in its place something asocial, marginal, or demonic. Hangmen and highwaymen, who often meet on the gallows, the death machine, are, at their respective moments of concealment, not persons, but powers symbolically external to the very society on which they depend for their livelihood. Orignally, hangmen wore masks to protect themselves from retaliation at the hands of friends and followers of popular heroes, but as Shalleck (1973:124) points out, the hangman later became a quasi-circusmaster, at which time he put a hood on the hanged man, ostensibly to keep him calm during the performance. The distance between hangings and circuses is not as far as one might think. Hangings present death-inducing acts; circuses, death-defying acts. Circuses, the physiologically odd; hangings, the socially marginal. Hangings, wild men; circuses, wild animals. Hangings, the misfit; circuses, the clown.

Masks to conceal seem rather consistently to appear in circumstances in which anomalous, asocial forces (dead people, deities, demons, wild animals, bandits) are breaking through classificatory grids or are being brought under social control. Culture is an arena in which are contained the masked champion and the masked antagonist in combat. Such masks are not "the self we choose" (Shalleck, 1973:3), but are roles broken loose from selves. As maskers who conceal, we become external to the culturally defined human; our externality derives from our kinship to animals, dead things, and supra- or infra-human powers. English prostitutes, the French "man in the iron mask," and the Ku Klux Klan have all employed masked identity-suspension to circumvent the legal-social order either for the purpose of attacking it or supposedly repairing it. And what they gain in power they lose in personhood.

MASKING AS EMBODIMENT

In the moment of concretion a mask is invaded from the outside, and potency assumes the form of a power-object. In the moment of concealment a mask is employed to gain power as a wearer steps to the boundaries of a culture. The term "embodiment" applies to those instances in which interior and exterior, inside and outside, are considered so in harmony as to be virtually indistinguishable. The moment of concretion is a paradoxical one; the moment of concealment is a dualistic one. And the moment of embodiment is a monistic one. Masking or, for that matter, any form of facial stylization is denied, and a claim is made for naturalness or spontaneity. A totally embodied mask would, of course, lose its dualistic relation to a hitherto trapped internality or a hitherto transcendent other. Embodied masking is frequently denied or else treated as a process of unmasking that strips off one's cultural overlay. This moment is an ecstatic one which clearly depends upon a prior iconoclastic movement.

The shell of a mask is either broken or removed not to create a space for an other, but to liberate a self that can be identical with its own body.

In the embodied moment of masking, the distinction between wearer and thing-worn is no longer made. Whereas I suggested that death masks illustrated concretion and hangmen's hoods were an example of concealment, I must now use the word "mask" in a more metaphoric sense to refer to the bodily and facial expressions we "wear." For an embodied masker, gesture and posture constitute the relevant exterior, and they are not taken off nor put on in quite the same way a wooden mask or a cloth hood is. So perhaps dance is an apt illustration of embodied masking, since a dancer must learn to stylize his or her own body to appear spontaneous.

Susanne Langer (1953:169,187) says that dance is the art most misunderstood and sentimentalized. Dance, she claims, is the art least divorced from its religious roots. She notes that the failure of dancers and its interpreters to understand the art is largely because they do not understand that it is not an expression of personal feeling or transcendent powers, but is an abstraction of imagined feelings. The feelings which are imaginatively abstracted in dancing are feelings of power. Dance is "virtual power," but dancers often forget its virtual or artistic nature. Of all the arts, dance is still the most closely tied to those aspects of religion we call "mysticism," or "religious experience." Dance has to do with the powers, though modern artistic dance is a constructed illusion of power; it is not a ritualistic arena for divine posession.

The notion of illusion seems to be integral to the embodied moment, but I distinguish two kinds of illusion, since two different interpretive points of view are at stake. Langer describes the sort of illusion which makes a virtual, formal power appear to be a transcendent one. A second form of illusion is one in which form appears to be formless, mask appears to be no-mask, and stylized facial gesture appears to be spontaneous.

I must be careful with the term "illusion" or I will bias the typology. An embodied moment is like a mystical experience, because it can only appear to an interpreter as a meaningful exterior. An interpreter of ritual has no direct access to interiority; one has only imaginative, indirect access. What appears to a wearer as either the naked power of an other or the bare power of selfhood can only appear to an observer as a stylization. Pure, ecstatic un-masking is, in this respect, an illusion. Whatever one says about embodied masking must depend upon imaginative observation and sympathetic re-enactment from an outside toward an inside. What appears as a meaningful mask to an interpreter is, a masker in this state would claim, no mask at all. Embodiment and concretion have in common their respective claims to immediate sources of power—the power of a totally immanent selfhood and the power of a holy other, respectively.

They both lay claim to ecstasy, but the ecstasy of selfhood, of course, is not identical with the ecstasy of otherness, and this difference is what separates the two moments. In concretion one puts on power by fixing it in a form; in embodiment one lays hands on power by shattering what fixes it.

Dancing and masking often occur together in a single performance. Lommel describes the conflicting unity of masking and dancing: "The effect of the mask lies in the deliberate opposition of a strict stylization and movement, often of a grotesque nature. That is to say, the 'masklike stiffness' of the face is opposed to the movements of the dance (1972:219)." Dancer and masker alike are actualizations of power. The latter suggests the fixity of sculpture and the dead. The former suggests the fluidity of winds which blow where they will. The masker puts on a mask. Though we may become deities, we are also put-ons, Wizards of Oz, tiny people hidden in rigid machines. We animate the powers that be only as a termite rides bored into a ship's beam, whereas a dancer appears to have tapped an inner power. The embodied no-mask of spontaneity, typified by the illusion of dance, is still a form of stylization and hardly a total unmasking. Dancing is not mere religio-cultural nudity, but is a dynamic form of masking.

Dancing and masking, doffing and donning, are ritualized flirtations with constitutive powers; they both long for consummation. Naked power, however, has neither rhythm nor form; so embodied masking offers rhythm, while concretized masking offers a solid form. The opposites demand one another.

MASKING AS EXPRESSION

The moment of stripping, of unmasking, is followed phenomenologically (not necessarily chronologically) by a moment in which the broken or denied mask is again tried on. Concretion gives substance to power, concealment is a hiding in order to maximize power, embodiment is the semblance of spontaneous power, and expression is the making transparent of power. Masking-as-expression does not treat a mask as a simple concretion of divine power, nor does it deny the power of masks culturally created. In the moment of expression we do not deny that we wear masks. We affirm their presence and value and accept responsibility for their functions. Furthermore, we may embrace both the concealing and embodying functions without attempting to substitute one for the other. I have taken the plaster or wooden mask as an illustration of the sensibility of concretion. I further suggest that dramatic make-up typifies the sensibility of expression. Concretion reaches its peak in magical and liturgical ritual; concealment, in ceremonies of civil enforcement; embodiment, in decorous, interpersonal encounter; and expression, in drama and celebration. One of these is neither better nor worse than any other. Each is simply a different moment in a process or a different level of a single performance.

Dramatic make-up displays its own concealing function during the same moment that it approaches the apex of expressivity. It is a transparent mask. It does not create the illusion of its own absence but expresses in illusion. Its basic function is to emphasize and thereby interpret. When masking appears as expression, it communicates information simultaneously about the wearer, our cultural roles, and the powers that constitute our cosmos. A transparent mask is one in which the inside and outside of self-awareness, social roles, and human-divine interaction are distinguishable, but articulated as a unity. Self does not replace role, nor does the divine replace the human. One thing does not displace, nor become a front for, another thing. A mask of expression is, like a meta-language, a form of communication capable of commenting on its own nature and presence.

Maggie Angeloglou's A HISTORY OF MAKE-UP (1970:7) illustrates vividly how canons of facial beauty—which include prescriptions about facial expressions, as well as formulas for hair color, eye paint, and lipstick—are condensations of socio-historical values and indicators of both an objective and subjective state of affairs. Cosmetics are barriers, but they are also codes. Strenkovsky says, "Man's face is really a microcosm" (1937:7). Of course, a great deal more investigation needs to be done before we can talk confidently about symbolic meanings of fashions and styles like the eighteenth century breast vogue, the late Victorian bustle, the leg of the 1940's, the post-Elizabethan milkmaid complexion, and the fourteenth century "demure puss." But it is already clear that make-up may express not only the personal, but also the cultural and religious, self as well—and all of this without denying that the whole performance is "made-up." Expressive masking is facial stylization done in a self-conscious and culture-conscious way. One uses the mask rather than being used by it. Of course, make-up is only a metaphor for this kind of masking process, because make-up, especially outside the dramatic context, can become a tool of either the concealing or concretizing sensibility. So we should not confuse physical transparency with the metaphoric transparency of make-up, which I am using to illustrate expressive masking. Stage masks, whether physically transparent or opaque, evoke a sense of transparency. The mask is "seen through" in both directions. The wearer perceives others through a persona; others perceive the wearer through a persona. In the moment of expression, no one wishes to arrive at the transcendent power of a deity or the naked actuality of some "real" self, because "reality" is both person and mask. And reality is not merely there; it is made up, created. An expressive mask is one in which face and head are decorated so as to communicate the character or power played and also to communicate the message, "This is a mask; this is artistic illusion." The concealing nature of such masking is seen critically, as it is in the moment of embodiment, but a different value is placed on illusion by wearer and viewer. Illusion is valued; it does not call for suspicion. Masking-as-expression is masking become clear to itself—become aware that it is put-on, yet effective put-on.

As I have characterized it, expression is a masking process; it presupposes a prior demythologizing, iconoclastic moment that dislodges the canonical power which divine or dead beings and cultural roles exercise over human exteriority. But it has also dislodged the absoluteness of the natural no-mask. It goes beyond unmasking to a creative use of masking. Expressive masking is a dialetical process in which we no longer are worn by a mask, no longer merely hide behind one, and do not tease ourselves into believing we can become maskless, but instead take responsibility for our masks and wear them so our face, society, and gods are seen through them, but not identified with them.

NOTES

/1/ Erich Herold (1967) distinguishes eight types of African masks: face masks, helmet masks, three-quarter masks, Niger Delta masks worn on top of the head, headdresses, shoulder masks, hand masks, and miniature masks.

CHAPTER 6

SITTING AND EATING

The human body is both "thou" and "it"—at once a distinctive, animate, socially aware subject and an object painted, broken, adored, abused, and examined. As a function of the body's intersubjectivity, its actions often communicate meaning and, therefore, present an interpretive problem. We not only speak English, we move and pose in English. We not only think as Buddhists or Christians; we also gesture "Buddhistly" or "Christianly." The body is in important respects text-like in its readability, and interpreting its communication is at least as complex as translating from Sanskrit to Japanese.

Gestures and postures are the smallest units to which a ritologist assigns meaning. Mere motions, unlike gestures and postures, are events occurring below the threshold of meaning; they are like the letters of the alphabet. Just as meaning arises when I organize letters into words and word s into sentences, so out of movements and placings of the body come gestures and postures. Out of gestures and postures come stylizations. Out of stylizations come ritualistic and dramatic processes. And out of these processes issue rites and ritual systems.

Symbolic actions vary in their levels of complexity, but they have in common that they are sometimes channels of communication. Overt bodily actions are not mere punctuation marks for verbal ones. Rather, they function as a "second language" articulated simultaneously alongside our words. Words are not necessarily primary.

Since religion is a complex system of symbolic processes, I resist the notion that it is reducible to a single, static essence. A religion is a style--a choreography of actions, values, objects, experiences, places, persons, institutions, words, thoughts, memories, fantasies, hopes, and feelings. In one religion a central building, for example, may be determinative of style; in another, a controlling institution; in another, a chartering story; in another, a seminal idea. Style is the "how" of our moving among these elements; hence, it is adverbial or verb-like despite our speaking of it as if it were a noun or a thing. Style is inferred from observed action. Even though every religion is a system of symbols, each religion has its own mode of moving from iconic symbol, to narrative symbol, to enacted symbol. It has its own way of hovering over one while tiptoeing past another.

Ritual studies, unlike liturgics, does not begin with a consideration of traditions and texts. It begins by attending to gesture and posture, the actual comportment of the body in interaction. A ritology is the ritual profile of a religion or people; it concentrates on a ritual's communicative, performative, and symbolic aspects. It treats a religion in terms of its most definitive stylizations. Furthermore, a ritology traces the process whereby a gestural motif is choreographed into the performative phenomenon we call a ritual and further elaborated into the macro-unit of ritual studies, the ritual system.

Here, for lack of space, I restrict my considerations largely to the ritological micro-units, gesture and posture. My purpose is imaginatively to reduce two ritual systems to what I take to be their definitive gestures and to show how their linguistic media (such as dogmatic formulations, theologies, and mythic stories) can be understood fully only when comprehended in connection with their gestural and postural styles. Since sitting and eating constitute the respective body-motion models of Zen and Christian practice, I offer a chart which outlines what I will have to say about zazen ("sitting") in the Soto tradition of Zen Buddhism and the Eucharist ("eating") in Roman Catholic Christianity.

SITTING AND EATING: A COMPARATIVE CHART

CATEGORY OF COMPARISON	BUDDHIST (Soto Zen)	CHRISTIAN (Catholic)
1. Gestural paradigm:	1. Sitting (zazen)	1. Eating (communion)
2. Gestural complement:	2. Breathing	2. Drinking
3. Facilitating gesture:	3. Walking (kinhin)	3. Receiving (by open hand or mouth)
4. Gestural Charter:	4. "Never from this seat will I stir, until I have attained the supreme and absolute wisdom."	4. "Take this, all of you, and eat it: this is my body which will be given up for you."
5. Gesture of obligation:	5. Being struck for encouragement (a discipline)	5. Making offerings (a sacrifice)
6. Gesture of gratitude:	6. Bowing with palms together	6. Praying, kneeling, standing
7. Mode of hierophany:	7. Discovery (enlightenment)	7. Transaction (atonement)
8. Formal quality of central symbolic action:	8. Sedentary posture: a stable, minimally moving subject following a process without object	8. Dramatic gesture: a group of mobile subjects consuming an object for a purpose
9. Metaphor of quality:	9. "Spaceful"	9. "Timeful"
10. Metaphor of quantity:	10. Empty	10. Full
11. Mode of time awareness:	11. Mindfulness of the present	11. Remembrance, anticipation
12. Unit of temporality:	12. The counted breath, the sitting period	12. The eon (New Age), week, the liturgical season
13. Mode of sacred identity:	13. Non-dual (identification)	13. Corporate (participation)
14. Locus of sacred space for paradigm gesture:	14. A side wall	14. A front or central altar
15. Mode of indigenous interpretation:	15. Bio-metaphysical	15. Symbolic
16. Aural context of gesture:	16. Silence	16. Words of Institution
17. Sensorium orientation:	17. Kinetic-olfactory	17. Gustatory-aural

The Christian charter to enact the most sacred of its gestures appears thus in the Roman Canon: "Take this, all of you, and eat it; this is indeed my body which will be given up for you" (THE ORDER OF THE MASS). One does not have to be a Freudian to argue that consuming the deity is the model, or paradigmatic, action of Christianity. Whether or not ritual cannibalism was the primal crime, symbolic eating in the context of a ritual meal is primary in Christian ritual.

The ritual moment signalled by these words was of such importance in the Middle Ages that crowds, milling outside the church door waiting for the preliminaries to be over, would rush in to see the elevated host. Bread became a power-object to be seen, touched, or manipulated. The term "hocus pocus" seems to have been a popular corruption of Hoc est corpus meum ("This is my body"). The ecclesiastical speculation was that some communicants were not eating their hosts, but reserving them for later use in rituals of magic, that is, for hocus pocus. In any case—whether in popular piety or learned theologies—sacred power was apprehended via the mouth. A gesture of ingestion provided the royal path down which holiness took occasion to enter human interiority.

The definitive appearance of the holy in Christianity was, of course, the moment of Jesus' embodiment, or to put it more theologically, incarnation. The way of sustaining that hierophany and making its sacral powers available lies specifically through the mouth, despite those few times in Eucharistic history in which seeing the host or merely desiring to commune was thought sufficient (Jungmann, 1955:364). Eating the broken bread-as-body is Christianity's gestural paradigm. Drinking wine-as-blood is its gestural complement. And the facilitating gesture of both of these is the action of receiving the elements with an open hand or mouth. Symbolically, Christians have their gestural mode of being and moving centered in their mouths; one is as one eats.

In Protestant Christianity the nearest gestural rival for paradigmatic status is the ritual act of speaking or proclaiming the word. This gesture is also of an oral mode, but one sometimes construed as the opposite of consumption: "Man does not live by bread alone, but by every word that proceeds from the mouth of God" (Matt. 4:4) and ". . . not what goes into the mouth defiles a man, but what comes out of the mouth, this defiles a man" (Matt. 15:11). It is not an overstatement, I think, to say that oral gestures constitute the bodily activity most characteristic of Christian ritual. They are to Christian ritual systems what a distinctive mannerism is to an individual or what a definitive doctrine is to a systematic theology. The Christian bodily style is fundamentally oriented around consuming and communicating.

A different gestural charter for Zen sitting (zazen) is found in the Introduction to the Jataka Commentary (I:68). The future Buddha has just circumambulated the bo tree, thereby symbolically turning the great worldwheel. He has considered three sides of the tree as places to sit--the southern, western, and northern:

> "Methinks," said the Future Buddha, "this also cannot be the place for the attainment of supreme wisdom"; and walking round the tree with his right side towards it, he came to the eastern side and faced the west. Now it is on the eastern side of their Bo-trees that all the Buddhas have sat cross-legged, and that side neither trembles or quakes.
> Then the Great Being, saying to himself, "This is the immovable spot on which all the Buddhas have planted themselves This is the place for destroying passion's net!" took hold of his handful of grass by one end, and shook it out there. And straightway the blades of grass formed themselves into a seat fourteen cubits long, of such symmetry of shape as not even the most skillful painter or carver could design.
> Then the Future Buddha turned his back to the trunk of the Bo-tree and faced the east. And making the mighty resolution, "let my skin, and sinews, and bones become dry, and welcome! and let all the flesh and blood in my body dry up! but never from this seat will I stir, until I have attained the supreme and absolute wisdom!" he sat himself down cross-legged in an unconquerable position, from which not even the descent of a hundred thunder-bolts at once could have dislodged him (Warren, 1963:76).

Buddhism, like Christianity, involves a multitude of symbolic acts, each of which in turn possesses a complex fan of meanings, but seldom do all symbols of a system or all of a symbol's meanings communicate at the same time. And the uniqueness, the style, of a religiously moving body depends on which gestures and meanings it chooses to enact at a given time and situation. There is within the canonical body of writings, sacred objects, and gestures always a smaller canon. Of all possible Buddhist gestures, the canonical ritual gesture for a Zen Buddhist is sitting. A Zen person is as he or she sits.

JUST SITTING

I assume at least a rudimentary familiarity with the Mass, but since zazen may not be familiar to Westerners, I will offer a fuller description of what it entails. Of course, my composite picture glosses some factional differences among Zen sub-groups.

When a Buddhist of the Soto tradition is doing shikantaza, he or she is only sitting. The sitter is not meditating on texts, waiting for visions, chanting mantras, practicing self--hypnosis, or concentrating on some image or idea. Zazen is not a preparation for anything, even enlightenment. There is to be no difference between practice and goal. In fact, to practice sitting with a goal in mind is to subvert zazen. One's goal is to sit without goals.

To sit "zenfully" is to sit with an aware, non-clinging mind. The usual facilitating gesture is walking, or kinhin. A forty-five minute period of stationary zazen is followed by ten or so minutes of "moving Zen." Both of these are complemented by the necessary occurence of breathing, which, as in many meditation traditions, has the quality of a gesture. Zazen is sitting, breathing, and walking; there is nothing else to do, nothing to remember or anticipate. Sitting, of course, takes a stylized form. Even the emptiness of "beginner's mind" (shoshin) must have a bodily form. One sits cross-legged with each foot on top of its opposite thigh. The back is held straight with the ear lobes and shoulders in line. The eyes are down, but the head is erect. The hands rest on top of one another, and they in turn rest on the ankles or lap, as the fingers and thumbs form an oval at the lower abdomen (hara). Breathing emanates from this spot. Breathing drops down low where the hands are. Sometimes these breaths are counted, particularly exhalations.

In one sense this is all there is, and the first reaction of those who have not tried it is, "There is nothing to it." They say more than they know, since continuing to do nothing is virtually impossible and excruciatingly painful both to the body and the ego. What Westerners call "the mind" wants to fly off or fill up, and the body wants to sleep or run--anything but sit emptily aware. Initially, strenuous effort is required. Eventually, however, effort itself disturbs the mindfulness of one's sitting. In fully developed practice the ego-strength required for effort is displaced in favor of the larger "self," sometimes called "Buddha nature," in which distinctions between self and other, practice and goal, dissolve. As Shunryu Suzuki (1970:29) puts it:

When we practice zazen our mind always
follows our breathing.   When we inhale,
the air comes into the inner world.
When we exhale, the air goes out to the
outer world.   The inner world is
limitless, and the outer world is also
limitless.   We say "inner world" or
"outer world," but actually there is
just one whole world.   In this
limitless world, our throat is like a
swinging door.   If you think, "I
breathe," the "I" is extra.   There is
no you to say "I."   What we call "I" is
just a swinging door which moves when
we inhale and when we exhale.   It just
moves; that is all.   When your mind is
pure and calm enough to follow this
movement, there is nothing: no "I," no
world, no mind nor body; just a
swinging door.

So when we practice zazen, all
that exists is the movement of the
breathing, but we are aware of this
movement.   You should not be
absent-minded.

What I have labelled with a single word, "sitting," is actually a
complex of actions including inhaling, exhaling, keeping the eyes
down, keeping the spine straight, and so on. As in any interpretation
of a gesture, a simple act has its meaning as part of a larger
actional complex.

Sitting is a juxtaposition of elasticity and rigidity.   The
awakened one is at once rocklike and fluid.   This dialectic is
symbolized in sitting by the rigidity of the triangle formed by
buttocks and knees and the deep flowing of breath. Physically, the
hip, knee, and ankle joints are stretched and then locked, while the
spine and shoulders remain erect. One's skeletal structure becomes a
hard frame to contain the soft flow of breath and the empty
mirror-mind. The highly formal and disciplined practice of zazen is
to create an uncluttered, and therefore utterly supple, mindfulness.
To be enlightened, to experience satori, the Zen mode of hierophany,
is simply to be fully awake. But moving from normal wakefulness to
being fully awake is as difficult as waking oneself willfully from
sound sleep.

Meiho, a practitioner of Soto Zen, says, "Identified with yourself, you no longer think, nor do you seek enlightenment of the mind or disburdenment of illusions. You are a flying bird with no mind to twitter, a mountain unconscious of the others rising around it" (in Stryk, 1968:368-369). The crossed legs symbolize stability and resolution in the face of ignorant mindlessness; the linked hands symbolize resistance to taking up tools or scriptures; the closed mouth symbolizes restraint from preaching; the half-shut eyes symbolize resistance to making distinctions; and the straight spine suggests a lack of dependence on leaning-posts. Seated on a cushion, the sitter is like Buddha in a lotus blossom or on a pedestal. But it is the seeing of one's own nature, not the symbolism, which constitutes the heart of Zen practice.

EATING

The gestural symbols of the Christian practice of breaking bread have quite a different ethos, since its roots lie in the meal and sacrifice. The Eucharist is a sacrifical meal in a very complex sense. The simple term "eating" is consistently avoided in Christianity in favor of more conceptually complex ones like "communion," "Eucharist," or occasionally, "love feast" and "the Lord's supper." I may not speak of "Christian eating" as I do of "Zen sitting"; nor may one speak of "eating Christ," but always of "consuming the body of Christ." The former phrase sounds too biological and literal to the Christian ear.

Christ was a sacrifice to end all sacrifices—at least animal and vegetable ones. Christians who eat the ritual body and drink the symbolic blood ingest power which resides in the elements as a result of the primal sacrifice and the subsequent priestly consecration of the elements. In return for this power consumed, devotees are to make their lives "a living sacrifice."

Action becomes transaction, or exchange, when, in view of Jesus' offering and the priestly repetition of the sacrifice, I make an offering prior to the actual eating and drinking. I give before I receive. What I offer or give up is returned to me transformed. What occurs is a highly spiritualized enactment of the do ut des ("I give in order that you give") principle. Even in Christian circles where bread, wine, and water are not offered by the people for consecration, the transactional character of the gesture remains. An offering, a cash gift deposited in a plate, or a "sacrifice of praise" is exchanged for the body and blood of heaven. Sometimes the requisite sacrifice is even further spiritualized. What is offered up is, for example, in some Protestant traditions, a life lived "in love and charity with your neighbor." The consumption of sacralized elements effects salvation, but what stamps the action permanently as a transaction is its cost. A price was (as precedent) and must be (as consequent) paid to continue the performance of the gesture. The qualities of a meal and a sacrifice are, then, integral to Christian eating and drinking, regardless of how symbolic and spiritualized the acts themselves become.

Whereas the Christian gesture of obligation (a prerequisite to participation in the paradigmatic one of consumption) is an offering of money, praise, or food, the gesture of obligation in zazen is being struck as encouragement or for inattention. The former is a sacrifice, the latter, a discipline. Appropriate gestures of gratitude accompany gestures of obligation. The Christian is grateful to be permitted an offering and speaks words of thanks with folded hands to God in prayer, while the Zen Buddhist bows (gasshos) gratefully to the godo for the sudden burst of energy and awareness and for the renewal of flagging attentiveness. In both sitting and eating, one is obligated and grateful to be allowed the performance of the paradigmatic action. And the hierophany which arises from these actions is, in the Christian case, a transaction or atonement, while in Zen it is an awakening to one's own nature (kensho).

The metaphors which issue from Christian and Zen gestural paradigms are different. Eating eventuates in the "fullness of time," sitting, in the "emptiness of space." At communion one eats to be filled with the spirit. In zazen one sits to be emptied of delusion. The Eucharistic meal is a commemoration ("This do in remembrance of me") and an anticipation of the eschatological banquet which will come in the "fullness of time."

The account of Buddha under the bo-tree emphasizes the spatial, not the temporal, context of his resolute sitting. Zen Buddhists remember and recite lists of their patriarchs, but the central action of sitting mindfully in a zendo ("zen-place") or walking in kinhin is dominated by a sense of present "spacefulness." Sitting is a ritual gesture pervaded by a sense of empty, present spacefulness, while eating Christianly is accompanied by a sense of "timefulness," tensed between the Lord's Supper then and the banquet to come. Insofar as zazen takes note of time, its primary units of awareness are the counted breath and sitting-period, rather than the aeon or liturgical season of Christianity. Christianity is often described as an historical religion, while most others are said to be natural ones. I suggest that the Zen alternative to "historical" is better described as "spaceful," not as "natural."

Christian eating is a corporate act. The gesture of sitting is a "non-dual" one. Christians gather to eat around a central or frontal table. Soto Zen people, on the other hand, face a side wall of the zendo or a screen put up specifically to restrict interaction. Practitioners do not face one another nor the statue of Buddha, which is likely to be present on an altar. There are certainly intense interpersonal encounters in Zen communities, but a gestural analysis of its central ritual actions shows that sitting is better understood as a "non-dual" action, that is, one in which separations among people are seen as illusory.   People are not individually alone nor corporately together, as in Christian traditions.   Rather, the distinction, individual/group, is itself thrown into question by zazen practice. To a Zen Buddhist, posturing and gesturing are such that no distinction exists between oneself and others. So one may say either "No-self, no other" or "In Buddha-nature all is one."

One might argue that the presence of the godo ("monitor"), who wields the stick, makes sitting into a social drama. We must not forget, though, that the sitter aims to be at one with the pain of the blow and does not experience it as done by some vindictive "other." In the practitioner's view, what occurs is not an interaction between distinct selves but simply an energy flux. The action is not an event of cooperation, as a meal is, but a surge like an incoming tide. Zazen begins with the ringing of a bell as sitters focus on its sound and gradually experience themselves as ringing. In a like manner they strive to become identified with the stick and the monitor, neither resenting, anticipating, nor differentiating.

SYMBOLIC AND NON-SYMBOLIC GESTURES

If a Zen Buddhist interprets an action of sitting, he or she typically does so bio-metaphysically. One speaks quite directly of the physiology of sitting, the pain in one's legs, a straight spine, and a tucked chin. These gestures certainly have symbolic qualities. For instance, the hand gesture (mudra) is sometimes said to symbolize a cosmic egg. But primarily, sitting is an experience, not a representation, analogue, symbol, or occasion for something else. The Zen Buddhist says that in sitting, body and cosmos are no different.

Christians, on the other hand, tend to interpret their acts as symbolic communications, albeit with various understandings of how fully present the sacred is to the symbolic medium. In any case, a Christian seldom talks about the physiology of digestion. Insofar as he or she speaks at all of eating and drinking as physiological acts, the concern is not biology but liturgized communication, that is, communion.

The history of Eucharistic ritual is replete with tendencies that not only press biological acts into symbolic ones, but actually conceal the consumptive act. The most significant, early modification of the primitive Lord's supper was the separation of the agape ("love") feast from the Mass. Also, there has been a longstanding tendency to withhold wine and serve bread alone. And, as I have noted, there have been times when gazing upon the host or even the desire to commune was considered sufficient. By enlarging what is interpreted as bread, Teilhard de Chardin's famous "Mass on the world" symbolically consecrates the whole world into one giant host. Biology is swallowed up by symbolic cosmology.

Whereas Christian communion has become increasingly symbolic and its sociobiological roots in meal-eating sometimes removed from what Victor Turner (1967:29) calls the "orectic" (physico-emotional) pole of meaning, zazen has taken another route; sitting is anti-symbolic. It is not basically a mode of communication at all, but of practice and motivation. Eating seems to demand interpretation as an integral part of its very enactment, but sitting does not "mean" anything. It is either mindful or scattered, but it does not "point," as a symbolic act does. Symbolization presupposes a distance between symbolic form and its referent, and insofar as the sitter makes such distinctions, he or she falls short of non-dualistic identity and lapses into being a striving ego.

The formal, aesthetic quality of sitting zenfully is pictorial, not dramatic, as in eating Christianly. Strictly speaking, sitting is a postural action, while eating is gestural in character. Zazen is analogous to painting, sculpture, and the plastic arts, while drama and the performative arts are modes of structuring more akin to the dramatism of Christianity's eschatological meal. The non-dramatic nature of Zen sitting is evident even in the handling of the kyosaku, the stick which symbolizes the delusion-cutting sword of Monju. When this stick strikes the shoulders of a sitter, an interpersonal conflict promising a social drama could ensue, but it does not. The action does not become interaction, as it must for drama to occur. Sitting is non-dramatic because it is non-teleological. Christian ritual, on the other hand, is essentialy dramatic, rooted as it is in conflict, history, and eschatological goals. Christian enactment tends to be action toward an end, while Zen action appears to be going nowhere. Even "moving Zen," kinhin, is non-teleological. In the case of Zen, a restrained, minimally interacting, unmoving subject follows without object a flowing process (breathing or walking). In Christian practice, a group of interacting, mobile subjects consume an object (bread, wine) for a purpose. In the ritology of Zen, the postural form is central, whereas for Christianity the gesture of moving toward the sacred object tends to overshadow static, postural dimensions. The meaning of bread and wine tends to attain as much importance as the gestures of eating and drinking. Sitting is a static posture providing "space" for a dynamic process, namely, breathing. Eating and drinking are dynamic processes focused on an object, namely, food-as-Christ. So gesturally considered, we can no longer make easy generalizations about the static quality of Eastern religions and the dynamic quality of Western ones, even though on a posture/gesture scale, Zen is more postural and Christianity more gestural. Rather, the difference is between a Zen posturing practice which has no object and a Christian gesture of communication which has the sacred as a direct object and the self as an indirect one.

Moving Zenfully and Christianly require different aural contexts. The sacred sounds silently in _zazen_. In the Mass the sacred appears among words, specifically the words of institution. The Mass is a communion, and communication is to be expected. _Zazen_ is a return to point-zero, a post-verbal state. If one is Catholic, on the other hand, the words must be said for the food to be efficacious. If one is Protestant, the food is an occasion for words. And if one is a Zen Buddhist, there is nothing to be said, though in the sound of nothingness much is supposed to be heard.

Ritual studies must also note the sensoria organization of a ritual style. The orientations of _zazen_ are primarily kinetic and olfactory, while those of the Eucharist are gustatory and aural. Buddhists and Christians do not experience their bodies, pay attention to sensory input, nor locate their psychosomatic centers in identical ways; consequently, their conceptual and verbal superstructures differ as radically as sound and silence. So whatever we do to deny differences between religions and to affirm the ultimate unity of religious thought, the ritologies, the profiles of enactments, of religions are their fingerprints; they are distinctive.

Someone once remarked to me that the main difference between Methodists and Anglicans was that the latter spend more time on their knees. Theologians might regard such a remark as naïve or superficial, but I wonder. Do kneeling and standing follow from theological differences? Or do theological differences follow from postural and gestural ones?

PARADIGMATIC GESTURES

I have, of course, been reducing two exceedingly complex religious traditions to their central kinesic features. Obviously, Christians frequently sit, and Buddhists often eat. Catholics observe moments of silence, and Soto Zen practitioners pound on drums or make noise with wooden clappers. So I have overdrawn differences and obscured similarities merely by painting ritological portraits. The distortion could be remedied, if I had the eye of a choreographer and the patience of a kinesicist and had the space in which to expand these considerations so sitting and eating might be seen in the full context of their respective ritual systems. My willingness to present gestures and postures so highly abstracted from their ritual contexts is partly inspired by the provocative work of communication theorists and micro-kinesicists such as Ray Birdwhistell, who have shown how 1 3/4 seconds of film (42 frames) is often enough to discover the gestural baseline of a person.

Gestures are metaphors of the body; they display the identifications I make and therefore am. A gestural paradigm leads me, for example, to feel strong while erect, but weak while slumped, aggressive in this stance, receptive in that posture. A gestural strength implies corresponding liabilities. If I sit too compulsively, I wrench my knees and ache between my shoulder blades. If I eat too much, I slump over a distended belly and have to search for breath.

Sitting and eating are not just activities of Buddhists and Christians; they are stylistic aspirations. Hence, they tend to modify, adverbially, as it were, related actions in the same ritual system and sometimes even actions outside the system. Not only do paradigmatic gestures lead to, or reinforce, particular values, liabilities, and lifestyles, they generate corresponding thought and feeling patterns. My mind and spirit become sated or whetted by what I eat or taste, just as they become sluggish or hyperventilated by what and how I breathe. So being able to discover authentic gestures and detect gestural lies, as well as locate gestural paradigms and imagine gestural liabilities, are of immense importance to ritual studies, communications, and psychosomatic medicine.

A popular image depicts a fat Hotei (the so-called "laughing Buddha"). Another depicts an emaciated Christ with a halo. This iconography is not what one might expect of sitters and eaters, respectively. The Buddha appears full, and Jesus, empty. The iconography seems to be the reverse of the ritology. Practitioners might explain the paradoxes in these ways:

The fat Buddha has not just finished a heavy meal; his belly is empty of food. Instead, he is centered in the fullness of his breathing. His stomach is not full of food. Rather his hara, a point just below the navel, is filled with the roundness of power.

The skinny Jesus has not forgotten to eat. Rather, he illustrates that he does not live by bread alone. Though he is empty of worldly indulgence, he is fully surrounded by the spirit, as is shown by his nimbus-encircled head.

I mention the postures of these two popular representations merely to illustrate how suggestive ritological considerations can be. Emaciation and obesity, the sedentary and the consumptive, fullness and emptiness, all seem to have possibilities for metaphorically condensing whole lifestyles. One might continue ritological reflection by asking whether the head as an organ of glory, the shrunken belly, and the spread-eagle crucifixion are metaphoric indexes to Christian cultures and whether the empty, inflated belly of enlightenment, the shaved head, and reclining on one's side (Buddha's death posture) adequately identify values of Buddhist cultures. Such questions take us beyond ritology to symbolic and cultural anthropology.

If we are to articulate the gestural distinctiveness, and thereby begin interpreting the symbolic actions, of the various religions, we must pursue in a more radical way what Paul Ricoeur (1967:3) calls "a sympathetic re-enactment in imagination." A ritologically focused approach to gestural communication will demand of us a bodily re-enactment. We cannot hope to translate postures and gestures, much less whole ritual processes and systems, without the help of mime, drama, game-playing, and the techniques of various therapies. These are necessary scholarly tools not just for teaching and communicating, but for interpreting and understanding the embodied dimensions of human religiosity. The body often understands, even against our own desires and thoughts; and what the body learns is a resource for ritual creativity.

CHAPTER 7

MODES OF ZEN RITUAL

"Sitting and Eating" was an imaginative reduction of Soto Zen to a single gesture. If I reverse the strategy and consider sitting in the context of affiliated gestures within the same ritual system, another sort of gestural profile appears—one in which sitting is not so much gestural essence as a moment in a fluid process.

"Ritual" and "Zen" are two words not often heard together in the West. Popular and semi-scholarly views, based largely on Westernized Rinzai lore, often treat them as opposites. In such views Zen is considered a type of mysticism, not ritual, and enlightenment is treated as a deep, formless, interior occurence. In this view Zen practice is a cult of spontaneity. With the gradual growth of Zen practice in North America, however, such stereotypes are beginning to crumble. Despite its proverbial iconoclasm and anti-ritualism, Zen is quite infused with ritual tradition. Meditation, enlightenment, and direct transmission do not preclude ritual; they presuppose it. The supposed absence of ritual in Zen is like the absence of scriptures. The tearing up of the sutras ("songs," "scriptures") only has power as a gesture if they are utterly essential, and ritual can be experienced as empty only if one is doing it.

The most obvious textual rationale for understanding the relation between Zen practice and ritual is the Heart Sutra, which is chanted regularly by Buddhists of both Rinzai and Soto schools. In the following passage "form" includes what we usually mean by "ritual":

> . . . Form is emptiness and the very
> emptiness is form; emptiness does not differ
> from form, form does not differ from
> emptiness; whatever is form, that is
> emptiness, whatever is emptiness, that is
> form, the same is true of feelings,
> perceptions, impulses, and consciousness
> (Conze, 1958:81).

In Zen emptiness is the absolute, the beyond, the spontaneous, while "form" refers to the extended, material aspect of the world. Ritual is formative action; it is how we prepare objects, spaces, and bodies to go beyond or attain themselves. Ritual studies attends to form, while the study of mysticism concentrates on emptiness. The point of this passage is that no dualism obtains between the changing forms of material life and the unchanging emptiness of transcendent life.

One mistake, in a view informed by the Heart Sutra, is to regard ritual form as a means to attain mystical emptiness. The identification of form and emptiness is a non-attainment, even though it depends on prajna paramita, wisdom born of effort-filled meditation practice.

In zazen, the central ritual practice of Zen, what I do with my eyes, nose, and other organs is carefully prescribed, yet according to the Sutra, ". . . There is no form, nor feeling, nor perception, nor impulse, nor consciousness. No eye, ear, nose, tongue, body, mind. No forms, sounds, smells, tastes, touchables. . ." (Conze, 1958:89).

These denials, of course, are not literal; otherwise, ritual, not to mention sentient life of any kind, would be impossible. Sitting (zazen) and other Zen rituals are thoroughly immersed in bodily processes; so the "no eye, ear" and so on, is an assertion that no sense has an existence separated from any other sense. Whatever bodily or psychological factors (dharmas) one engages during ritual practice, all are marked with impermanence, suffering, and lack of solidity. The implication for ritual is that even if the same form is repeated over and over again, it is not the same gesture that it was during its original performance. Repeatability is an illusion, since the constituents of every pattern in life, including ritual patterns, are composed of impermanent skandhas ("heaps"), temporary aggregates.

What I have said so far about ritual in Zen is implied by its most widely used text. My comments are a rudimentary Zen "theology" of ritual, insofar as theology is the product of reflection on normative texts. However, the "ritology" of Zen, that is, the view of ritual elicited by fieldstudy, participation, and interviews of participants, proceeds in another direction. In North American Zen centers and monastaries ritual is more likely to be discussed as the practice of mindfulness than as an example of the form/emptiness dialectic. My fieldstudy, visits, and practice in five Zen centers (two Canadian, three U.S.) across the past six years lead me to think that such notions as "ritual as symbol system" (Geertz, 1966:1-46), as useful as they are in the study of Western and tribal rites, may miss an essential point about Zen ritual, namely, that many of its gestures do not "mean," refer to, or point to, anything. To be sure, Zen has symbols. The mokugyo, for example, which is a small drum beaten during chanting, is a stylized goldfish, a symbol of never-sleeping, wakefulness. The eating bowl is symbolic of Buddha's head, and the zagu ("prostration cloth") symbolizes the traditional four quarters and ten directions. But all these symbols are far from central to North American Zen practice, as well as Japanese practice, though, of course, they are more fully elaborated in the latter.

A commonplace of ritual studies is the discovery that people who practice rituals often cannot say what a specific gesture or object means. Sometimes even the specialists do not know, or the reply to an inquiry about meaning is, "This is how we've always done it." In Zen centers one meets what I call "exegetical silence." There is nothing to say about what is done, no story, no exposition. But the silence is not of ignorance, mystification, or forgetfulness. The silence is intentional. Sometimes there really is nothing to say.

Of the frequent rituals in Western Zen, meal-taking is often the most elaborated. The gestures are precise, even minute in some centers, yet few of the gestures stand for anything else. They have histories, of course, but the point is not to do them in order to remember or re-present some primordial event. The point is simply, fully, mindfully, to do them. Unlike the Catholic idea of doing with intention, which involves some thought and moral commitment to the meaning of a ritual gesture, in Zen one "just eats." If I think, "I am just eating," while eating, this is not "just eating." Nor is "just eating" a "natural" feast in which one does whatever feels spontaneous with a chopstick or bowl. A mindfully performed ritual action is neither whimsical nor thought-filled. Decision-making and reflection, two staples of most Western views of culinary rituals, inhibit the full presence expected of participation in Zen ritual. Attending to the connections between symbols in a system is what one does not do during Zen ritual gestures.

Zen people seldom speak of Zen "ritual" or "ceremony"; they speak of "practice." In its narrow sense, "Zen practice" is a synonym for zazen, sitting meditation. In its broader usage, anything, for example, striking a bell or drum, leading a chant, or working, can be a practice for someone. The term "practice" does not connote in Zen circles something preliminary to something else, as the terms "baseball practice" or "piano practice" do. These suggest actions that precede public playing. In Zen the practice is the play. The whole point of Zen practice is to eliminate the split between practice and play, preparation and execution, symbol and referent. In Zen a gesture is just a gesture; the mistake lies in looking for more. In the end—which is right now—a mountain is surely a mountain and form is just a form. The action of embracing the form in its emptiness, without the suspicion that it points to some mystical meaning, is essential to ritual processes in Zen.

BREATHING: ZEN RITUALIZATION

In the third chapter I outlined six modes or phases of any ritual action: ritualization, decorum, ceremony, liturgy, magic, and celebration. I will interpret the rituals of North American Zen centers in terms of this model.

Ritualization processes, I have said, are grounded in our psychobiology; hence, they are largely preconscious. Ritualization is the process during which animal life, including our own, begins to form by the sheer process of surviving and being alive together. "Ritualization" is the name I have given to elemental, formative processes which drop below the threshold of our conscious intentions. They elude our full control over them. Ritualization is the most "natural" element of ritual; no ritual is without it.

Analytically, the natural and cultural elements of an action are difficult to distinguish. Even the neonate is socialized before birth; a child is "formed" in the "emptiness" of a womb. So how shall we regard ritualization processes in adult ritual? The simplest way is to consider elementary stylization of basic psychobiological processes.

Since breathing is more pre-intentional than sitting, it is probably the best example of a ritualization process in Zen practice. To consider breathing a ritualization process is not to deny its obvious biological function, but to recognize that any action, no matter how practical or survival-oriented, can become symbolic. Breath is symbolic for Zen, not in the sense that it was, say, for ancient Hebrews; it does not point to the spirit, divine or otherwise. One might say that the "how" of breathing, rather than the sheer act of breathing, is symbolic. In Zen how I breathe is how I am in the world.

Ritual is fundamentally rhythmic. In our practice we sometimes find and follow rhythms. At other times we create them. We follow the drift of things. Then we allow processes such as breathing to follow our intentions. Ritualization occurs on the threshold between sheer passivity and manipulation. It is natural—but not quite. It is—in elementary practice at least—cultivated naturalness.

In zazen a person sometimes counts breaths, especially in the early phases of meditation. This practice cultivates attentiveness and concentration. To refrain from pushing inhalation and exhalation is difficult. So we also follow our breath, but even following is hard to do naturally, especially if we have some idea what "natural" is supposed to be.

The stylization of breathing is most often preconscious to us. We are not aware of it, though with effort we can be. Respiration feels so simple—in and out, that is all. Yet the rhythm, depth, and rate are culturally and personally distinctive, sometimes intentionally so, particularly in traditions which maintain strong meditative rites. Awareness of breathing in Zen practice is not always preconscious, as is the case in non-meditating traditions. But neither is it accurate to regard breathing as intentionally stylized. Zen breathing does not occur under a "breathe naturally" dictum. Trying to breathe naturally is self-contradictory. The very intention modifies our breathing patterns. So "just breathing" is not intentionally natural, nor is it stylized in some specifiable way. Following the respiration cycle with awareness means following it through all kinds of waves, jumps, dispersals, and condensations, all of which are marked by varying degrees of naturalness and stylization.

Breathing in <u>zazen</u> is breathing, period. Breathing also has a meaning, though intellectually contemplating this meaning is not part of <u>zazen</u>. As a ritualization process, breathing expresses how I flow from connectedness and symbiosis to isolation and solitude. The extent to which I press it or let it go symbolizes how I am situated in the ebb and flow of affiliation and disaffiliation. And where the breathing centers itself—high in the nose or chest or low in the abdomen (<u>hara</u>)—bears a message indicating the depth at which I am laid hold of by basic rhythms. To discover this by talking about it is inessential to Zen ritual. The proper articulation of the "message" of breathing is in the performed deed, and the words I speak about the meaning of the deed are at best a demonstration of, and at worst a deterrent from, breathing itself.

Breathing, we might say, is "selfing." It is how we flow into being without solidifying into selves, egos, souls, or other forms of clinging. But even breathing can rigidify. Even though it occurs at a level deeper than habit—we are compelled to do it and cannot really choose it—breathing patterns can habituate. Habituation is the opposite of mindfulness; it is inattentive action. Mindful breathing, despite its being done repeatedly, is a gesture of de-habituation. It is a way of emptying and forming.

BOWING: ZEN DECORUM

The decorous layer of a ritual process emerges from face-to-face interaction. It feels less "natural" than ritualization and is concerned not with "genetic culture," as ritualization is, but with polite culture. Decorum is less dependent upon rhythms such as seasonality, aggression/withdrawl, or inhalation/exhalation, and it focuses on social transitions, for example, leaving or entering a room, meeting a superior, or expressing gratitude and respect.

In Zen practice the most obvious instance of decorous ritual is the gassho ("bow with folded hands"). In North American zendos bowing is one of the first gestures learned by practitioners. It is also the one most likely to lead people quickly to discover the "physiology of faith" (Dixon, 1979). Christians and Jews who practice Zen sometimes confess that, even though they are no longer theists, they find themselves resisting bowing. Two of the issues at stake are that bowing feels idolatrous, and it is experienced as ego-dissolving. The latter effect is intended in Zen, but the former is more a product of the differing gestural histories of Asia and North America. What one thinks a gesture is supposed to mean, or remembers that it once meant, influences what it means now. It does so despite verbal reminders that, in bowing to a cushion or Zen master, one is not idolizing or worshipping anything.

I bow to the Zen master, the cushion, other practitioners, and statues. When the two palms meet and the head or upper trunk bends, what were two becomes one. We are no longer different from one another. Yet, if the feeling "This is bowing to idols" persists, we remain separate and apart. So body and mind must learn together. If I am split, you and I are alienated. This is the Zen view.

Decorum tends to be culture-specific. So bowing, like eye decorum, which rules that the eyes not wander but remain directed toward the floor, may be felt by North American practitioners to be more "Japanese" than "Zen." The meaning of a gesture is not identical with what is said about it by people who do it. What is felt about it and during it, as well as what is done alongside it, also constitute the meaning of an action. The gassho is done not only in respect for persons but for objects such as the zafu ("cushion") and in response to actions such as being struck with the kyosaku stick. So it can serve as a gesture of humility, as well as one of greeting or conclusion. And for those with Western kinesthetic heritages, it may also suggest piety, since the position of the hands--palms together--is associated with Christian acts of piety such as waiting in line to receive communion.

Although "ritual" is not definable as "empty gesture," as ordinary usage would have it, I do not consider it wrong to attend to the empty dimensions of rituals. And decorous rites, such as saying "Good morning," inquiring after another's health, or commenting on the weather, are especially interesting because of their emptiness. They seem necessary and empty at the same time. The various bows in Zen practice are empty in the sense that they may be done without our thinking about their meaning, but they ought not be, by Zen standards, empty in the sense that they are rote or unattended. I ought not contemplate the gesture's meaning, but neither ought I be absent from my own action.

Gasshos and bows in Zen ritual function as commas and periods to mark transitions between ritual phases. Bowing is a bending beneath the flow of time and change (samsara). I bow; I also rise back up—the motion of bamboo in the wind. However, since I bow on cue, for instance, hearing the sound of a bell or entering a zendo, performance of the gesture carries a lightweight "ought." I do not bow merely because my nature is to bow. I also bow because people expect it of me when the bell rings at the end of zazen.

Bowing ritually insures that sociability itself is recognized. Zazen is not merely sitting on a cushion, alone, despite the presence of others in the room. It is also a sitting-with. The bow formalizes this "withness," which is what the sangha ("fellowship of those who follow the Zen way") is about. I sit on a cushion alongside others. Bowing condenses these "social prepositions" by formally recognizing the fabric of connectedness which is above, below, and around me.

HITTING: ZEN CEREMONY

Ceremony is constituted by ritual actions which establish a group as a group. Its most obvious forms are civil, tribal, and racial. A few examples are national holidays, inaugurations, totemic enactments of solidarity, and courtroom ceremony. Whereas decorous actions are face-to-face and are "proper," but not quite "official," ceremonious ones have imperative force. They certify social dramas or define historical and cultural groupings.

If I were considering Zen ceremony in Japan or Korea, I would have to say something about its political and civil functions, much as one has to do with Christian or Jewish elements in North American "civil religion" (Bellah, 1974). Zen, of course, does not serve these functions so obviously as Shinto and other forms of Buddhism in Japan.

North American Zen centers are just beginning to be established in their respective local communities; so community, not nation, is their major civic focus. And community contact is mediated largely through decorum (teas, social service, being neighborly) rather than official ceremony.

Therefore, the best way to illustrate Zen's ceremoniousness is to consider exemplary gestures which illustrate the specifically Buddhist quality of Zen or those which distinguish leaders and followers in Zen communities. Ceremony establishes, with varying degrees of hardness or softness, we/they distinctions, and few religions are without them—even those that insist on the fundamental unity of all people. In Zen when we bow, there is no difference between us. But ritologically considered, he is still master, and I am still follower.

The ritology of being a master or senior disciple is unmistakable. Doans and jikijitsus have specially designated positions in zendos; they lead the chants, maintain order, and in some places administer the kyosaku stick. Zen masters share and transmit authority, and no matter how "eyebrow-to-eyebrow" this transmission is, it usually is also formalized externally by symbols such as prostration cloths, robes, and ceremonial ordinations. North American practitioners new to Zen are sometimes shocked at the elements of Buddhist piety which characterize Zen ceremonies. They soon realize that even though a Zen master may be an enlightened person, he or she is also a Buddhist pastor and priest bearing ecclesiastical authority from both a teacher and the sangha. Some North American centers and monastaries operate semi-democratically, and practitioners share the responsibility for fund raising, work, scheduling, and daily administration, but the master still retains authority to certify attainment (or non-attainment) and examine practice in dokusan ("formal interviews").

An obvious example of a ceremonial gesture which establishes ritual otherness is the administration of the kyosaku stick. In North America the practice varies from zendo to zendo. In some only the master strikes the sitter's shoulders. In others senior disciples share the responsibility. In some a person is hit only when he or she asks for it by bowing as the kyosaku bearer passes, and in others the stick is used whenever those authorized to do so feel it is useful or necessary.

Hitting establishes authority, even though this is not its stated purpose. One of its intended purposes is encouragement. The blow releases energy, re-focuses awareness, and spurs a person on. Hitting is a precipitant. Nevertheless, the elementary ceremonial facts remain: I do not strike myself, and we do not exchange blows. My teacher reminds me that only my ego makes such observations; only my ego construes this moment as having a you-versus-me quality. I do not disagree. However, I know that the loss or minimization of ego-determined actions depends, first of all, on the establishment of the master's authority. The distinction between the master and me must be ritually recognized before transcending the distinction is possible.

What striking ritually might establish, namely, social drama (Turner, 1974a:23-59) and concomitant lines of power, bowing ritually abolishes. Hitting says, "You and I are different." Bowing says, "You and I are the same." And it is not important to think about the question whether you and I are different or the same.

Zen is sometimes anti-authoritarian; it is also authoritarian. Enlightenement is attainment; therefore, it has its badges and banners. And it is non-attainment; it is nothing special. The badges and banners are empty of power except for those who need to revere or submit. Zen practitioners hope to use ceremonial authority against authority in order to dissolve the heteronomous quality of authority.

Ceremony is implicitly conflict-laden, but it also contains symbols of conflict-resolution or conflict-denial. The feelings of comfort, contact, and fear elicited by the quiet, slow walk of the kyosaku bearer are accompanied by shivers of pleasure and pain. A meditator sits in this rift. On those occasions in which the stick just falls and there is no clinging, anticipation, or meta-pain (pain about undergoing pain), there is--to put it in Zenlike language—neither striker nor struck, only striking, being struck, and "selfing."

CLINGING: ZEN MAGIC

Zen is the most fully anti-magical ritual tradition I know. Still, stories and attitudes around zendos are sometimes implicitly magical despite the intentions of Zen masters. The presence of magic lies more in attitudes than overt practices. I know of no magical rites as such in American Zen centers.

Stories of enlightenment are often heard and repeated by disciples, though it is not decorous to do so. The accounts become tales of great spiritual prowess to which novices aspire. Even though aspiration to spiritual heights is deemed illusory, it appears in statements like, "I sit because I want to find peace" or "My goal in meditating is to calm my nerves so I can work better."

Magical thinking is causal and transcendent: one aspires to rise above the broken round of ordinary living and enter a state of tranquility and spiritual recollection. Practitioners aspire to enlightenment, but Zen masters regularly attack this notion of enlightenment as the most tenacious of illusions. However, they also use such spiritual goal orientedness, hoping to re-direct it. They recognize its worth as an initial motivation for meditating, but they deny it a place in the most advanced practice.

Magical rites are grounded in desire. Desiring material goods or spiritual ones are of the same status by Zen standards. Desire leads to clinging, and clinging, to suffering. So Zen practice aims to cut the nerve of desire, because it leads to actions which are attached to goals. However, desire is not supposed to be repressed; otherwise, we will be trapped by counter-magic. Rather, desire is allowed to rise in meditation without being either nurtured or resisted. Desire, in the Zen view, will never reach, much less own, its object. So Zen magic is nothing particular that one does; it is an attitude one has. As long as one has it, anxiety is inevitable, and every action, even sitting, will be pervaded by it. Sitting because I desire to be enlightened is ultimately a form of makyo ("illusion"). In Rinzai Zen this pursuit is more openly acknowledged than in Soto circles, but even in the former, clinging to enlightenment must be thrown overboard at the last moment. Magical rites are transcendently oriented, but Zen aspires to be "mysticism without transcendence" (Nordstrom). The Zen critique of transcendence is that it is a form of alienation, even though it is one that is spiritually high-class. Zen ritual is implicitly anti-magical, because it would deflate both spiritual aspiration and the use of transcendent means for empirical ends.

Zen rhetoric is full of denials of transcendence, and they must be taken seriously. But so must the affirmations. Zen has little interest in the kind of transcendence which would lead beyond the natural toward the supernatural or the sort that would abandon ordinary life and consciousness for the visionary and dream-filled. But teishos ("lectures-as-demonstrations") are replete with positively valued goals such as "just" doing, centeredness, non-clinging, enlightenment, and compassion.

A gesture useful to consider for its magical perversions is kinhin ("walking meditation"), which typically follows zazen. Practitioners often view kinhin as a type of "extended" zazen. Kinhin is the first ritual departure from the extra-ordinary action of sitting still for forty minutes. It is the first step toward re-entering the ordinary world. Zen teachings insist that sitting itself is ordinary, that one never really leaves the world (samsara). Nevertheless, sitting this way is not ordinary in the ordinary sense of the word. So kinhin is, ritologically considered, a step toward re-entering the world that most North American practitioners find ordinary. And this world is pragmatic. It would put Zen meditation to use curing its own ills; such a move would transform moving Zen from a meditative action to a magical one.

The way one walks during kinhin varies--typically slower in Soto-influenced centers, faster in Rinzai-influenced ones--but in all cases it is stylized, not the way we walk down a street. It is meditative and ritualistic; but it does not get me to the grocery store.

Kinhin ritually links my liturgical action, sitting, with my ordinary actions. When I sit, my knees and back hurt, and my nose drips. But I am sitting, so I sit with the pains and pressures. I do not go anywhere, except in my imagination. In kinhin I begin to pay more attention to practical matters. I walk to renew the circulation in my legs. I walk from here to there; it suits my American sensibility, my myth of mobility. I feel that I am going somewhere, whether I am or not. Walking clockwise in a circle at least allows me the illusion of progress. And I am certain that I have made progress when I bow out of line in order to visit the urinal. I am not allowed to break sitting for this, but I can break walking for it.

Kinhin is the most ritually orthodox gesture of moving Zen. Another is work, ordinary work. One sometimes sees in Zen center workshops signs such as, "Work mindfully: leave no trace." Kinhin symbolizes what I think is becoming the most distinctively Western contribution, and danger, to Zen practice, an emphasis on moving Zen. Ritologically considered, a gestural-postural path leads from sitting through walking to the various "arts of"--motorcycle maintainence, archery, running, seeing. The list goes on.

Magic is ritual usefulness. If Zen practice is viewed as beneficial to everyday life, if it contains therapeutic possibilities, and if I can live a more fruitful or centered life because of my practice, I am engaged in magic, because it puts meditative rites in the service of work. Magic is mindful of empirical consequences and would produce them by transcendent means.

SITTING: ZEN LITURGY

As I use the term, "liturgy" refers to rituals done in a cosmic frame of reference. Liturgies are performed because they accord with the way things most fundamentally are. Liturgy follows the flow of cosmic rhythm (logos, tao) without attempting to redirect it or put it to use. The two most fully developed kinds of liturgical rites are worship and meditation, both of which eschew the transcendent pragmatism of magical rites. Receptivity, rather than active desire, is characteristic. So the tone of liturgy is reverent, and often quiet, rather than expansive. In liturgy we attend, inquire, petition; we do not demand or exclaim.

Liturgy falls in a category between magic and celebration, inasmuch as it is neither transcendent work nor ludic festivity. Liturgy is work only in the sense that it consists of discipline or regular practice, not in the sense that it aims to produce goods, spiritual or otherwise.   Therefore, I regard zazen as the basic liturgical act in Zen, comparable to the Christian Eucharist but devoid of theistic worship.

To the Western knee, back, and buttocks sitting does not feel like liturgy. Our ritual history leads us to identify liturgy with the kinesthetics and acoustics of vocal worship, ritual meal-taking, and symbolic sacrifices. We also have linked liturgy to a theistic belief system in which a worshipper bows before a god who is other than oneself. But liturgical ritual is not restricted to these forms.

The essence of a ritual is determined not only by what actions are done in it but also the place these actions hold in a ritual system. Zen people eat and drink tea together, but decorously, not liturgically. Christian and Jewish people sit, but do so decorously; they eat and drink liturgically.

When I sit, I am shaped like a triangle. I am stable, though not rigid. I am vertical, with a triangle of two knees and buttocks under me. My chin is tucked. I do not sway or slump. The triangularity of my skeletal system is a structure for the circularity of my respiratory rhythm. I become a living embodiment of structure and process, stasis and flow. And in Zen experience and aspiration, there is nothing else to be found beyond this one, differentiated action, because this is the way things are cosmically. Enlightenment has simply to do with how I sit here. If I sit slightly outside my self and situation, I have a goal to attain, and sitting is magical. If I just sit here, neither inside myself in introversion nor outside myself in fantasy or thought, I am liturgically empty. Since the nature of things, in the Buddhist view, is emptiness, I am in accord with my true nature. To be in accord is the essence of liturgy.

In Zen centers one's intention is to go beyond intention during zazen practice and to extend this way of being present to every action in ordinary living. For this reason, sitting in a formal position—usually full or half lotus—is the paradigm gesture. Sitting is stylized and, due to its length and stillness, experienced by Westerners as highly formalized and unnatural. Nevertheless, ordinary sitting is so elemental as to be unavoidable for most humans. As human animals we just do it. Even though breathing is biologically more fundamental than sitting, zazen is called "sitting," not "breathing." So sitting is the generative gesture, the matrix of all others in the Zen ritual system. It is the last one Zen people would give up. It is sacred.

ENLIGHTENMENT: ZEN CELEBRATION

The celebrative process of any ritual system is constituted by its playfulness. When the gesture is an ultimate one, it no longer aspires to anything. Goals and origins are not in sight; just the processes are. The ultimate gestures of most religions are the most ordinary ones: eating bread, drinking wine, sitting, giving away, getting, entering conflict. Celebration occurs when aspiration is no longer necessary.

Celebration is ludic and "spontaneous." The quotation marks suggest, however, that spontaneity does not arise apart from form or training. It is cultivated. In Soto Zen it is said that sitting is enightenment. Therefore, a separation between Zen liturgy and Zen celebration would be regarded as a penultimate or analytical distinction and an indication that one's practice is lacking. Ideally, sitting is unmotivated; one "just" does it.

If I become attached to moments of joy or occasions of spontaneous breakthrough, as if they are better than the routine or painful ones, I am trapped. So celebration, properly understood, does not look like anything special, as it might in some other ritual system. It should not "smell of Zen." In the allegorical Zen ox-herding pictures the gesture of an enlightened one is called "entering the city with bliss-bestowing hands." His hands are not raised in exaltation nor held in a formal <u>mudra</u>. Rather they "leave no trace." In the Zen view any action which leaves a trace is put-on. And what is put on can be peeled away like a mask.

Ritual studies would have no way of speaking about Zen celebration if enlightenment literally left no trace. I would not claim that enlightenment is reducible to a set of gestural or attitudinal traits, but I do maintain that observers can discern in the demeanor of Zen masters a way of walking, sitting, listening, and so on, which differs from that of novices. Perhaps I cannot say this way is enlightened, but it is, I think, a reliable indicator of who is advanced in practice and who will, therefore, be emulated.

Zen masters test a student's <u>kensho</u> ("seeing one's own nature"). This fact, along with the existence of enlightenment stories, suggests that a trait, if not a trace, of some sort is assumed. Enlightenment is not invisible, even though it is not reducible to a set of visible characteristics.

Celebration in Zen is not limited to enlightenment, though it is epitomized by it. Other occasions such as ordinations or parties include celebrative elements, but their expression should be derivative from the moment of insight into one's own true nature. Ultimately, every ordinary moment is also a celebrative one. Celebration, as they say in Zen, is "nothing special."

PART III

THEORIES OF RITUAL

INTRODUCTION

Rituals are complex phenomena with such a difficult symbolic logic that interpretation of them is still in a rudimentary stage, much as it is in the interpretation of dreams. Only since the advent of anthropology in the nineteenth century has there been sustained theorizing about it. Before that time, reflection on it took the form of considering specific rituals either for polemical or apologetic purposes. Theorizing is a peculiar activity, not at all a universal one. Narrowly conceived, it is a creature of the physical and social sciences, which are modern, Western enterprises linked to canons of evidence, probability, and predictability. But insofar as theorizing is simply the most general reflection of which we are capable, it is an ancient, widespread activity virtually identical with philosophizing and its standards of coherence, parsimony, and comprehensiveness.

The most general claims for ritual have been that it: (1) maintains contact with the sacred, (2) helps bind a society together, (3) is a symptom of unresolved neuroses, and (4) is indissoluably linked to myth. These are the traditional religious, Durkheimian sociological, Freudian psychoanalytic, and Cambridge school theories which have dominated modern ritual theory. Most others have been variants of these until the advent of structuralism and the work of Claude Lévi-Strauss.

Some of these theoretical positions concentrate on different aspects of ritual and so are not necessarily mutually exclusive. Much more systematic work needs to be done before any theory can claim even to treat, much less explain, the various facets of ritual. Any theory which hopes to do so, will have to draw on contributions from several fields, ranging from musicology to kinesics, symbolic anthropology to religious studies, psychosomatic medicine to aesthetics.

In the eighth chapter I consider the theories of Gotthard Booth, a psychiatrist and physician, and in Chapter 9, those of Theodor Gaster and Victor Turner. These are examples of theorists whose writings bear gleaning for insights into ritual theory.

CHAPTER 8

A PSYCHOSOMATIC THEORY:

GOTTHARD BOOTH

Few people have been as concerned about developing a hermeneutics of the body as the late psychiatrist, Gotthard Booth. Booth's research concentrates on symbolic processes in illness and healing and draws as heavily on poetic and metaphoric structures as scientific ones. His intention was to uncover the grammar of bodily language, especially the language of illness.

Although Booth did not write directly on ritual studies, he worked closely with pastors and had an abiding concern for religion and therapy. Ritual studies has much to learn from both medicine and therapy, since illness of any sort is a crisis of the connections between values and the body. Ritual, no less than medicine and therapy, translates and affects psychosomatically rooted symbolization. If ritual studies becomes preoccupied with embodied paradigms to the exclusion of ritual pathology, that is, gestural "sins" or "lies," it overlooks a primary area of body language. Volney Gay (1979) has shown that Freud does not prove that ritual as such is pathological. Booth, who was influenced by Freud but not really a disciple, provides a theory for interpreting pathology as a gesture. His insights provide a useful, but tentative, first step toward a ritual criticism based not on theological criteria, but on psychosomatic ones; these can be of use to liturgics, theology, and ritual studies, as well as the healing arts.

The view of health as an "ecology of relation" (my phrase) serves Booth as both his most axiomatic assumption and primary value. Health, in his understanding of psychosomatics, is not merely a state of some organ or organism, but is a quality of relational symbiosis obtaining among multiple factors: hereditary predisposition, familial-social environment, specific organ systems in the body, the conscious self and its goals, and the unconscious. Each element is an expression of the quality of relation among the others. Our bodies are ecological systems.

A basic thrust of Booth's psychiatric work is his critique of the speciously independent self. To this effect, he is fond of quoting Rioch, "The mind is a function of two or more brains and not the property of one" (cited in 1963a:24). Social and environmental elements are not factors merely tacked onto our biological selves. Rather, they constitute us from the very beginning. For Booth there can be no natural/social dichotomy, since being social is natural. Nature, insofar as it is represented, for example, by animals, is such that a disruption of rituals, symbols, or values can kill or make ill as surely as deprivation of food and shelter, since symbolic behavior is genetically derived from purposeful, living relationships between living beings. A characteristic of human beings is that they will sacrifice survival itself for the sake of a lifestyle, value, or symbol. Since being in relation is natural, Booth takes the Christian confession that "there is no health in us" to mean there is no health in individuals, only in the interconnectedness of things. Religion is wholeness, ecology in its fullest sense. "Healing occurs when an organism finds a satisfactory relationship with its environment in all spheres of existence" (1962a:13). "Disease is always the product of an encounter between a genetically determined inner motivation and a frustrating external situation" (1975:427).

Booth's axiom of the ecology of relation demands that he reject dualistic and demonological, as well as mechanistic and causal, interpretations of disease. The latter interpretation is but a secularized version of the former. Both views project the agency of disease as an enemy which invades the inner sanctum of an organism. Such views fail to recognize that in important senses the "enemy" or "cause" is already within a person and situation. To recognize this fact radically changes our dualistic split of subject/object, health/disease, interior/exterior. By implication, all diseases, not just selected ones, can be construed as psycho-social-somatic: when "I" am sick, the whole of things is ill within/as me.

THE ECOLOGY OF RELATIONS: PURPOSIVENESS

A second axiom grounding Booth's hypotheses is that having purpose is as natural as being fundamentally related. The purpose of a living organism is to interact. The goal and process of living are identical (see 1967:102). At first this view seems a truism, until we recognize that by maintaining it Booth intends to reject the view that the fundamental purpose of living beings is to prolong their own lives. Instead, he argues that the will to live is less fundamental than the will "to maintain our innate way of relating to the environment" (1962b:312). Not being alive as such, but living one's life and death in a specific way, in accord with one's own symbolic forms and psychogenetic constitution, is life's goal and motive (cf. Dixon, 1979:46). Every organism has its own style, and style symbolizes purpose.

> Organisms, however, are different   from machines .   They stay healthy only so long as they can interact with their natural objects. The finitude of the organism's life is more comprehensive than the life span.   Finitude also means that organisms live only as long as they attain their biological and psychological ends.   End, finis, telos mean not only conclusion but also purpose" (1975:420).

For organisms to have purpose means, in Booth's thought, two things: (1) that they are by nature oriented beyond themselves toward causes or others—toward transcending their encapsulated egos--and (2) that they choose their own forms of going beyond themselves. Both of these, not mere survival, are the fundamental activities of living and dying.   Health is the by-product of purposeful relation.

I suggest that, if Booth is correct in maintaining that style is as determinative as genetics or social environment, ritual has to be seen as ecologically essential (cf. Rappaport, 1971).   It is essential, not merely because it communicates ecologically significant information, but because it influences our very mode of bodily encounter with the environment.

THE DISEASED RELATION: ORGANIC SYMBOLIZATION

The connection that Booth makes between these axioms and specifically medical hypotheses constitutes the controversial cutting edge of his thought and practice. He claims that he and others have demonstrated scientifically that certain diseases have consistent, if not predictable, relationships to specific lifestyles./1/ The choice of a given lifestyle, or pattern of relationships and choices, entails a specific disease liability and hence a predictable mode of death. Booth says:

> The body speaks a very basic and very honest language through the healthy and unhealthy functioning of its organs.   Our expressive gestures, the color of our skin, and the behavior of our heart and bowels, of our lungs and our genitals, unequivocally spell out our existential situation.   The lie detector, reading the body directly, triumphs over the faculty of words to hide the truth (1967:96).

To state the claim simply, we choose the mode of our illness and death. Although Booth's hypothesis does not typically posit a simple causal relation between a personality type and a disease, he is still making a claim which is verifiable or falsifiable in principle; so perhaps it is best to say, as social scientists sometimes do, that a given personality type and a specific disease co-vary significantly./2/ A change in one implies a corresponding change in the other, so they exist in true systemic relation. Booth sometimes insists that he is not arguing for the pscyhogenesis of all diseases, only that psychosocial and symbolic elements are constitutional factors among others in diseases such as cancer (1963b:16).

When a relation between us and the objects or other persons of our environment becomes dislocated, we become diseased, not in mere random fashion, but in our "dominant biological function" (1966:420), for instance, my muscles and bones if I am a hunter, my lungs if I am a romantic. The notions that each person has such a "dominant organ system" (1957a:17) and that it is natural to lead with one's strongest function (1962a:23), much as one might be dominated by right-handedness or right-"eyedness," lead to Booth's typological categories.   He identifies at least the following: cardiovascular, cancer, tubercular, and locomotor types. Persons of each type are genetically and existentially prone to succumb in specifiable organs or organ systems to certain predictable diseases. Therefore, organic disease is a symbol, voice, or message, which conveys to an interpreter (oneself, a pastor, psychiatrist, physician, or friend) the lifestyle of the patient and signals that the organism is imbalanced toward some dominating function./3/ Somatization is what happens when psychological processes become symbolized in the flesh, and these psychological processes are, in turn, expressive of the style and telos of the organism.

The locomotor type, for example, is prone toward Parkinson's disease or rheumatic disorders. If I am this type of person, I have a constitutional disposition toward action and am "bound to succeed." In the face of overwhelming odds, I assert myself. I have a tendency to use my muscles and bones, not merely for locomotion, but to express myself in pleasure. Having identified myself as a child with the dominant parent, I am quite self-assertive and apply myself fully to my work. In addition, I am scrupulously honest.

When the symptoms of Parkinson's disease become evident, they symbolically caricature this lifestyle. The posture becomes rigid. Muscles tighten, bending the limbs and causing tremors when sleep or purposeful action is absent. The disease symptoms are a gestural and postural parody of the controlled but active biography of the person. According to Booth, "The personality regresses from realistic satisfactions to a level of merely symbolical satisfactions" (1957a:16).

The cardiovascular, or vasomotor, type includes people most prone to diseases of the heart and arteries. Such a person is characterized primarily by collectivistic and conformist tendencies. The blood stream, according to Booth, is the symbolic internalization of the environment. The blood stream is to human beings what the sea was to primitive organisms; a person is a "bit of encapsulated sea water." If I were of this type, I would identify strongly with my cultural group, as I once did with the conforming parent. High blood pressure is a somatization, a fleshly symbolization, of a lifestyle typified by an overdeveloped sense of responsibility to the group. Sometimes a very competitive person, the cardiovascular type is preoccupied with time and scheduling. In contrast to the first type, the cardiovascular patient undertakes physical activities only as a way of complying with social demands. Such a person is always in search of a supportive milieu, and since a circulatory system is a somatic milieu, this type will be likely to suffer in it. "The organ of action becomes the center of self-expression, and its pain becomes a heightened form of self-experience" (1967:106).

The tubercular type's primary orientation is toward the establishing of a mutual relationship--not the relationship of an individual to a social group, as in the case of the cardiovascular type, but a face-to-face relationship with another person who is as highly valued as the self. This is the typical romantic, oriented toward the pursuit of love and friendship. Booth, following Freud, describes such a person psychoanalytically as a "genital type." If I am a tubercular and I become ill, my striving for union regresses to a new form of symbiosis, namely, one with the Koch bacillus. My affectionate needs, which may at one time have led me to pursue my loves in the face of strong social disapproval (which would stop a cardiovascular type), lead me in times of illness to express those needs symbolically in the form of an infectious disease—a sublimated way of becoming identified with another in the form of its internal symbol, the parasite within my own body.

A fourth type, the one with which Booth's later writings are most preoccupied, is the cancer-prone. Booth sometimes refers to this kind of person as "neoplastic" or, in Freudian language, "anal". The cancer-prone person is strong willed and characteristically forms brittle object relations. Like Kierkegaard, such a person identifies purity of heart with willing one thing.

As a cancer type, I am latently in despair and secretive about my frustrations. I am too busy pursuing some object or goal which is the highest one in my life. Unlike the tubercular, I, as a cancer personality, want to control my desired object. I am a "sadder but wiser" person who avoids mutual symbiosis for the sake of domination. As Booth notes, the cancer-prone person's model is, metaphorically at least, a digestive one: "animate and inanimate parts of the world are transformed into materials which can be used for personal survival without creating new organisms" (1967:113).

When the desired object is lost, either by being removed or obtained, a symbolic substitute object, the cancer itself, is generated in the dominating somatic function. Cancer cells are "asocial" (1962a:20; 1967:111). They do not interact, as an infectious parasite does. Hence, they, like their host, strive for autonomy.

Typically, cancer patients have great difficulty changing the object of their strivings; yet they feel considerable guilt because of their betrayal of relatedness and because of their idolizing some separated, external thing, which now threatens to take them over from within. They who would control, now become controlled.

FRAGMENTS OF A RELIGIO-MEDICAL HISTORY OF DISEASE

The boldness of Dr. Booth's work becomes evident when he suggests that the types themselves have a history. As I have sketched the types, they are in a chronological order of diseases symbolizing major value systems. In Booth's view, locomotor diseases typified early hunting-shamanic cultures; cardiovascular diseases, planting-priestly cultures; tuberculosis, the pre-industrial era; and cancer, the modern, technological era./4/

He argues that hunters were typically individualists in pursuit of game. Ritually, they were shamanic, hence their courting of personal power and spontaneous visions. Their characteristic mode of sacrifice was to sever fingers or toes, to inflict injury on the motor system. Booth regards prophetic or shamanic people as coincident with the locomotor type, since they share a common need for individual action and consequently have an identical disease liability.

When hunting cultures began to subside in favor of agricultural ones, the priest (argues Booth following Joseph Campbell) replaced the prophetic shaman, and the value of group solidarity displaced the extolling of individual prowess. Priestly religion and culture, with its conservative emphasis on group and order, are correlated by Booth with his cardiovascular type. The same anxiety about social expectations underlies a priestly planter's human sacrifice of individuality and a business person's coronary: the individual is sacrificed for the sake of the group.

Booth never claims to have outlined, much less written, a complete religio-medical history of disease; so the religious and cultural correlates of tuberculosis are not very clear in his writings, though he obviously thinks the typicality of tuberculosis began to subside in the nineteenth century with the rise of the machine age. He never says what the cultural system of this disease is, as he does in the cases of locomotor and cardiovascular diseases. However, he does seem to think these three belong to "the old type," (1967:109) in contrast to cancer, which is a modern type. In the old type people identified themselves symbiotically with their objects or environments—hunters, with animals; agriculturalists, with plants; and tuberculars, with other people. But in cancer symbiosis is absent.

The latest chapter in the religio-medical history of disease is what Booth regards as a "cancer epidemic" (1979). Cancer symbolizes the emergence of a new personality type, technological personhood. Like our lifestyle, our disease takes the form of over-differentiation and a false, destructive sense of domination over the environment. Our cancer is to us what we are to the surrounding milieu.

All the older diseases corresponding to early religious value systems persist, because the genetic predispositions and certain of the social conditions persist. Whereas the transition from locomotor to cardiovascular liability seems correlated with the religio-economic shift from hunting and shamanism to planting and priestly ritualism, the shift from tubercular- to cancer-proneness is symbolized by the industrially, technologically inspired substitution of bottle-feeding for breast-feeding. Booth insists that the turberculosis epidemic of the early nineteenth century turned into a cancer epidemic at the time when depersonalization with nursing bottles began (1974:114).

DIAGNOSTIC AND THERAPEUTIC SYMBOLIZATION

For Booth disease is situational. He prefers this more relational, existentialist term to the reductively biological notion of an "instinct" (1975:418). Disease is situational, not merely somatic, nor even narrowly psychosomatic. It is the symbolization of genetic factors, unconscious needs, and conscious choices, as well as interpersonal, social, and environmental factors. Booth usually tries to avoid medical and psychiatric reductionism. Nevertheless, he is willing to assert that some of these factors co-vary with sufficient regularity to be of diagnostic and predictive value. By projective testing with Rorschach ink blots, Booth is able to differentiate the various disease liabilities. In responding to the ink blots, people express typical choices which symbolize disease liabilities. To cite only two examples, cancer patients tend to see in the blots isolated organisms, while the tuberculosis-prone are likely to see socially interactive ones. Tuberculosis patients are inclined to be flexible and unstable in their responses; cancer patients, willfully singular in theirs (1979,ch.2).

Booth thinks that art, specifically the Rorschach test, allows us to bypass verbal barriers, thus providing a direct look at an artist's or patient's highest values, which in Western symbolic modes will be projected on the center or axis of the painting. Knowing these values, we in turn can project the disease liability and the path toward death.

Booth is modest in his claims about the therapeutic possibilities of his findings and hypotheses. Healing is the re-establishment of wholeness. Easily said, but how are we to do it? Booth thinks we can become wise to our bodies' messages. The faith and knowledge which arise from interaction between patient and healer often set in motion a person's freedom; though we must remember that choice is only one factor, perhaps not even the most important one, in re-establishing ecological balance. One of our most important actions as diseased persons is learning to embrace our own weaknesses. For Booth, "Be ye perfect" means that we should not despise our own weaknesses nor try to follow only our virtues (1962b:317). What we cannot afford is moralism toward our diseases. Booth does not think we "ought" to be healthy. Health is a by-product. Neither it nor the love which generates it can effectively be pursued as direct goals. Love is not usable as a means to health. Booth thinks those who accept his views may do considerable damage if they try to make holistic medicine itself a cure-all.

Therapies, both primitive and modern, generally employ ritual sacrifice as a means of restoring diseased relations. Whereas wholeness cannot be pursued directly without its becoming a mere objectified goal, it is pursued indirectly by our offering up our most cherished organs or possessions. Modern surgery, Christian communion, and tribal scarifice are ritually equivalent. For example, Origen is said to have sacrificed his excessive extroversion by self-castration; Tertullian, his overdeveloped mind by concluding, "I believe because it is absurd" (1962b:315). Some cherished part of our lives is traded for the more cherished whole. The exchange, however, is seldom directly acknowledged as such, lest it lose its effectiveness. We say the gods desire it or the surgeon recommends it. Both of these expressions may be true, but that we desire to make sacrifices is likewise true. Therapy, whether surgical or psychoanalytic, takes the form of a ritual destruction of the "guilty" organ (1962a:16). New life comes only after a symbolic, sublimated, or substitute mutilation or death. So Booth seems to conclude that the most we can do in a therapeutically deliberate way is to ritualize the healing process, which means becoming actively receptive to what is occurring within and among us. Our most healing action is a ritualized enactment of passion. Whereas the ancient Greeks sketched the dialectic leading to wisdom thus: action (poiema), passion (pathema), knowledge (mathema), Booth takes us from the knowledge of our illness to an action which is fundamentally "passionate," or receptive, in nature. The implicit model is that of Christian ritual.

A CRITICAL RESPONSE

The breadth of Booth's view is as wide as the ecosystem itself; so it needs to be both appreciated and criticized from a variety of perspectives, particularly medical, psychological, and religious ones. Being unqualified to comment on the first two, most of my responses have to do with the religious, specifically, the symbolic and ritualistic, implications of Booth's studies. Crucial to all these fields, however, are problems of scope, definition, classification, and causality, which I will outline before proceeding to the religious issues.

I find it difficult to know whether every occasion for treatment, including accidents, childhood diseases, and birth defects, are to be included in Booth's hypotheses. Since some diseases seem more typical of childhood, and others seldom lead to death, should we speak of these as "ways toward death" and take them as messages in the same sense we do tuberculosis, cancer, and cardiovascular disease?

Booth, of course, could not in a single lifetime have done research on every disease. Nevertheless, we need to know what might warrant extending his views to every disease, unless he is making an axiomatic assumption not subject to disconfirmation, as I sometimes suspect he is. If disease is dis-relation, then, as Booth recognizes, it is ubiquitous. Like sin, in the theologian's view, it is everywhere and is expressed, though latently, in every relationship.

A related problem is knowing how to differentiate types. Booth admits that the characteristics of the types overlap, but insists that in projective testing a person's basic disposition becomes clear. Perhaps this is so, but there are obviously undercurrents and countervailing tendencies—one may be predominantly a cancer type, but also have significant tubercular tendencies. What social factors might elicit the recessive tendencies so they overwhelm the dominant predisposition? If such a transformation is possible at all, a type is at best a useful heuristic device. If a person's type can change, say, from cancerous to tubercular, then a type is better regarded as a phase, not a constitutional disposition. And if a type cannot be changed, how useful is knowing what path we have "chosen"? Booth, I think, is not clear which variable is the strongest, the genetic or the socio-historical.

Not only might one cross the boundary of a type, the principles of delineating the types are only partially clear. Is a type defined by an organ system or a disease? How do we classify cancer of the bone marrow? Does this disease typify a locomotor or a cancer type? Is the tubercular type better interpreted as a respiratory type? What are we to do with diseases that are not organ-specific?

If the scope of Booth's theory is ever to be broadened to include the psychosomatic dimensions of every disease, I would expect a concomitant expansion of the number of personality types. Instead, his four types are sometimes reducible to two, individualist and conformist, or anal and genital. Instead of more precision, we sometimes find less. If we are to account for disease as such, descriptions of personality traits need greater elaboration and accuracy.

The classification problem in Booth is especially acute when he begins making cross-cultural generalizations, for, as Ray Birdwhistell (1970) and other kinesicists have shown, symptomology is highly dependent upon regional variations in gesture and verbalization. Booth, I think, is not sufficiently aware that the body can lie and its message be misunderstood. Deciphering body language, and that includes disease, is more difficult than decoding verbal messages. A doctor can as readily project him- or herself onto patients' bodies and psyches as the patient can project onto inkblots. Medical anthropology has shown that we must be wary of thinking we can identify a disease from an ancient or culturally foreign description. So even though I find Booth's historical claims interesting, I suspect they derive more from his axioms and, to cite one example, from an assumed analogy between the lifestyle of modern individualists and ancient hunters than from demonstrated coincidence of ancient lifestyle and ancient disease.

Other dimensions of the classification problem are Booth's notions of dominant function and organ system. A person is supposed to lead, for example, with the lungs or heart, and disease is supposed to strike this leading function. Why, then, is a genitally oriented tubercular type affected in the lungs rather than the genitals, and the anally oriented cancer patient in functions other than excretory or digestive ones?

I suggest that the connection between disease and lifestyle is metaphoric rather than literal or causal. The "a-social" cancer cell expresses the independent, goal oriented cancer patient. The circulatory system expresses the congenial social circulation of the cardiovascular type, and so on. If Booth were only arguing for expressive analogy, and not also for psychosomatic co-variance, I would have no problem with his theory. But to give up arguing for co-variance (complex causality, as opposed to simple causality) would take the teeth out of his research. Even on a symbolic level Booth sometimes mixes his metaphors. For example, breathing, hence the lungs, are how we express our independence and freedom (1972:5); yet the tubercular patient expresses a need for mutual dependence by living life, as it were, through the lungs. Such problems as this illustrate how Booth's initial classification and description eventually dictate, and thereby clarify or confuse, how he interprets messages of the body.

A final problem is his view of causality. Booth criticizes simple, or mechanistic, causalism and reductionistic psychogeneticism, though he sometimes indulges in reductionism (e.g., 1962b:313; 1972:3,5,8). But he is not content merely to list factors (psychological, genetic, social) of disease. He insists that by knowing one factor we can infer another, for example, from high need for mutual relation, he infers tuberculosis liability. Yet, at one moment of his argument the most significant (he would not say "independent") variable is genetic, especially when he is aware of the danger of moralizing; at another moment, interpersonal (for instance bottle feeding), when he wants to account for the generation gap; at another, conscious choice, when he wants to emphasize responsibility and the possibility of healing; and at still another, cultural factors (such as planting or hunting), when he needs a situation which expresses a disease. This constant shifting of hermeneutical ground without explicit warrant leaves those of us who might follow and extend Booth's work either free to choose the significant variables however we wish for whatever purposes we deem desirable, or it obligates us to systematize his views so they become genuinely methodological, that is, scientific, in the broadest sense of the word. Those who consider either diagnosis or predictability important might go the latter route. Those with ethical, religious, or poetic motives will most likely pursue the former.

THE END OF RITUAL

In my view, an organ system does express a lifestyle, but it does so only for the interpreter who sees the metaphoric connection in the same way he or she would see it in a poem. To perceive that a cancer is a microcosmic lifestyle is not different from perceiving, to paraphrase Blake, infinity in a grain of sand.

Some interesting possibilities emerge when we accept the notion that both rituals and somatic organ systems express metaphorically a person's or culture's highest values. Somatic symbolization is common to ritual, drama, and medicine.   Meaning has an exteriority. Furthermore, exteriority is an embodiment of value. Values do not reside merely in ethical systems, linguistic formulations, or rational choices, but also in bodies, blood, bones, lungs.   The body has a wisdom of its own; "it" often knows before "we" do.

Walter Ong (1967) has argued that it is not enough merely to note that ideas come via sensation; this is obvious.   What is not so obvious is that cultures and individuals have relatively unique, therefore expressive, ways of paying attention to the bombardment of sensory data.   This, Ong calls "sensorium organization."   Ong distinguishes, for example, oral-aural from visual cultures.   A culture, he thinks, emphasizes certain senses, just as Booth thinks a person leads with some specific organ.

Booth suggests that technological, "cancerous" society's model is a digestive one. I am tempted to view Western society's consumptive model as an expression of Jewish and Christian ritual. However, the relationship between ritual, symbol, and cultural value is seldom direct or merely reflective.   Often the relationship is one of inversion.   A useful starting assumption is that symbols, including symbolic actions mask value-contradictions; so we can never establish the meanings of such actions before articulating their place in a specific system or process. We cannot always assume that symbols are analogous to their referents, since symbol and meaning often appear in metaphoric tension, rather than analogical parallel, to one another.

Rituals and symbols can become sick, just as organs can. In fact, some psychologists, along with a few anthroplogists and religionists, have suggested that symbolism and ritual as such are pathological.   Even Booth, who seems to appreciate religious expression, implies that symbolic expression only occurs when "real" fulfillment of need is blocked. In his view, indirection is the result of blocked directionality. This understanding of symbols leads Booth, like theologian Paul Tillich, to develop a "protestant" principle, whereby the tendency to absolutize a single symbol or an isolated somatic function is protested as "idolatrous." Booth speaks of a "natural valuing of one   somatic   function" (1963a:25,28); yet this natural tendency is the source of disease. It is the "original sin" of the body.

Viewed in this light, healing takes the form of a de-symbolization or de-ritualization process. The disease of autonomy is treated when symbols become, in Tillich's terms, "broken" or "transparent." Booth comprehends, I think, the implication for therapy, namely, that de-ritualization of an idolized function is itself a ritualized, hence bodily, process. Booth knows that actions are needed, so he mentions the symbolic sacrifice of surgery, as well as communion and unction (which are preceded by their own kinds of ritual sacrifice). The latter, he thinks, restores an isolated person to a symbiotic relation with a larger whole.

I suggest that, though restoration of symbiosis may be the intended theological meaning of communion and unction, their ritological, that is, somatic, gestural, and postural, predilections may be different or even contradictory to this meaning. The ritological significance of a symbolic performance is to the theological meaning of an action what a Rorschach assessment of personality is to an introspective one. And what it means, say, for a cancer-liable person to be annointed ritually with oil would differ from the meaning apprehended by a cardiovascular-prone person.

We must show, not merely assume, that a specific symbolic action genuinely redresses the somatic imbalance of a given illness. So, I conclude with the suggestion that a sacrifice-communion ritual, based on ritological exchange and consumption, plays into, rather than therapeutically counterbalances, the psychosomatic dynamics of the cancer personality. The "eschatology" of the rite is a symptom of, not a symbolic cure for, the goal orientedness of cancer-prone, technological humanity. If there are genuinely therapeutic responses to cancer perhaps they lie in the more receptive, less teleological rituals of the East and in the ritual possibilities of meditation and play, because in these activities goals are not so easily separated from processes.

NOTES

/1/ Booth thinks nature is genuinely creative and not always predictable, but its creativity is sufficiently regular to be subject to scientific study based on probability and the laws of physical interdependence (see 1963a:23 and 1957b:1).

/2/ Booth says genes do not "cause" pathology, but "excessively favor" the use of one biological potential over another.

/3/ Booth's debt to Jung is clear in both his search for typological symbols and his claim that their appearance performs a conative, compensating function (cf. 1957a:18; 1962b:315).

/4/ The hunter/planter distinction is taken from Joseph Campbell (1979). Booth's characterization of the socio-history of tuberculosis is chronologically less clearly demarcated than the other types.

CHAPTER 9

RELIGIOUS AND ANTHROPOLOGICAL THEORIES:

THEODOR GASTER, VICTOR TURNER

Two of the most provocative theorists of ritual are Victor Turner, an anthropologist, and Theodor Gaster, a religionist. Each is regarded by his colleagues as something of a creative maverick in his field, partly because of the sweeping, interdisciplinary swaths cut by his theories. I find their views especially crucial to ritual studies; each man has grounded his theoretical formulations in large amounts of carefully studied data without becoming lost in them.

I want to offer here a critical comparison of the two figures with a view to ferreting out their contributions to ritual studies. I do not intend merely to present, compare, and contrast; I have a special agenda. I am neither an Africanist nor a Semiticist; so I will not rehearse the works of Turner and Gaster in their respective fields of specialization. They are prone to what Turner calls "extended case studies." My interest is specifically in the principles which inform these extensions; hence, I persist in asking the two theorists what they have to teach us about the hermeneutics of symbolic action. I want to know: in what units ritual is to be studied; what it has to do with drama, myth, and symbol; how it can be described as a religious phenomenon; what one must know to interpret it; and what difference it makes if performances are ancient, "folk," or "primitive"; in short, what is expected of a scholarly interpreter in the face of a symbolic act.

Some obvious differences between Gaster and Turner are initially apparent.   Gaster is trained in classical philology, folklore, Semitics, and ancient Near Eastern studies.   Consistently, his writings concentrate on the texts of Mesopotamian, Canaanite, Egyptian, and Hittite religion or Judaism and the Old Testament. He also publishes on folklore, myth, and ritual. Turner, on the other hand, is trained in English literature and social anthropology and first published in the area of African studies.   His persistent interest is in ritual symbols. More recently, he has written very widely on "liminal" (threshold, borderline) phenomena such as religio-political movements and pilgrimages in England, Ireland, and Mexico. Both Gaster and Turner have done very detailed micro-studies on texts and tribal rites, respectively, but have made further forays into that cluster of phenomena usually lumped together under the label, "symbol, myth, and ritual." Despite the difference between their historical-philological and socio-anthropological methods, both have pursued myths, rituals, and symbols in the context of a keenly developed interest in folk and popular (as opposed to philosophical or theological) religiosity.   And both have an abiding interest in artistic, particularly literary, culture.   What strikes one whose interests are more contemporary is the adeptness with which they link their data from ancient and tribal cultures to contemporary post-industrial concerns.   This facility is undoubtedly responsible for earning them their reputations for provocative, but rather unorthodox, stances.

GASTER'S THEORIES

Among Gaster's writings the theoretical implications for ritual studies are most explicit in his THESPIS, "Myth and Story," "Myth, Mythology,"MYTH, LEGEND, AND CUSTOM IN THE OLD TESTAMENT, and "Errors of Method in the Study of Religion"./1/ Though Gaster is intent on breaking the sway of literary criticism over the interpretation of myth and ritual, his methods are philological and literary-critical for the simple reason that his data are texts for performances, not directly observed rituals. One of his most fundamental contributions is his argument that certain ancient texts bear the marks of what he calls alternately the "Seasonal Pattern" and the "Ritual Pattern." In THESPIS he is specifically interested in demonstrating that ancient Near Eastern texts reflect this pattern (as do the Rig Veda, Greek tragedy, the Elder Edda, ancient Chinese folk songs, grail romances, and English mummers' plays). The four moments of this pattern are as follows (1961:26ff.):

(1) Mortification--a state occurring at the end of a seasonal cycle which precipitates a state of suspended animation and is marked by

fasts, austerities, abstinences, self-denial, ululation, and weeping; in this moment roles and the normal order of things are suspended or inverted.
(2) Purgation—a process whereby pollution, evil, and contagion are drained off or neutralized by ritual actions like exorcism, scrubbing, burning, explusion, or aspersion.
(3) Invigoration—the moment of maximized ritual effort whereby power is procured; typified by mimetic combats, races, sacred marriages, sexual activity, and rites of incorporation or rebirth.
(4) Jubilation—the celebrative moment when the ritual work is accomplished; marked by feasts and joyous celebrations./2/

Gaster contends that this fundamental pattern characterizes both ritualistic and mythic texts in the ancient Near East. The bulk of THESPIS consists of texts and commentary offered as illustration. Some of his ritualistic examples are: the Babylonian Akitu (a festival of the New Year), the Hebraic ritual complex, Asif-Kippurim-Sukkoth ("Ingathering-Atonement-Booths"), Attis celebrations, the Hittite Puruli Festival, the Egyptian Memphite Creation Play, and the Egyptian Ramesseum Drama. Among the mythic texts he uses to illustrate his pattern are: the Canaanite poems of "Baal," "The Gracious Gods," and "Aqhat" ("The Story of the Divine Bow"); the Egyptian "Coronation Drama"; the "Edfu Drama"; the Babylonian "Epic of Creation" (Enuma Elish); and the Hittite "Snaring of the Dragon."

The criteria for categorizing texts as "ritualistic" or "mythic" are by no means simple. Gaster claims that not only the content of these texts but also their forms reflect seasonal dramas (1961:99). This is true, he argues, even of cases in which a text shows clear signs of poetic re-casting (1961:83). So whether a text is mythic or ritualistic is an irrelevant consideration in deciding to what extent it follows Gaster's seasonal pattern. Some of the texts are explicitly divided into two sections, one ritualistic and one mythic, for example, the Hittite Yuzgat Tablet, "The Snaring of the Dragon," and the Canaanite poem "The Gracious Gods." In these cases the texts may have served as prescriptive "orders of worship." So even though Professor Gaster explicitly denies that he is claiming all of the texts considered are "libretti of liturgical dramas or the spoken accompaniments of ritual acts" (1961:12), he is, nevertheless, working with data, some of which are still sufficiently close to their origins in ritual as to be actual "books of words" or retain clear survivals of such.

One of Gaster's main contributions is his typology. The fourfold pattern which I have outlined is, as Gaster recognizes, a composite picture. As he interprets specific texts, he characterizes them typologically according to the chords they strike in his ritual pattern; the result is five types:
(1) The comprehensive type is typified by the Canaanite poem "Baal," since it includes all the moments of the seasonal pattern.

What is of theoretical importance about Gaster's interpretation is that his comprehensive model allows him to clarify meanings, fill in lacunae, and lend coherence to fragmentary narratives by extrapolating from what he takes to be a cross-culturally typical pattern of folklore and comparative mythology. He feels that he can get behind words to referents: ". . . words are, at best, the mere shorthand of thoughts, and . . . folktales originate in the mind rather than in the mouth or from the pen" (1961:109). If one has a comprehensive type which directly reflects the minds of its creators, one may, Gaster implies, infer what was intended when the data are unclear or incomplete. This is the axiom which Gaster uses to warrant his full but controversial translations and comparative commentaries. Extrapolation from known pattern to unknown lacunae is at the heart of comparative folklore.

(2) The combat type, his second one, emphasizes the moment of invigoration from the Seasonal Pattern. Gaster knows that typologies account for similarities better than for complex differences and that some parts of his pattern are more vestigial in certain myths and rituals than in others (1961:92). So even though the Hittite Puruli Festival contains several elements of the pattern, Gaster chooses to classify the text of the Puruli myth under the combat type. The differences between the comprehensive and combat types are not absolute, since Gaster views combat so broadly. In this type of myth and ritual, conflicts occur between old and new years, rain and drought, summer and winter, life and death (1961:267).

(3) Although Professor Gaster does not say so, I suspect that the disappearing god type, his third classification, emphasizes the moment of mortification, since what predominates is a pregnant absence, a suspension which promises rebirth. To cite one example, Demeter searches the earth for lost Persephone, for the fructification which only certain seasons bring. The fact that the Telipinu myth, however, illustrates a type does not prevent it from containing all the moments of the ritual pattern (1961:299).

(4) The coronation type is one of the most interesting and problematic, because in illustrating it Gaster rearranges the material of Egyptian ritual-dramas to support his view of the relation between "punctual ritual and mythological drama" (1961:377). In reworking the Egyptian processional scenario of the Ramesseum Drama, he distinguishes ritual action from mythological interpretation and interjects his own explanations to "trick out the original wording." In this instance I find distinguishing rubrics, indigenous interpretation, and Gaster's glosses quite difficult. But even overlooking the confusing conflation, I wonder why a sentence like "The ceremonial barge is equipped," constitutes "mythological interpretation," while "Horus requests his Followers to equip him with the Eye of power" is a "ritual action." I should mention one further problem raised by the coronation type. In it Gaster uses a formal

list of dramatis personae, as well as a division into scenes; yet he does not make explicit why the Egyptian Ramesseum Drama is to be regarded as drama at all. One wonders what criteria distinguish ritual and drama. If in an Egyptian performance the king is Horus, is this ritual or dramatic action?

(5) The burlesque type, Gaster's last one, is "a degeneration from the original sacer ludus" (1961:413). Historically, myths and rituals of this kind occur when drama has lost its functional significance, which means for Gaster that it has lost its role in the renewal of seasonal power. What is offered as illustration of this type is the poem "The Gracious Gods," with its curious parallels to the ribald, off-color joking and acting of folk drama, mummery, and popular entertainments. Apparently, this type does not represent an emphasis upon a particular moment of the ritual pattern so much as a devolution of the pattern itself, with a concomitant change of function from magic to entertainment.

I have said enough to indicate Gaster's basic outlines of the ritual pattern and ritual types, respectively. The former is a composite view of the moments of an intra-ritualistic process, while the latter is a taxonomy of whole rituals and myths./3/ Both the pattern (I would prefer "process") and the typology are cross-cultural and wedded to some important historical, sociological, and phenomenological assumptions.

Gaster's most significant historical thesis is implicit in what I have already said, namely, that there occurs an evolution or devolution from primitive ritual to literary composition. This process leaves a deposit of survivals which bear marks of their ritual origins (1961:326). A corrolary argument is that, in addition to this poeticizing, the rationale for ritual sometimes shifts from seasonal to historical-political, for example, the battle of dryness and wetness becomes a battle of rival groups (1961:38-39). A third related historical thesis is Gaster's suggestion that, in the course of time, what was done ritually by a whole group comes to be focused upon one representative of that whole, namely, the king (1961:17,48). The agents of such developments in the history of ritual seem to be three: artists (like Euripides), the "irrepressible and playful inventiveness of the common people," and urbanization (1961:18,83). Gaster argues that eventually natural processes lost their urgency in urban life; hence, seasonal rites were no longer functional and only survived fragmentarily because of their artistic or customary appeal. Dramatic ritual becomes, then, either drama or literary motif; "the pattern of the ritual becomes the plot of the drama" (1961:83). Gaster implies an even further devolution by suggesting that the loss of a functional, seasonal rationale catapults performance not only into drama but into crude, popular entertainments.

At issue in Gaster's historical generalizations is the phenomenology of ritual, drama, and myth. For Gaster rituals are functional, "punctual," and seasonal. They punctuate a moment in time and an area in space as an effort to rejuvenate what he calls a "topocosm," that is, "the entire complex of any given locality conceived as a living organism" (1961:17). And what ritual does punctually, myth does duratively, or ideally. Gaster construes myth and ritual in terms of a spatial metaphor, that of two parallel planes; he is quite critical of Eliade and Malinowski, who conceive of it according to a temporal metaphor. In this latter view, myth is said to narrate the primordial, archetypal deeds of the gods, which are then subsequently enacted (1954:207). "Presentation then becomes representation; the ritual turns into a drama" (1961:8), and both myth and ritual are altered in their essence. So Gaster insists that we view myth and ritual as simultaneous planes or levels instead of cause and effect of one another. I am unsure whether he thinks that treating them as sequential is something that occurs only in poorly considered models of ritual studies or in the actual evolution and practice of ritual as well, in other words, whether this view is a methodological critique or a historical thesis.

Whereas Gaster conceives the relation of ritual and myth "spatially," he sometimes views ritual and drama processually and temporally. Occasionally, he implies that drama is the outcome of a change in the nature of ritual and myth. At other times he seems to view the relations phenomenologically, for example, "The interpenetration of myth and ritual creates drama" (1961:17). This insistence that the ritualistic and dramatic are concurrent levels of the same act is, I think, more consistent with his related claim that the mythic and ritualistic are parallel planes. However, I still wonder what drama is, since the interpenetration of myth and ritual is usually called "religion," not "drama." Are all representative acts dramatic ones? I doubt that the difference between ritual and drama hinges on the criterion of whether what is being represented is conceived as above, in a parallel plane, or behind, in a primordial time. Implicit in some of Gaster's other comments is another criterion, namely, role. Correspondence of punctual and durative, ritual and myth, is contrasted with impersonation (1961:79); the latter suggests a dichotomy which marks the dramatic consciousness.

It seems that the dramatic consciousness (though not drama per se) is latent in myth, since the ritual performer enacts the mythic ideal. Gaster thinks that when myth and ritual occur together, participants are at once having a direct experience and impersonating other characters such as gods (1961:77). Since myth adds a second layer /4/ to ordinary, empirical experience or to ritual experience, religion is not only latently dramatic, but is a latent double entendre (see 1954:205); and one would expect burlesque theater, the union of punning and pretending, to be its outcome (as for Gaster it is). If we begin with an ideal/real distinction, we may expect a dramatic or comic worldview once the literal-functional aspects of seasonal performances have deteriorated.

I take it, then, that drama is two steps removed from ritual, myth constituting the intermediate phenomenological level by its introduction of memesis ("imitation of action"). My inference is that in Gaster's view we become actors the moment we mythologize our rituals (see 1961:24). Phenomenologically, ritual, myth, and drama co-exist simultaneously. This contention I take to be Gaster's most basic and overt axiom. However, I think there are grounds for inferring a secondary thesis, which is that, historically considered, the religious consciousness emphasizes in sequence: ritual, myth, and drama. Myth and ritual are "spatially" parallel, but ritual is temporally prior./5/ Drama is the latest historically, since it is what is left when the ritual act ceases to be a direct experience and becomes mimetic, imaginative, and impersonatory; a ritual form becomes a mere convention.

When Gaster outlines the history of myth's development, he suggests four stages (1954:200ff.): (1) the primitive, a postulated stage in which a story is a direct accompaniment of a ritual performed for "purely pragmatic purposes"; (2) the dramatic stage, in which a performance is an enactment of a myth which functions as a script; (3) the liturgical stage, in which a story is performed as a recitation in an order of service; and (4) the literary stage, in which the myth becomes a tale or an artistic product. Since Gaster is here tracing the evolution of myth, not of ritual, he ends in recitation and literary art, not in dramatic art, which has become a form in its own right. This accounts for the difference between the implied chronology of THESPIS and the one in "Myth and Story."

As I see the broader implications of Gaster's work on ritual, the central theoretical issue is the same as that which myth, ritual, and drama themselves attempt to symbolize, namely, continuity and change, or metaphorically considered, space and time. Methodologically, these pairs parallel the differences between the phenomenology and history of religion or social-systems analysis and social dramatism. From a variety of materials and from diverse cultures and times, Gaster infers a ritual pattern. This structure he projects, despite himself, chronologically; it is the "original." So he transforms history of religion into phenomenology of religion, but only to argue once again that the essence, the seasonal pattern of ritual, "comes first." Myth, "then," is a projection on a durative plane. This is why he speaks not of a mythological pattern but of a ritual pattern.

Gaster's basic intent is to resist any view of myth and ritual as developing sequentially. Essentially, myth and ritual are for him co-substantial (1954:187), and he explicitly rejects Robertson Smith's thesis that myth is a mere offshoot of ritual. I say "essentially," because Gaster does, in fact, know that specific myths and rituals have sometimes been expressed in sequence. For Gaster there is a difference between ideal and actual myths and rituals. Actually articulated myths /6/, called "mythological stories," are "inevitably compromised"; they are "reductions" of the essential Mythic Idea (1954:103). What in THESPIS is called "punctual" and "durative" is in "Myth and Story," a later article, the "basic mythic idea" of an "intrinsic parallelism between the real and ideal," which Gaster takes to be implicit in the very process of apprehending and interpreting. If such a parallelism is actually the case, myth and ritual, durative and punctual, are elements of a fundamental epistemology, not mere data in religious studies.

Gaster says he wants to remove the study of ritual and myth from the study of literature, art, and imagination (1954:199); but in elevating punctual and durative to the status of necessary epistemological categories, I do not think he can avoid implying a theory of perception and imagination. Gaster's punctural/durative, or real/ideal, schema is a metaphysic and thus not challengeable by definition (see 1954:208). It is a metaphysic rooted in spatial metaphors, specifically, the metaphor of two parallel planes. The difficulty with such a root metaphor is, of course, classic. It is the problem of specifying how the two planes intersect. The planes provide us with the statics of a method for ritual studies, but what are the dynamics of the interpenetration of myth and ritual? For Gaster the dynamics seem to be located in the psychological-ideational realm.

In response to critics who contend that Gaster's patterning is itself a bit of durative fictionalizing which overlooks the diversity of cultures and rituals, Gaster says he is making "psychological," not historical, statements. Some would call Gaster's patterns "structural" or "archetypal," but whatever the terminology, his statement of the status of his schema seems clear enough:

> What it asserts is that a certain type of story is <u>au</u> <u>fond</u> a literary (or, more neutrally, a verbal) expression of the same situation as is expressed 'behavioristically' in ritual, and that the two things therefore run parallel, the sequence of incidents in the one finding its counterpart in the order of actions in the other. In short, what we are discussing is a parallelism not between an actual <u>recitation</u> and an actual <u>performance</u>, but between a <u>pattern</u> of narrative and a pattern of ritual, or—to put it more broadly--the ultimate relation of a <u>genre</u> of literature to a <u>genre</u> of ceremony (1954:211).

Gaster's schema itself has the qualities he attributes to myth; it is durative, metatemporal. It is used to explain certain historico-temporal phenomena, though it is not itself explainable or inferable from them. It articulates an ahistorical ideal in terms of which actual phenomena, in this case, mythic stories and ritualistic performances, are only approximations. In short, the "Mythic Idea" and "Ritual Pattern" must be written with capital letters to indicate their durative character.

I do not mean to reject Gaster's theses by referring to them in this way, since I think a homology of data and method is important. His work is strongly comparative in tone, and the ultimate ground for any comparison usually remains somewhat mysterious, axiomatic, and impregnable because of its "meta-" character. Insofar as Gaster believes in a basic conceptual unity of human religious practices, the concepts grounding that unity are functionally akin to myth—not insofar as myth articulates a ritual act, but insofar as it lifts the locally punctual to a pan-human level. Because of this scope, Gaster, like Frazer and Eliade, has been accused (as Eliade accused Frazer) of "confusionistic comparativism" (Eliade, 1963:42)./7/ Gaster might protect himself (with more success) as Eliade did: by claiming that "the historical context of each example we give is implied." For Eliade historical context is implied; for Gaster the pattern is "psychological," not historical. Comparativism, phenomenology, and structuralism (all methods pervaded with spatial-static metaphors) share a common intention which permeates Gaster's work, namely, to "recognize the permanent truth behind the changing forms" (1953:x). The assumption I question is that truth is what does not change--that truth has only a durative and not also a flowing character.

Linguist that he is, Gaster knows that people of ancient cultures did not express themselves as we do; there are differences between us and them (see 1953:5). But he sees these as mere differences of expression, not of essence, and one can arrive at essential continuities by translating the specifically local into the general:

> When an ancient Hebrew said that God spoke with Moses on the top of a mountain, what he was really saying, in the only language then available, was that any code of laws which professes to set up a universal standard of human living must represent a link between the human and the divine--that is, must derive its authority from man's apprehension of what the basic scheme of the universe really is. Today, thanks to the progress of philosophy and theology, it is possible to express this idea in more rarefied,

metaphysical terms; we can speak, for instance, of Natural Law as the ultimate source of human legislation, or of the general interpenetration of the punctual and the durative, the temporal and the eternal. But the fact that three thousand years ago, men used more primitive terms does not make the idea more primitive; at most, it makes the language antique (1953:6-7).

Gaster then goes one step beyond this demythologizing. He re-mythologizes (1974:192) the general conception in terms of the local idiom of some contemporary Western cultures, for example:

The Messiah is today simply a particular symbol for a general and perennial idea, and the fact that this symbol sprang out of the conditions of a distant past is completely unimportant. Indeed, our own alternative image of the Golden Age issues, in precisely the same way, out of ancient Greek mythology rather than out of our contemporary environment, while the French symbol of liberation during the Second World War was the cross of Joan of Arc! Viewed in this light, the Messiah is no more inappropriate as a symbol than are, for example, Cupid, Santa Claus or the Minute Man (1953:8-9).

Gaster posits a fundamental, intercultural continuity underlying a surface of diversity and change. This is what allows for his controversial reconstructions, extrapolations, and strikingly idiomatic translations such as THE OLDEST STORIES IN THE WORLD and THE DEAD SEA SCRIPTURES. Only such an axiom would permit, for example, a translation of the name of the Hittite god, Hahhimas, as Jack Frost (1961:273).

One might wrongly assume, because Gaster renders "religious overtones" in translations that sound like "popular undertones," that he Platonically exhalts the ideal and general and denigrates the "minute particulars." For him the particulars, both historically and culturally, are the real. Hence, when responding in the epilogue of FESTIVALS OF THE JEWISH YEAR to the query why Jews do not simply trade in their peculiar institutions and festivals on more familiar ones if they all are simply exemplifications of universal ideals, Gaster retorts that the <u>living</u> experience itself resides in the <u>distinctive history</u> of Jews (my emphases). Simply because Independence Day and Passover are both concretions of the same universal ideal, does not mean that Gaster thinks one can be substituted for the other. So especially when the issue is his own religious tradition, what is important for Gaster is not only the "permanent, continuous truth" (1953:11), but the lived experience in historical time. In short, Gaster does not go all the way with Plato despite his punctual/durative distinction, because for him "real" and "ideal" are dialectical opposites, not synonyms. The real is the punctual, though it must be ever renewed by contact with the ideal-durative.

Before I proceed further, I would like to provide a synoptic chart that summarizes what I have said about Gaster's implied model and anticipates what I will say about Turner's. Neither writes so systematically as such a chart might lead the reader to believe; the chart is my construction. It distorts their research by eliminating too much of each man's definitional playfulness and, perhaps, by attaching too high a level of generalization to their comments on "minute particulars," but I think it fairly indicates their continuities and differences.

A COMPARISON OF THE THEORIES OF THEODOR GASTER & VICTOR TURNER

CATEGORY OF COMPARISON	GASTER	TURNER
1. Academic field:	religious studies	anthropology
2. Areas of specialization:	ancient Near East (also modern Judaism and history of religions)	Africa (also modern Christianity and history of religions)
3. Early scholarly influences:	James Frazer Gilbert Murray Francis Cornford	A.R. Radcliffe-Brown E.E. Evans-Pritchard Arnold Van Gennep
4. Mode of cross-cultural study:	comparative folklore (motif study)	comparative symbology (extended case study)
5. Primary sources of data:	texts, inscriptions, archeological remains	field study as participant-observer
6. Context for treating ritual:	historical (derivations)	sociocultural (co-variances)
7. Usual topic cluster:	myth-ritual-drama	ritual-symbol-drama
8. Ritual viewed as:	punctual enactment of durative-ideal (typically natural-seasonal in character)	transformative performance revealing major classifications, categories, and contradictions of cultural processes

9.	Drama viewed as:	mimetic (representational, impersonatory), playful, entertaining, conventional	conflictual, teleological (climactic), role-employing, before an audience, rhetorical style, single set of rules
10.	Myth viewed as:	narration of ideal-durative	form of indigenous exegesis, treating of origins but derived from transitions
11.	Types of ritual usually considered:	1. comprehensive (seasonal) 2. combat 3. coronation 4. burlesque	1. life-crisis (rites of passage) 2. rites of affliction 3. pilgrimage 4. festive
12.	Formal sub-units of intra-ritual study:	pattern; act, scene	symbol; phase, episode
13.	Formal unit of comparative ritual study:	type, pattern	symbol
14.	Pattern of socio-ritual processes:	1. mortification 2. purgation 3. invigoration 4. jubilation (ritual pattern with social implications)	1. breach 2. crisis 3. redress 4. reintegration (social pattern with ritual implications)

15. Modern, post-industrial parallels:	survivals (meaningless customs, figures of speech, poetry, drama)	liminoid phenomena (festivals, counter-cultures, revolutions, pilgrimages, the arts)
16. View of historical process:	evolutionary-devolutionary	political-conflictual
17. Basic dichotomies:	ideal/real durative/punctual myth/ritual	structural/liminal ceremony/ritual hierarchy/communitas
18. Root metaphors of model:	spatial (e.g., parallels, planes, "topocosm," "punctual")	temporal (e.g., processes, social dramas, becoming, development, growth)
19. Stages of myth:	1. primitive--direct accompaniment to ritual 2. dramatic--script for performance 3. liturgical--recited in order of service 4. literary--tale or artwork	
20. Underlying philosophical presuppositions:	idealism	empiricism, vitalism
21. Levels of meaning (of a symbol):	1. exegetical 2. operational 3. positional	

TURNER'S THEORIES

Turning from Gaster to Turner is a shift from a modified idealism to a modified empiricism, a move from the ethos of Plato to that of Heraclitus, or from Hegel to Marx. The emphasis now is upon what flows and changes; innovation, not duration, becomes the keynote. For my purposes, the most important works of Turner are THE RITUAL PROCESS and DRAMAS, FIELDS AND METAPHORS, as well as THE FOREST OF SYMBOLS and a large number of articles.

In Turner's view, if we analyze a ritual into its constituents, we find symbols; and if we inquire into its context, we find arenas of social conflict, or "social dramas."/8/ So his work is Janus-like. Theoretically, it faces two ways, on the one hand, toward semantics and semiology (or "comparative symbology," as he prefers), and political anthropology or "processualism," on the other. And just as Gaster's generalizations about myth and ritual arise from tightly focused textual studies in the ancient Near East, Turner's broader forays into ritual and symbol develop from early anthropological field studies in Africa among the Ndembu of Zambia.

The continuity of ritual is, in Turner's treatment, not conceptual but dramatic; hence, ritual is best viewed as a process, not an enduring system or set of types. Even though the Latin root of "rite" connotes a way or mode of ordering, Turner notes that its Indo-European origin suggests a flowing (1968a:269); this flowing character is the crux of Turner's contribution to ritual studies. Turner's dramatism depends on perceiving the similarities among dramatic performance on stage, ritualistic enactments, and public crises. These have in common: (1) the playing of roles, (2) the use of rhetorical style speech, (3) an audience, (4) knowledge and acceptance of a single set of rules, (5) and a climax (1968a:274; cf. 1957:xxiv).

Social dramas are phased processes in which paradigms are contested (1974a:17)./8/ They are "units of aharmonic or disharmonic processes, arising in conflict situations," and they typically follow the pattern of breach, crisis, redressive action, and reintegration (1974a:37,38-41). Ritual typically functions as a mode of redressive action in this process of accelerated social transition. It at once masks social contradictions and enacts them, thereby providing a symbolic unification which temporarily bridges factionalism and schismatic rifts. The symbolic unification which ritual provides is, of course, an ideal one which lies, as it were, on top of very real divisions (see 1957:330). Here Turner's view is quite different from Gaster's. For the latter, ritual is the punctual-real correspondent to the ideal-mythic, while for the former, ritual is an ideal or symbolic layer of real social processes. The two views are in agreement insofar as ritual is treated as occurring in a rift, though for Turner the rift is in time, not space, as the case is with Gaster's "topocosm."/9/ Furthermore, despite their differently locating the "real," they agree that in the study of ritual we should not divorce consideration of ideal and real, synchrony and diachrony (see Turner, 1957:xxiv).

The motto of Turner's first major book, SCHISM AND CONTINUITY, is important: "General Forms have their vitality in Particulars, & every Particular is a Man" (William Blake's JERUSALEM). Ritual symbols are focal points for mediating bipolar dichotomies: general/particular, ideal/real, schism/continuity, diachronic/synchronic. So even though drama is a temporal flow, it does issue in a climax, a telos, which provides "a limited area of transparency on the otherwise opaque surface of regular, uneventful social life" (1957:93). When Turner looks through, behind, or below the surface, he tends to find multiplicity, conflict, or flux; whereas, Gaster tends to find unity, cohesion, and stability. The difference is due in part, I think, to Gaster's concentration on symbolic language and Turner's focus on symbolic action as their data.

The differences between Gaster's and Turner's ways of interpreting ritual's relation to drama are illustrated by their actual procedures in THESPIS and CHIHAMBA THE WHITE SPIRIT, since the subtitles of both works indicate that they are studies in "ritual drama." Enough has been said already about the view of drama expressed in THESPIS, so I will concentrate on CHIHAMBA. Turner participated as a candidate in the Chihamba rite and collected indigenous accounts of other performances. He reports that there is no canonical version of the ritual; no two performances of it are alike. So the account he offers is no more an "order of worship" than most of those translated and interpreted by Gaster. Formally considered, what seems to make the Chihamba ritual dramatic is its division into episodes. Functionally considered, Chihamba appears to be a ritual drama because of its restatement of indigenous values in such a way as to perform a redressive task in a larger social drama (1957:316). There is, of course, role playing, mimesis, a climax, and an audience, but Turner's dramatism seems to depend less on actually operationalizing these criteria than on his discovery of conflictual social interaction growing out of contradictory roles and statuses. In other words, the drama of a "ritual drama" like Chihamba depends less upon formal qualities of the performance itself than upon the connection of a ritual enactment with a "social drama."

Both Turner and Gaster present their respective ritual dramas in scene or episode form. I have some reservations in both cases about the sub-divisions, especially with Gaster who does not always say whether the informant or interpreter makes such divisions. But I do not consider mine a serious objection, since the dramatism of both men seems to depend on criteria other than internal subdivision into acts, scenes, and episodes. What is fascinating about the dramatism of

Gaster and Turner is the tension between their views. For Gaster, ritual becomes dramatic insofar as it loses its functional values and becomes playful or entertaining and people no longer believe that it will affect the seasonal process. For Turner, a ritual is dramatic insofar as it represents and redresses a public conflict. In considering ritual drama, the two of them insist that the ritualistic and dramatic sensibilities belong together; yet Gaster is quite sensitive to the possibility that ritual can degenerate into mere entertainment, and Turner knows that ritual can easily become a mere condensation of local politics.

Behind Gaster stand Gilbert Murray and James Frazer. Behind Turner stand Radcliffe-Brown, Evans-Pritchard, and Arnold Van Gennep. I say "behind" because neither is an uncritical disciple of his mentors. Most important to understanding Turner's view of ritual is Van Gennep, particularly his notion of the limen, or threshold, since much of Turner's most creative work is an extension and transformation of this idea. In analyzing rites of passage, Van Gennep outlined a ritual process the stages of which he designated: (1) separation (pre-liminal), (2) transition (liminal), and (3) incorporation (post-liminal). For Van Gennep, a spatial passage across a threshold symbolized social passage through life crises such as birth, marriage, social puberty, and death.

Liminality, in Turner's works, is a moment of social limbo which is similar in some respects to Gaster's "mortification" stage. It is an anti-structural moment of reversal which is the creative fond not only for ritual, but for culture in general. As ritualists cross the threshold, they temporarily exit from the status system and find themselves in immediate, non-hierarchical contact with their compadres. A prime quality of liminality is an I-thou ethos which Turner calls "communitas." In this moment distinctions of wealth and class are suspended in favour of equality, poverty, and homogeneity./10/ Turner uses the term "liminal" much as religionists have used the term "sacred," except that it has socio-temporal rather than theo-spatial connotations. "Liminars," or "threshold people," are in a temporary state of wholeness, which is, from the point of view of structure, or the status-system, as dangerous as holiness is for homo religiosus. Consequently, it is hedged with taboos and restrictions.

Originally, in Van Gennep's THE RITES OF PASSAGE, liminality was a place and moment in life-crisis rituals of pre-industrial societies. In Turner's writings, liminality designates the generative quality which lends motion to a society, forcing it out of a rigid system and into flowing process. Among the liminoid phenomena considered by Turner are rituals, myths, pilgrimages, millenarian movements, revolutions, fiestas, and public celebrations. Liminars are metaphorically identical with the dead or the infantile (1967:96), since they are unclassifiable; they are located at the interstices of things.   In Van Gennep's study, liminars (Turner's term) were "initiates" (Turner prefers the term "initiands") undergoing rites of passage.   But as he extends the concept of liminality to include post–industrial, non–ritual phenomena, he coins the term "liminoid" to apply to functional equivalents, to hippies, artists, pilgrims. Pilgrimages are to historical religions what rites of passage are to tribal ones (1974a:65).

Turner's theory of liminality leads him to stand the anthropology of ritual on its head.   Ritual is no longer a Durkheimian collective representation which reflects society and insures social solidarity. Ritual is not a bastion of social conservatism whose symbols merely condense cherished cultural values.   Rather, ritual holds the generating source of culture and structure.   Hence, it is by definition associated with social transitions, while ceremony is linked to social states: "Ritual is transformative, ceremony confirmatory" (1967:95).

Though Turner has written more widely on ritual and symbol than on myth, he opens his article on myth and symbol in the INTERNATIONAL ENCYCLOPEDIA OF SOCIAL SCIENCES with a very liminal sounding statement, "Myths treat of origins but derive from transitions" (1968b:576). He radically challenges the usual assumptions of social anthropologists and historians of religion such as Malinowski and Eliade, who would interpret ritual and myth solely as presentations of static paradigms, rules, grammars, or structures. He and Gaster are unified in their dissent from these two great mentors of anthropology and religion because of their emphasis on the backward–looking nature of myth and ritual (as illustrated by Malinowski's "charter" and Eliade's "illo tempore"). Rituals and symbols do not simply point us backward to a timeless origin, but, Turner might say, to the ever–present source which was, and is now, originating culture. For Turner, this source not only moves us, it is itself moving. Ritual is usually interpreted in the light of its conserving function; Turner wants us to perceive its creative function.

What Turner wishes to reject in the study of ritual are asocial and atemporal methods, and his grounds for doing so are epistemological and methaphysical:

> The social world is a world in becoming, not a world in being (except insofar as 'being' is a description of the static, atemporal models men have in their heads), and for this reason studies of social structure as such are irrelevant. They are erroneous in basic premise because there is no such thing as 'static action.' That is why I am a little chary of the terms 'community' or 'society,'

too, though I do use them, for they are often
thought of as static concepts. Such a view
violates the actual flux and changefulness of
the human social scene. Here I would look,
for example, to Bergson rather than, say, to
Descartes, for philosophical guidance
(1974a:24).

Ritual cannot be divorced from the changing pattern which is
society; it shares society's processual, dramatic form. To be sure,
there is pattern in the flow, but the patterning occurs as a phasing
process, not as a set of systemic grids. In attacking the
timelessness of structural functionalism, Turner points to the
threshold of transition, liminality, but says of it, "In this no-place
and no-time that resists classification, the major classifications and
categories of culture emerge within the integuments of myth, symbol,
and ritual" (1974a:259).

Turner has rejected acculturalism and atemporalism in method only
to rediscover it in liminoid phenomena, which not only are experienced
as "moments in and out of time" (1968a:5), but are cross-cultural,
universally human. Liminality is transcultural. Of course, Turner
knows quite well that what is liminal today will be part of the status
system tomorrow.   In fact, he distinguishes three kinds of
communitas—spontaneous, ideological, and normative (1969a:132), the
latter of which is a coincidence of two opposites, liminality and
status system. Despite his recognition of the temporariness of
liminality-communitas, he still views this experience as essentially
the same in widely differing times and places. It seems that one must
in some sense stand on atemporal ground to discuss temporality. We
found this to be true with Gaster as well.

Ritual has its home in time, so harmony and unity can only be its
goal, not its presupposition.   As Turner notes, "The pathos of the
ritual situation arises from human antagonisms which may themselves be
provoked by the very rules which men make to establish peace among
themselves" (1968a:273). Despite the at-oneness of communitas,
conflict is hidden deep in the fabric of symbolic performances.

There is in Turner's writings, I think, a deep ambivalence, and I
am unsure whether to attribute it to him, to ritual itself, or to
both.   Ritual, as he characterizes it, particularly in earlier
writings, has a strong agonistic quality, while in his later works it
has just as pronounced a ludic quality. Of course, he could resolve
this tension easily enough by appealing to the metaphor of game a la
Huizinga, but he explicitly rejects game theory as a model for
understanding social drama, and I assume he would do the same for
ritual drama (1974a:141). If I might hazard a speculative guess, I
would suppose that Turner might locate the primary agonistic impulse

in social drama and the primary ludic one in ritual drama. Ritual is at once worklike ("ergic"), playlike ("anergic"), and combatlike; it is worklike in liminal, pre-industrial settings, playlike in liminoid, post-industrial ones, and combatlike insofar as it is an active force in the crises of social dramas (see 1974b:83). Turner and Gaster are in agreement that ritual may at once be both work (social and seasonal, respectively) and play (novelty-via-inversion and entertaining burlesque, respectively). For Gaster, the ludic element of ritual issues in folk customs, literature, and "survivals"; for Turner, revolutions, countercultures, artistic creativity, and other liminoid phenomena.

Turner and Gaster both comment on the relations between drama and ritual, but Gaster turns toward myth as a third focal point, while Turner shifts toward symbol. Myth and symbol can both be linguisitic units, but symbol is, so to speak, a smaller atom./11/ Whereas Gaster's units of cross-cultural comparison are the ritual type and the ritual pattern, Turner's is the symbol, particularly what he calls a "dominant symbol." The centrality of symbolism to Turner's theory is indicated by the naming of his enterprise "comparative symbology" (see especially 1974b). This subfield is broader than either symbolic anthropology or ritual studies, but narrower than semiotics (1974b:56), and is intended to include a processual-temporal emphasis which is missing from what some religionists and anthropologists are currently calling a "symbol systems approach." Despite his insistence that symbols must be studied in their temporal context in relation to other events of the social process (1967:20), Turner thinks it is possible to do comparative, morphological, and cross-cultural studies of dominant symbols (as distinct from "instrumental" ones), since they condense social norms and are indigenously regarded as ends in themselves (1967:32,45). Turner quite often pursues a dominant symbol through its ritual context, to the wider one of the whole cultural system of symbols, then through a whole culture area, and finally, toward a cross-cultural assessment. Such a method is possible, he thinks, because dominant symbols have a kind of autonomy in their respective rituals that instrumental symbols do not possess. For instance, symbols of whiteness in Ndembu ritual seem to have this characteristic, hence Turner's comparison of it with the whiteness of Moby Dick and white symbolism in the resurrection narrative of Matthew 28. Turner notes:

> One of the marks of a viable ritual symbol may be said to be its capacity to move from society to society without marked change in form but with many changes in meaning. Though referents are lost in transference, new referents are readily acquired. Certain

symbols arouse an almost universal response,
much as music does. This is a problem that
would repay investigation in terms of a
detailed comparative study (1967:291).

So although Turner's theory is certainly not archetypalist in
either a Jungian or Eliadean sense, it aims at a high level of
cross-cultural, transtemporal generalization.

Professor Turner makes a variety of observations about ritual
which have a definitional quality. Ritual is "an aggregation of
symbols" (1968a:2); a "quintessential custom" (1968a:23); a "patterned
process in time" (1967:45); "prescribed formal behaviour for occasions
not given over to technological routine, having reference to beliefs
in mystical beings or powers" (1967:19). Of all these succinct
statements, the first receives the most sustained attention. The key
to understanding ritual lies in the dynamics of symbols, since they
often epitomize whole domains and condense entire systems.

Symbols are multivocal units which become centers of interaction
and interpretation. They are "blazes" (chijikijilu in Ndembu,
1969a:115) which link known territory to the relatively unknown.
Characteristically, they unify disparate significata, condense
meanings, and polarize meaning around ideological (normative) and
orectic (sensory, affective) poles (1967:28). They usually have three
levels of meaning, which Turner names "exegetical" (indigenous
interpretation), "postional" (the relations between symbols of the
same system), and "operational" (what people do in relation to the
symbol (1967:50)./12/

"Drama" is a term Turner uses to connote the conflictual,
timebound, "processual" quality of ritual, while "symbol" is the word
he employs to suggest something more stable and cross-temporal.
Turner's "symbol," like Gaster's "myth," is "durative." The symbols,
not so much the phases (or what Gaster would call the "patterns"), of
ritual can be compared, once their role in differing cultural contexts
is understood. But we must not push the distinction between ritual
drama and ritual symbol too far, since Turner warns:

My intent here has been to show how symbols
are dynamic entities, not static cognitive
signs, how they are patterned by events and
informed by the passions of human
intercourse, in friendship, sexuality, and
politics, and how paradigms, bodied forth as
clusters and sequences of symbols, mediate
for men between ideals and action in social
fields full of cross-purposes and competing
interests (1974a:96).

Symbols, the "molecules of ritual" (1969:14), are most exposed in liminal phases of a ritual process or in liminoid moments of a social drama (1974a:252). During liminoid phases, symbols are exposed as nodal points which join classificatory planes to one another (1969a:41-42). Symbols cluster about such interfaces, and as liminars cross chasms, they see what they imagined to be axioms broken down into more fundamental units. What appeared solid now is shown to be a cluster of symbolic "particles" that could have been recombined in other ways. Grotesque masks, costumes, and body-decorations, which appear in liminal rites such as Mardi Gras or Halloween, are a ludic recombining of symbols in order not to destroy structure, but to expose its parts so they can be assimilated as gnosis, or deep knowledge. Paradigms are broken up to teach initiands how to generate other viable schema from the same fundamental symbols—a skill which social and environmental change will demand (1974a:256; 1967:105).

Even though symbols manifest what is mysterious and axiomatic in a ritual and culture, and thus seem "structural" or "systemic," they nevertheless have an active side. Since a symbol is "multivocal," it can speak one way on this occasion and another on that. The meaning of a symbol is not static, but shifts radically when the context shifts./13/ Symbols attract and lose meanings, and further, they have a dynamic of their own which enables them to operate as active factors in ritualistic, artistic, and political arenas. So what we might call Turner's "anthroplogical vitalism" pervades his view of symbols, as it does his treatment of drama and ritual. As he himself recognizes, the root metaphor of his method is an organic-biological one: things grow, develop, become (1974a:24). Such "living" things as dramas, rituals, and symbols have static or atemporal structures only "in actor's heads" (1974a:13, 36), and even then, mental processes themselves have a "processual" character. Far from being rooted in an atemporal, collective unconscious, symbols have their origin and goal in temporal flux.

Of considerable importance to ritual studies is Turner's resistance to sociological reductionism. The ritual symbol, he insists (1962:86, 91; cf. 1974a:57), has its own formal principles and ought not be reduced to a function of some other principles, though the essences of dominant symbols and ritual plots must be articulated together. But above all, ritual symbols are not to be cast as mere reflections of social contexts, since they are so often the fonds of culture. What is distinctive about human ritual, in contrast to animal ritualization, is that the formal principle of ritual is symbolic, and these isolable "parts" have a languagelike capacity for combination and recombination that allows them to generate new meanings and be culturally creative (1969b:8). Ritual symbols are not simply expressive, but epistemologically and sociologically constitutive, units (1968a:7).   This is why a ritual is viewed as typical, modal, or quintessential for the society in which it appears. Dramatistically considered, symbols are the real actors in a Turnerian view. Like stage actors, they move from scenario to scenario—from myth to ritual to epic to a juridical scene (see 1974b:55; cf. 1967:44). This migratory quality forces the interpreter to follow a symbol's career not only through ritual, but through a variety of genres; hence, symbology is of necessity comparative and cross-cultural.

SOME CRITICAL QUESTIONS

The theories of Gaster and Turner epitomize the academic fields of each. Insofar as their models have limitations, they are often symptomatic of those fields—religious studies, in its preoccupation with language and ideas, and anthropology, in its bent toward social processes. Gaster exerts himself to avoid reducing ritual to a mere expression of theological ideas, and Turner must continue to resist the temptation to shrink a performance to its operational or functional context. I have chosen the studies of Gaster and Turner because I think they have succeeded the most fully in avoiding these pitfalls and because, better than most, they have avoided both vague generalizations and excessive particularism in the study of ritual. Their success depends on their consistent wedding of static and dynamic forms--Gaster's punctual/durative and Turner's liminal/structural distinctions. It also depends on their maintaining the tensive trialogue among ritual account, indigenous exegesis, and scholarly commentary.   These are essential to ritual studies.
I want to make three observations on points at which I differ from their views. First, I think ritual studies should be grounded in hermeneutics, and from this point of view, both Turner and Gaster pay too little attention to the cultural and religious horizon of the interpreter. The result is that we are often left with what threatens to become a dualism of ancient-primitive versus modern-industrial. Both men eschew theological apologetics in the study of ritual, and I agree with their decision.   However, I am not satisfied that contemporary symbolic acts are best regarded as either "survivals" or "liminoid," since both concepts seem to locate the primary phenomenon elsewhere. Gaster's and Turner's categories are partly a function of their study of ritual in ancient and pre-industrial contexts. From these perspectives, contemporary symbolic acts must be viewed as reflections, likenesses, or remnants of earlier or simpler ones. Ritual studies should, I think, begin with the relationship between performer and audience-observer.   This, and not indigenous interpretation or extrinsic frameworks, is the beginning of ritual

studies. Gaster's retelling of the "oldest stories in the world" and his debates with Henri Frankfort and others (cf. 1955) over the "pre-logical mythopoeic" mentality of ancient people, along with Turner's accounts of his relations with informants, are beginnings in a truly dialogical interaction frame for ritual studies. The theoretical underpinnings for the study of observer-interpreters need more explicit formulation. Such questions as these need fuller handling: To what extent do ancient or primitve performers view their rituals as dramatic, as socially functional, as literally effective? To what extent are contemporary interpreters outside the actional frame of ancient and primitive rites? For post-industrial cultures, drama and civil ceremony are the ritual counterparts of demythologized myth. How does this affect our sense of ritual?

Another general response is that ritual studies should more systematically pursue the various dramatistic metaphors: act, actor, scene, audience, role, script, direction, and plot. Gaster and Turner have dramatistic elements in their models, though they are more fully pursued by Turner. Nevertheless, the dramatism of both is mitigated at points by the substitution of linguistic metaphors and methodologies more appropriate to exegesis, semantics of symbols, and etymology. The result is that gestural action receives little attention from either. And sustained attention to gesture would require both theoretical and technical attention to film as a medium for the study of ritual, as well as dance and sculpture, because they provide comparative data for use in the interpretation of gestures.

The third way in which I think ritual studies differs in emphasis from Turner and Gaster is in paying more attention to the formal level of meaning. Both Turner and Gaster tend to move rapidly from etymological, exegetical, or philological interpretation to comparative (and, in Turner's case, "action field") study without sufficient attention to the internal development of the ritual. They tend to describe formally and interpret comparatively. Despite their mention of episodes, phases, acts, and scenes internal to ritual performances, little is made of them interpretively. Gaster typically moves from philological exegesis to precedents and parallels, while Turner widens his hermeneutical circle from symbols to social co-variances, then to parallels. Both minimize what has been the strength of liturgics and what must be integral to ritual studies, namely, careful attention to the internal movement of a single rite and to the connectives between rituals in the same system.

Finally, I would in brief form raise some less important questions for further dialogue on issues where I find conflicting signals. Of Gaster I would ask the following: (1) To what does the term "punctual" most properly apply--a specific performance of a ritual, a ritual text, or an historical event, for instance, the Exodus? (2) Is not a ritual performance or text already a "preterpunctualizing" of an event? If so, why is a ritual any less durative than a myth? (3) Does myth itself constitute the durative "long view" or is it the vehicle and means to such? If the latter, to what does a myth point—a central idea? (4) What is the relation of types and patterns to motifs? (5) How can the tension be resolved between the view that drama is a degeneration of ritual and the view that both qualities occur together as different dimensions of the same thing?   (6) How are stages of myth related to types of ritual?

Of Turner I would query: (1) Is ritual necessarily oriented to divine beings? (2) Does ritual "break the cake of custom" (1967:106), or is it "quintessential custom"—is ritual typical or compensatory? (3) Is every act and word in a ritual symbolic? If not, what should we call nonsymbolic elements? What is the connective tissue between symbols? (4) Is a symbol recognized by common, conscious consent, or are there elements which are unconsciously symbolic? (5) What is the "location" of the static element in symbols and rituals—in actor's heads, in "space," in interpreter's ideas, in root paradigms? (6) How would one cross-culturally compare rituals per se, instead of ritual symbols?

It has been but a short time since religionists such as Gaster helped break the hold of Christian theological liturgics, and anthropologists such as Turner, the grip of reductionist social anthropology. Questions such as mine are attempts further to consolidate the autonomy and integrity of ritual studies as a discipline.

NOTES

/1/ A full bibliography is available in "The Gaster Festschrift," THE JOURNAL OF THE ANCIENT NEAR EASTERN SOCIETY OF COLUMBIA UNIVERSITY 5(1973):446-453.

/2/ Though not formally part of this pattern, two other phenomena are noted as "constant elements" by Gaster: the return of the dead and communal meals (1961:44). He does not say why these do not become moments in the process which he outlines and illustrates.

/3/ Though he does not develop it fully, Gaster also offers a table of motifs (1961:150-151), i.e., a comparative unit of "plot" content.

/4/ Gaster's rather consistent layering of phenomena into "religious overtone" and "popular undertone" is, perhaps, another twofold outgrowth of his basic ideal/real distinction.

/5/ Also metaphysically prior, since one "ascends" to ritual (1954:210).

/6/ A myth differs from a tale, inasmuch as the former is linked to a cultural performance (1954:198).

/7/ Contrast the metaphor Turner uses to describe the accusation that one might aim at him: "incursive nomadism" (1974a:17).

/8/ In view of the scope of the term "social drama," Kenneth S. Carlston suggests that Turner use the term "constitutive conflict" to designate such processes (Turner, 1974a:102).

/9/ Even his notion of the limen ("boundary," "threshold") is de-spatialized to connote transition in time.

/10/ See the chart in 1969a:106-107 for a full list of the qualities.

/11/ For Turner, a symbol is "a thing regarded by general consent as naturally typifying, representing, or recalling something by possession of analogous qualities or by association in fact or thought" (1967:19). A symbol is distinguished from a sign by the latter's pointing to what is already known. Hence, for a ritual specialist symbols tend gradually to become signs.

/12/ In 1974b:53 he makes rough equations between these terms and Charles Morris' "semantic," "syntactic," and "pragmatic," respectively (see Morris, 1938).

/13/ In ritual proper, the "voices" are confused; many things are said at once. In divination, however, the means are brittle, segmented, and distinct, says Turner.

PART IV

RITUAL AND THEATER

INTRODUCTION

Theologians frequently reflect on theologies instead of living religious practice, just as novelists sometimes write in the ambience of other literature rather than lived experience. Reflexivity, which is reflection upon one's own self or task, is a mark of the post-modern era that affects both the practice of ritual and scholarship on it. Nothing is wrong with reflexivity unless it becomes merely self-serving. Theorizing can easily degenerate into a closed circle when theorists write only about other theorists. To say that theory and practice belong together is a truism. Of course they do. Who could disagree? But in what proportion and under what circumstances? How do they belong together? Do we apply theory to practice, or do we infer theory from practice? Or do we merely derive theories from other theories?

A series of steps leads from practice to theory in ascending degrees of abstraction: (1) pre-reflective participation in a ritual, (2) reflective participation such as that of a priest, rabbi, or educated layperson, (3) sympathetic participant-observation as a field researcher might provide, (4) detached observation and description, (5) taxonomy, classification, comparison, or categorization, (6) theoretical explanation, and (7) reflection on theories or theorists.

Each of these steps on the theory-practice scale has its strengths and weaknesses. Different cultures and eras have emphasized different steps and ways of connecting them. Ours, I think, is characterized by a strong, split emphasis on number one and number four. Whether this is true or not, ritual studies is best characterized as an effort to center on number three and then reach in both directions in order to mitigate the cleavage.

Now I turn from theoretical considerations to fieldstudy materials on ritual, particularly as it relates to theater. The tenth chapter is the only one in Part IV that depends largely on written sources, interviews, and lectures; it concentrates on Grotowski's he remaining chapters draw mainly on fieldwork. Chapter 11 is about Grotowski's activities after he left theater in order to conduct experiments with actions resembling meditation and ritual. In Chapter 12 I consider an example of a performance by Actor's Lab, describe the its most basic form of training, and then look at a pararitualistic event designed by its members. The thirteenth chapter is a comparative analysis of two public celebrations. The fourteenth is a description of a public celebration designed by Welfare State International of England. And the concluding chapter is about contemporary efforts to appropriate shamanism as a model for unifying educational, dramatic, therapeutic, and religious practice.

CHAPTER 10

GROTOWSKI'S "POOR" THEATER

Ritual and drama are dance partners. Whether observed historically, in terms of their origin and development, or phenomenologically, in terms of their structures and dynamics, ritual and drama circle one another in a dialectical two-step characteristic of coinciding opposites. The Western world's post-medieval segregation of church and stage was only a moment in a process; it was not a permanent state of affairs. The recent emergence of ritualized theater belies any such simple oppositions by laying bare the fundamental impulses toward stylization, mimesis, and transformation which are characteristic of ritualistic and dramatic impulses. Because of its forays into ritual, experimental theater is of significance not only to the history of drama and culture but also to religious studies, specifically to the hermeneutics of symbolic action (ritual) and religious experience (mysticism).

Experimental theater, much of which is ritualistic in form and ethos, breaks off sharply in some ways with "modern" theater. As characterized by Tom Driver, modern theater ends in the mid-1950's.

. . . Its principal growth has been toward an ever more pervasive irony, by which is meant the maintenance of an attitude of affirmation and negation toward whatever is in the field of vision and the accompaniment of this

attitude by accute self-awareness. The
ironist is not always sure that what he
sees is real, but he is sure that he
sees it. He knows that the reality he
seeks lies neither in the subject nor
in the object alone but in the
interchange between them (1970:346).

Modernity, says Driver, culminates in the plays of Samuel
Beckett, Luigi Pirandello, Bertolt Brecht, and Jean Genet and reaches
its destructive fulfillment in the theater of cruelty of Antoin
Artaud. Despite their many striking differences, Driver finds in
these playwrights what he calls "theatrical positivism," the theater's
"strategy of regarding itself as the one, sure, positive reality"
(348), and a tendency to construe the theater as an imitation of a
self-enclosed consciousness (368). Such theater is constituted of
acts rather than imitations of action; it concentrates on its own
positive techniques and existence. When theater pursues autonomy by
imitation of itself, when it becomes drama about drama, it is headed
toward theatricalism and formalism.

POST-MODERN THEATER

Jerzy Grotowski's role in the shift from modern theatrical
positivism to the ritual theater of the late 1960's and early 1970's
is a leading one. By "ritual theater" I intend what Peter Brook calls
"holy theater," Grotowski, "'poor' theater," and others, "theater of
masks." Some of its best known representatives include Grotowski's
Polish Theater Laboratory, Andrej Gregory's Manhattan Project, Richard
Foreman's Ontological-Hysteric Theater, and Peter Schumann's Bread and
Puppet Theater. One might include elements of plays like "Hair" and
"Dionysus 69," as well as Peter Weiss' "Marat Sade" and Peter
Shaffer's "Equus." Characteristics of the ritualizing of theater
include: an abiding interest in the use of masks, gesture, Asian
spirituality, and drama; use of indigenous folk drama and
storytelling; an emphasis on the sounds, rather than the discursive
qualities, of words; little emphasis on playwrights; heavy reliance on
the interaction between actors and directors; a tendency to experiment
with audience-inclusion in the performance; an eclecticism of form and
content; and sometimes a borrowing from popular entertainments,
circus, puppetry, mime, and tribal dance.
Recent theater of ritual is no mere return to primitivism or
archaic piety, since its holiness is radically profane. Even though
"Dr. Faustus" (as directed by Grotowski), "Waiting for Godot" (written

by Samuel Beckett), or "Les Cenci" (written and directed by Artaud) may employ themes and forms from classical, medieval, or even Aztec ritual-drama, the holy stage they generate survives by negation of the conventionally sacred. As Brook notes, it works "like the plague, by intoxication, by infection, by analogy, by magic" (1968:44). The holy theater has a consuming interest in silence, incantation, and chant, which sets it in contrast to the various theaters of the word. Gesture is its medium of "statement," and it prefers exclamation to declaration. Repetition fills its "plots." And masks overlay the "characters" even when they strip off all their clothes. This theater-become-religion is to drama what Blake's poetry and engraving were to him—an art so practiced and conceived as to be a lifestyle, an ethic, and finally, a cosmology.

On first consideration, such theater appears to be the very antithesis of theatrical positivism, which cuts away everything non-theatrical from the stage; but it contains a deep irony and thus continues the modern, ironical, self-conscious ethos by treating reality itself as theatrical. What is post-modern about it is its lack of historicism, which Driver takes to have been essential to modern drama. Whereas historicism typically insists on a radical distinction between nature and history, the theaters of ritual insist on an organic link between the two. The deterioration of historicism paved the way for a new theory of the origins of drama which locates its matrix not in seasonal rites (a la Frazer, Cornford, Harrison, and Gaster), but in shamanic performances (see Kirby, 1975).

In post-modern theater irony continues in the form of ritual profanation; the sacred is invoked against itself. Historicism seems to have begun crumbling under the impact of Asian and native spirituality and ecological consciousness; hence, history as the arena of human and sacred interaction can no longer be meaningfully detached from the animal, vegetable, mineral, and astronomical dimensions of nature. So the developing stream of ritual theater is more richly religious than modern theater was, but at the same time it is more profoundly anti-Christian. It is a polytheistic or non-theistic theater which embraces Christian forms only insofar as they can be shorn of exclusivism, verbalism, and historicism. Contempory theater of ritual insists on wedding any theology of history to a ritology of nature and embodiment.

The rejection of literary theater parallels in significant ways the ritualizing of theology. With the ecstatic proclamations of God's death, the celebrative invitations to play, and the clarion calls to revolution, the systematizing word of theologians is now going the way of the drama of texts and ideas. The theologian, like the drama critic, now is pressed to become at least an observing participant in performance. In ritual theater there are many performances but few texts, so interpreters are having to learn to read gestures where they once read only words.

GROTOWSKI'S "POOR" THEATER

Jerzy Grotowski, director of the Polish Theater Laboratory, epitomizes the ritualizing ethos of post-modern drama better than any playwright I might name. This fact is symptomatic of the shift away from playwrights and dramatic texts toward the performative process.

Grotowski's productions such as "Akropolis," "Dr. Faustus," "The Constant Prince," and "Apocalypsis Cum Figuris" have not influenced so great an audience as his actor-training workshops have; audiences for his performances have been quite small and primarily Polish. His seminars, workshops, and special projects, however, have been conducted and attended more internationally. The result has been that a half-understood Grotowski has become the inspiration for most ritual-drama of recent times.

What occurs between a director like Growtowski and his actors is as important as what occurs between actor and script; so we must understand his methods of actor training, the most ritualized aspect of the theater of ritual, or we miss the crucial point--that in it, process supercedes product. In Grotowski's poor theater practice takes precedence over performance. In actor training one anticipates performing only in the sense that the actor knows someone will eventually see the action. Practice is no mere prelude to be regarded as less real than performance because the former lacks an audience. Actor-training is more akin to religious practice than to the usual modes of rehearsal.

Grotowski's theater, like that envisioned by Antoin Artaud, is hieratic, but with the important difference that poor theater is highly disciplined. The difference between their forms of theatrical mysticism is that which marks the distinction between meditation and possession. Both pursue a "theater of the invisible-made-visible" (Brook, 1968:38), but the price of Grotowskian myth, ritual, and meditation is poverty and self-examination.

When Artaud, the ecstatic prophet of the theater of cruelty, said, "Actors should be like martyrs burnt alive, still signalling to us from their stakes," Grotowski reacted:

These signals must be articulated, and they cannot be gibberish or delirious, calling out to everything and nothing--unless a given work demands precisely that. With such a proviso, we affirm that this quotation contains

in an oracular style, the whole problem
of spontaneity and discipline, this
conjunction of opposites which gives
birth to the total act (1968:125).

In search of a theater of holiness, Grotowski upsets both
theatricality and religiosity. "Theater" as a word, perhaps even as a
reality, is, in his view, dead (1973:113,124,126); so is the church.
What is indispensable is something more fundamental that is the ground
of both religion and drama, something he calls variously a "holiday,"
"not hiding," "meeting," "bodily sincerity," "disarmament," and
"doing" (as opposed to mere "skill"). What Grotowski trains for, and
experiments with, in his "laboratory" is anti-theatrical inasmuch as
it aims to cut the nerve of "publicotropism" and exhibitionism; it is
anti-religious inasmuch as its form of holiness consists of
transgressing the most sacred rites and symbols of the Western world.
From Grotowski we learn a great deal about profanation. It is not
mere disbelief nor simple rejection of religious forms, but a
disciplined, ritualized act of negation carefully aimed at releasing
spiritual energy.   For Grotowski acting is an occurrence of
self-sacrifice in the arms of a once-sacred tradition of myth and
ritual.

His actor-training exercises, like those of Zen training, do not
aim to impart any positive technique from master to pupil, but
constitute a thorough-going via negativa aimed at eliminating
resistances of the actor's psyche and body. The aim is to enable one
to act without conflict of "body and soul, intellect and feelings,
physiological pleasures and spiritual aspirations" (1968:131).   A
total act is done disinterestedly in relation to the other, but never
for that person.

The essentially totalistic, and therefore religious, nature of
Grotowskian theater is evident in the director's concern to engender
an artistic ethic. Poor theater is neither a temporary lifestyle nor
merely a formal dramatic type. Rather, it is a way of self-knowledge
and a mode of being with others. Grotowski denies that his exercises
(exercises plastiques) constitute a method of teaching people to
perform in front of others. Instead, his goal is to elicit the
self-revelation of a disarmed person who refuses to perform. Such
action arises from "contact," the non-resisting encounter with another
in which the fullness of one's memories and associations are the
conditioning factors. Grotowski says:

One thing is clear: the actor must
give himself and not play for himself
or for the spectator.   His search must

be directed from within himself to the outside, but not for the outside. When the actor begins to work through contact, when he begins to live in relation to someone--not his stage partner but the partner of his biography--when he begins to penetrate through a study of his body's impulses, the relationship of this contact, this process of exchange, there is always rebirth in the actor. Afterwards he begins to use the other actors as screens for his life's partner, he begins to project things on the characters in the play. And this is his second rebirth. Finally the actor discovers what I call the "secure partner," this special being in front of whom he does everything, in front of whom he plays with other characters and to whom he reveals his most personal problems and experiences. This human being--this "secure partner"--cannot be defined. But at the moment when the actor discovers his "secure partner" the third and strongest rebirth occurs, a visible change in the actor's behavior (1968:247).

In such a view, ethical, technical, and religious dimensions are one. Grotowski's performers are told that they must "surpass themselves" and "do the impossible." They work in virtual silence without the usual laughter, lounging, and small talk. Self-penetration, which Grotowski also calls "trance," is an "excess"; therefore, it needs a form. If one is to become "without defense" before another, a formalization must frame such an act each time it occurs. I am reminded of the Zen paradox: emptiness is form, form is emptiness. On the one hand, the actor learns with Grotowski to avoid the theatrical trick, to skirt cliché and stereotype, and on the other, to exercise the body-soul-mind as a precisely expressive organism. Grotowski's single most important aim is negative: to avoid blocking. He has nothing else, nothing positive to teach, he says. All else is magic, stage-trickery.

Director and actor cultivate a way strikingly similar to the wu wei of Taoism, a resignation "not to do," that is, to act vigorously with a deep internal passivity. Like Zennists and Taoists,

Grotowskian actors aim to "stop the cheating," to find the authentic impulse"(1968:250). But unlike those two ways, which depend upon a body of handed-down formalities that one learns to do passively, or emptily, the Grotowskian actor treats a performance as a "confession," a profoundly Catholic view. To act is to express in an articulate, structured fashion what one usually hides. All acting ought to be confession, and all confession which is merely friendly is still masking, not revelation. What the actor aims for is not to illustrate "acts of the soul," but actually to accomplish them. Therefore, the director and actor assume an obligation of discreetness about each other's struggles and an attitude of respect toward the terminology and place of their practice. The "purity" of the Grotowskian actor has little to do with moralism. Rather, it consists of an effort to eliminate the superfluous; it is an "aesthetic asceticism." Grotowski's actors are "poor" and "pure" in a religious sense: they are shorn of extraneous movements and motives. Grotowski, by claiming that he has nothing to give actors, that he only takes away, is providing an alternative to Artaud's theater of cruelty.

The total act to which Grotowski aspires, unifies opposites in the face of the demons of blockage and stereotype. An actor learns at once to avoid imitating actions, including those of other persons and of himself on other occasions and to resist considering results such as pleasing or offending audiences or gaining recognition. The actor refuses to "canonize one's burdens" (1973:115). This process—elimination (of resistances and blocks), revelation, and articulation (through signs)—most students of religion will recognize as a pattern similar to that of a mystic's ascent. Director and actor seem strikingly like master and disciple, spiritual director and novice. Grotowski's accent falls heavily on the first step: unknowing, unlearning, not doing, eliminating.

THE ACTOR'S RESEARCH

How Grotowski actually succeeds both in training actors for such self-abandon and precision and for producing plays of genuinely ritualistic significance is difficult to describe. Furthermore, his methods are evolving rapidly. At one time he tried using yoga for training purposes. He was also influenced by Peking opera and Japanese theater (Noh and Kabuki); he also has had an interest in India's Kathakali drama. Some Asian elements were visible in his exercises, but he no longer thinks it possible or desirable to try appropriating them. Other influences have been the methods of Russian director Stanislavsky, as well as those of Meyerhold, Dullin, and Delsarte. All of these sources have been so transformed that describing his style and some typical exercises, as we might have learned them in his poor theater phase, is more useful than cataloging influences.

There is much silence. Exercises begin: walking with knees bent, hands on hips; squatting curled up, jumping, landing in the same position; walking rhythmically while the arms and hands rotate. These exercises are not merely a gymnastic prelude. Eventually, people associate every detail of the exercises with a remembered or imagined image.   Grotowski watches carefully to see if the actor has resistances; he looks for malleability and flexibility in movement, rigidity and strength in support.

Do without thinking. Do not prepare, says Grotowski. He calls attention to mental planning and rehearsal whenever he sees them. Bodily activity is first, then vocal expression, and both without forethought.

Now participants do an exercise, "the cat," involving the vertebral column. They lie face downward. One person described the exercise this way:

> The legs are apart and the arms at right angles to the body, palms towards the floor, the "cat" wakes up and draws the hand in towards the chest, keeping the elbows upwards, so that the palms of the hands form a basis for support. The hips are raised, while the legs "walk" on tiptoe towards the hands. Raise and stretch the left leg sideways, at the same time lifting and stretching the head. Replace the left leg on the ground, supported by the tips of the toes. Repeat the same movements with the right leg, the head still stretching upwards. Stretch the spine, placing the center of gravity first in the center of the spine, and then higher up towards the nape of the neck. Then turn over and fall onto the back, relaxing (1968:135).

Afterwards, people continue the research. Grotowski insists that actors are not merely practicing, repeating in order to find a technique which, when mastered, becomes the best way. They are searching and researching for hidden resources. One might be doing the same thing by accomplishing headstands in Hatha Yoga. In assigning these positions, Grotowski does not aim at minimizing thought, breathing, and sexuality—a traditional Hindu goal. Rather, he is researching how a change in one part of the organism influences the rhythm and tension of the other parts.

Remembering sensations of flying from dreams, participants do another exercise. They squat, hop, sway; their hands are wings. They swim into the air, leap forward, land like birds. Shamans have long done it. Grotowski leads them to associate images with, and locate resistances to, their bird-selves.

As if to test resistances to bodily contradictions, he takes participants through exercises that employ movement in opposite vectors. People's right sides become graceful, their left, clumsy. Hands become angry, feet, joyful. Hands quarrel; bodies are astonished at the fight. Knees become greedy; shoulders cry.

Grotowski's students experiment with gestural ideograms, but without codifying them, as is done in Asian dance and drama, in which one always uses the same gesture for a conventionalized meaning. They become trees; they blossom, wither, die. They become tigers and cows and find their centers of vitality.

The work proceeds without comment or private reflection to what Grotowski calls the "resonators." In these exercises, the whole body, not merely the tongue or larynx, learns to vibrate. Voice is as material as body, Grotowski insists. He shows trainees how a flame vibrates when put near a resonant spot at the back of the head and how a glass shatters upon vocal assault. People vocalize at the wall, and Grotowski tells them, "If you expect an answer from the wall in the form of an echo, your whole body must react to this possible answer. If you give me an answer, you must first do so with your body. It is alive" (1968:197).

In voice training, as in the training of extremities and trunk, the whole body must adapt itself to every movement. Actors do nothing for which they cannot account. They assume responsibility for each action by locating its connection to their centers, to vital impulses. Participants utter every inarticulate sound possible. They moan, scream, twitter animal sounds. Grotowski kneads bodies and feels chests and abdomens to release new resonances. Actors never practice diction; they "do." In doing, one finds that the image—lying in a warm river, being a tiger—requires its own kind of breathing and voice. People are not learning a system, but are making contact—with an imagined someone, with the environment, with their own centers of power. In the exercises the vital impulses are allowed to originate from the center of the trunk (spinal column, abdomen, loins) and radiate to voice and limbs.

Grotowski asks an actor to sing a song while associating it with an axe, a tiger, a snake; others note the changes in sound that follow the respective images. Next, they try to contact a spot on the ceiling with their voices. They try to sing sheets of paper out of his hand.

The exercises of Grotowski's actor training are far richer and more complex than I can convey with mere description, and much depends on his own powers of observation and charisma. But perhaps this sketch will permit me to enumerate some of his crucial principles as follows: (1) the quest for contact; (2) avoidance of mental rehearsing and planning; (4) insistence on a concrete, associated image at the moment of execution; (5) adaption of the whole body and psyche to every movement; (6) action from bodily centers outward to extremities and voice;   (7) surpassing fatigue, chatter, self-indulgence, and masks for the sake of revelation.

The relationship between Grotowski and actors is a "profane" form of spiritual training—profane in the etymological sense, "before the temple." It is akin to forms of meditation and therapy in the sense that it does not aim to raise the more purely aesthetic question of Stanislavsky's "method" acting, "What would you do if . . . ?" but asks, "What do you want to do with your life; and then—do you want to hide or reveal yourself, do you want to discover yourself, in both senses of the word: discover—uncover? It does not matter whether literature—as a point of departure—is indispensible for you in this" (1973:116).

FROM RESEARCH TO ACTING IN GRACE

In the exercises, Grotowski leads actors to unblock so they can be free of "performance." Nevertheless, a work of performative art does eventually occur in the presence of people other than those of the Theater Laboratory itself. "Performance" is what Grotowski calls acting for the sake of an audience or acting with tricks and methods; "doing" is what occurs in the presence of others without tricks and armament.

If Grotowski refuses to canonize a standard method of training, he also refuses to treat a dramatic text as having canonical status. As in the mystical and meditative traditions of some religions, a text is often a context, sometimes a pretext, for visionary interpretation. Grotowski says that every great artist is a priest or pontifex, a bridge; so parts of a text will be eliminated if actors can neither agree nor disagree with it. Little is interpolated; much is stricken or rearranged. The result is a dramatic-poetic montage, the purpose of which is a meeting of self and text. Grotowski sometimes uses classical plays, for example, those of Marlowe and Calderon, but his "Apocalypsis Cum Figuris" is a montage of texts, including the Bible, THE BROTHERS KARAMAZOV, and selections from T.S. Eliot and Simone Weil.

An acting score of fixed elements evolves out of the research and contact which actors make in the presence of scripts. Then what occurs is an event neither merely religious nor purely theatrical. A Polish Lab performance typically leaves audiences awed by the precision, flexibility, and power of the actors, particularly that of Ryzard Cieslak. Josef Kelera, a professional theater critic, commented after seeing "Constant Prince":

> Until now, I accepted with reserve the terms such as "secular holiness," "act of humility," "purification" which Grotowski uses. Today I admit that they can be applied perfectly to the character of the Constant Prince. A sort of psychic illumination emanates from the actor. I cannot find any other definition. In the culminating moments of the role, everything that is technique is as though illuminated from within, light, literally imponderable. At any moment the actor will levitate. . . . He is in a state of grace. And all around him this "cruel theater" with its blasphemies and excesses is transformed into a theater in a state of grace (cited in Grotowski, 1968:109).

The audience is often seated very close to the action, sometimes in the midst of it. Grotowski at one time tried to elicit the direct participation of an audience, but decided later he was exercising a tyranny, since the actors were prepared, while the audience was not. Now, if he involves the audience directly, he does so by extending who they are. They become "witnesses." Such a performance may include the possibility of their active or passive witnessing. In a performance of "Dr. Faustus," for example, Faustus, an hour before his death, offers a last supper to his friends, the spectators, who sit around long tables, as he remembers and enacts his story. In "The Constant Prince" the audience looks down on the action as if they are students witnessing an operation on the table below.

Typically, the themes are mythic, the action ritualized, and the faces sometimes frozen into masklike gestures. The theological perspective is profane, aiming to invest with power by transgressing. The audience feels, perhaps, that it is witnessing an ecstasy or that it has unwittingly stumbled into the midst of a sacred rite.

RITUAL THEATERS

Grotowski's is certainly not the first theater to ritualize. If we compare what E.T. Kirby, echoing Richard Wagner, calls "total theater" (gesamkunstwerk) with Grotowski's poor theater of ritual, some interesting continuities and contrasts appear. Total theater includes many theatrical forms ranging from opera to happenings. It aims to be the locus of an intersection of the arts in synthesis (Kirby, 1969:xiii). Total theater looks to the reunification of what Wagner took to be a primal, undifferentiated unity of the arts and of the senses. So certain "primitive" qualities are characteristic of total and poor theaters, but the former typically ends in a spectacle, while the latter ends in sparsity—in theatrical monasticism. Both evoke a sense of mystery, but the mystery of total theater resides in the means—effects, lighting, music, and so on, while in poor theater it is a quality of the actors. The two theaters have in common a de-emphasis on literary and narrative aspects of drama and a strong concern with environments of action.

Poor theater has a pronounced participatory ethos, but total theater is less aggressive in involving audiences directly, except when it merges with ritual theaters as, for example, in Schechner's "Dionysus 69." Total theater tends to retain Wagner's "mystic gulf" between stage and audience. Both theatrical styles are what Kirby calls "hieroglyphic" (1969:xxxix); they involve multiple ways of knowing and communicating which are not characteristic of the realistic stage.

Though total and poor theaters are related in much the same way as St. Peter's compares with an early Franciscan monastery (the former displaying grandeur and the latter demanding radical commitment), both pursue archetypal images in search of a myth of cosmological proportions. Whereas total theater seems content with the most fully blown image, poor theater strains toward the unmediated breakthrough to which neither stereotype nor archetypal gesture is ultimately relevant. Total theater pursues mystification and semi-darkness; poor theater's rituals aim for nothing less than the pure light of revelation and contact. The drama of Richand Wagner, Max Reinhardt, and Vsevolod Meyerhold presses totality into the service of the marvelous and grotesque; theirs are theaters more for directors than actors. Grotowski wants "saints," while the theatricalists wanted

Übermarionettes ("superpuppets"). Saints and superpuppets are visionary images from related, but fundamentally opposing, religio-dramatic traditions. Saints penetrate their masks to the point that exteriority becomes transparent to pure interiority. Superpuppets, on the other hand, rid themselves of ego; so they appear to be totally responsive, hollow exteriorities. Total theater lives by expansion, addition, and inflation of the ordinary; poor theater lives by negation, resignation, and reduction. Both are theaters of ritual, but the rituals of total theater are magical (they enact power over the Other at a distance), while those of poor theater are mediative-mystical (they enact the coincidence of interiority and exteriority).

The religious import of Grotowski's theater of ritual lies in its effort to create what traditional religions claim is only discoverable. He does so in a time and cultural setting in which there is a radical plurality of symbols and little consensus of values. Ritual has traditionally drawn upon cultural consensus. Grotowskian ritual-drama depends upon an inversion of, or assault upon, what once constituted this consensus./1/ The events Grotowski directs are celebrations of difference and plurality; they are also symbolic modes of creating unity. The language with which Grotowski discusses theater is thoroughly and profoundly religious, though profanely so. His theater laboratory is not a religion or a sect, but it does have a "monastic" relation to the theater at large. It is a place where disciplined self-examination, ritualized expression, and mystical revelation can occur with unusual intensity. Like those of the great mystics and masters, Grotowski's methods evolve rapidly, and "heresy" is an ever-present cry threatening to erupt even from friends and followers.

If we do not insist that rituals, by definition, arise collectively from cultural consensus, we must admit that Grotowski is doing what some religionists and psychologists, Eliade and Jung, for example, seem to think is impossible, namely, discovering and creating rituals which are not mere private obsessions nor means of cementing culture into a whole. They are mid-range, neither private nor universal, appealing to small affinity groups, particularly young, disaffiliated actors and the secularly religious. To visit the Polish Theater Laboratory or participate in one of their special projects is to make a pilgrimage of communitas:

> . . . The theater and the church are dying. Although the two phenomena are very different, in spite of some affinities, I feel that in both of them something is drawing to an end.

Men shared bread and thought they
shared God. They shared God. And we
feel the need to share life, share
ourselves, as we are, whole, unveiled,
uncovered, share brother--and if one is
brother--share not like candy, but as
bread. One must be like bread, which
does not recommend itself, which is as
it is and does not defend itself. In
this there is already a great faith.
How to go, how to refer to brother as
to God? And then--How to become
brother? Where is
my--brother's--birth? (Grotowski,
1973:124-125).

These sentiments form the bridge over which Grotowski walked as
he left the theater and entered the Polish forest--a transition which
is the subject of the next chapter.

NOTES

/1/ A good series of critiques on Grotowski can be found in Brecht
(1970). The remarks of Donald Richie (205ff.) are the most useful in
understanding how Grotowski's theater differs from ritual theater in
Asia. For further documentation and critique, see THE DRAMA REVIEW
(issues T24, T27, T35, T41, T45).

CHAPTER 11

GROTOWSKI'S THEATER OF SOURCES

Although we have rightly given up asking what are the pre-historical origins of ritual, the urgency of discovering its sources has never been more pressing. The search and research for ritual matrices is nowhere more imaginatively and responsibly directed than in Jerzy Grotowski's Theater of Sources Project. Because rumors of his association with a Haitian Voodoo group threaten to cloud the project for both participants and the interested public, I want to offer an interpretation of the Theater of Sources, having participated in it in Poland during the summer of 1980. The urgency of clarification is considerable. Theater people still insist on being mystified by Grotowski's having left theater; and North Americans profoundly misunderstand Voodoo, viewing it as fundamentally concerned with magical death, witchcraft, and zombies. In addition, the project has profound implications for both the practice and study of ritual.

HOLIDAYS AND BEGINNINGS

Grotowski's work is commonly divided into three phases, best chronicled in GROTOWSKI'S LABORATORY (Burzynski, Osinski, 1979): (1) the "poor" theater phase (1959-1970), (2) the "paratheatrical" phase (1970-1975), and (3) the "active culture" phase (1976-present). His TOWARDS A POOR THEATRE (1968) is the best summation of the first phase, which I have described in the preceding chapter. "Holiday:

The Day that is Holy" (1973) reflects the paratheatrical phase; ON THE ROAD TO ACTIVE CULTURE (Kolankiewicz, 1978) chronicles responses to it. And "The Art of the Beginner" (1978) is the most readable of Grotowski's programmatic statements about the intention of his present research.

Members of the Polish Theater Laboratory Institute insist that the Theater of Sources, consisting of explorations in "active culture," is not to be confused with the paratheatrical work, which was interpersonal in tone. Meeting what is "other," rather than meeting other people, is central to the "active culture" phase. Whereas in "Holiday" (1973:114) Grotowski had said, "What matters is that, in this, first I should not be alone...," in the Theater of Sources one is "alone with others." Even though people work alongside one another, they are in solitude.

In both the paratheatrical phase and the Theater of Sources, the forest, not a theater, is the scene of action—action not acting. But what is uncovered, or discovered, differs between the two projects. In the former, the goal was to disarm oneself in the presence of others. The search was for "bodily sincerity" (1973:118). In the latter, what is "other" than the interpersonal—call it nature, God, spirit, or do not name it all—is the presence before which one searches out "the movement which is repose" (1980). "Holiday" (1973) is couched in interpersonal language: "Body and blood—this is brother, that's where 'God' is, it is the bare foot and naked skin, in which there is brother. This, too, is a holiday, to be in the holiday, to be the holiday" (1973:119).

The paratheatrical work developed a bodily ethic of trust among one's "own kind of people" (1973:121). Sincerity and trust in the Tree of People, one of the paratheatrical projects, were drawn beyond mere sincerity of words toward action which was revelatory. The paratheatrical work seemed to be a search for likeminded people and for ways of meeting which did not create audiences or depend on acting. "Meetings," not "performances," occurred.

In "The Art of the Beginner" (1978) Grotowski continued to articulate the interest in un-training which was present even in his theatrical period. The article does not describe what is actually done in the Theater of Sources, any more than "Holiday" described the paratheatrical work. Rather, it sketches Grotowski's understanding of the process of reaching below the "techniques of sources" (spiritual disciplines such as zazen, yoga, Sufi whirling or shamanic healing) to the "sources of the techniques of sources" (1980). By facilitating an interaction among representatives of old and young cultures, he wants to nurture intuitions which are the basis of meditation, celebration, and healing. He is searching for an original, pre-cultural sense of beginning. This source or beginning is present here and now, not hidden away in some primitive culture. It is no lost golden age, but is a capacity for a perpetual sense of discovery. Grotowski is not interested in imitating archaic disciplines, but in finding simple actions to carry on the "work with oneself" (1978:9), the "opus-process." Grotowski refers to his project as a "journey to the East," (1980) but "East" does not mean that he intends to borrow either Asian, primitive, or mystical techniques. It means that he wants to find out how any action begins. East is the direction of sunrise; it is a symbol of any zone that is formative of culture.

WORK WITH GROTOWSKI'S INTERNATIONAL STAFF

In the Theater of Sources there were four groups: invited participants, a small group from India (including a Baul), Grotowski's international staff, and part of a community of Haitians. No one, not even Grotowski, could describe everything that occurred during the Theater of Sources. By design no person saw every action. Even though Grotowski "directed" the dozen or so staff people, each was typically accompanied only by a few invited participants. About fifteen people were in my group, only a few of which were present for a given activity. Usually, one of Grotowski's staff led from two to fifteen of us. And eventually, by consultation, selection, and decision, we each concentrated on working in only a few of the ways introduced to us. So any description is partial--the result of personal choice and limited perspective--and at best only illustrative. Therefore, I will describe only those actions in which I participated.

"Action" is, perhaps, an abstract, awkward way of referring to the things we did. But Grotowski and his staff deliberately refrained from labeling them "events," "exercises," "rituals," and so on. In this respect, our activities were highly abstract, but in another, they were utterly concrete. So I use "action" because our guides used the term and because it is the least prejudicial way to designate research into the sources of action.

One action consisted of long walks, during which we paused at transitions in terrain or foliage, honored the sounds of animals, clung to trees, lay on the earth, crawled under dense pines, watched fish, ran through thickly entangled forest at night, and walked under waterfalls. The ethics of participation required silence, lightfootedness, non-pollution, careful imitation of the guide, and no movements disruptive of forest life or the group. We experienced a full range of emotions in the midst of such walking: loneliness, fear, elation, weariness, embarassment, amazement, simplicity, boredom, disgust. A dominant response was a sense of attunement. I do not mean by this a sentiment of group kinship or nostalgia for unity with the forest. Rather, I mean a letting go of both feelings and thoughts as the center of awareness. We "just did" things. We responded.

That was all. And it was enough. The staff clearly and overtly discouraged romantic attachment to "the beauties of nature." We lay on the earth, quite simply; we were not to imagine making love with it.

Another kind of action was a stylized step done clockwise around a tree to the rhythms of solid-log drums. One might have called it a dance. We moved for very long periods, always in the daytime, always without innovating or improvising. The sense of monotony was profound. Some found it grounding; some found it boring. The sameness and repetitiveness of the step, like the simple monotony of the drums, provided meditative potentialities once the technique had been learned. The "dance" was neither free-form nor creative. While doing it, our feet replaced our eyes in searching the ground before stepping.

Often, following this activity were indoor sessions in which we were instructed to find and repeat some simple gesture to a slightly more complex beat. Again, the periods were quite long; so whatever interest there might have been in performing or displaying one's abilities, it soon withered. As with all the actions, they remained essentially uninterrupted, unnamed, and unexplained. There was minimal group ideology; so entering, continuing, or ending an event depended almost entirely on personal, unspoken motivations. We tested the actions as actions, not as concretions of some shared ideology, not as preludes to anything else.

Whirling was another of the actions. We whirled at a crossroads in the forest. Some fell, some vomited, some got up again. We whirled in one spot. We whirled while running in the woods. Sometimes we whirled in one direction; at other times we alternated directions. We had to attend to both centrifugal and centripetal forces while whirling and running as a group. Clinging with one's eyes or attention had disastrous consequences. The whirling was not of the formal Sufi kind. It was more extroverted, rougher, exploratory.

Several of Grotowski's people taught a series of movements that I would call "spiritual exercises." "Spiritual" connotes a way of being in one's body, rather than a way of exiting from it. Comparisons with tai chi and yoga were inevitable, but the movements were neither. Grotowski does not encourage the importation of techniques, especially those imbedded in long, rich, cultural traditions. Rather, staff persons coming from those traditions are encouraged to find some new action that is then tested to see whether it can be shared.

Because of the complexity of describing gestural sequences, I will not recount individual movements in the series. Emphasis was upon keeping our eyes open yet unfocused. Diffuse attention was paid to vistas framed by our postures, for example, watching the sky through our hands or legs. The movements oriented us to the horizon surrounding us--to the sky and the earth. Vision was always to be outward, mobile, and flowing--not introverted, static, or choppy.

The exercises were, for me, a generative grammar of the other actions of the Theater of Sources. The exercises were a summary of the "gestural competence" of the project, in the way that katas constitute a "grammar" of karate competence. I felt they contained the kinesic seedbed out of which other events sprang as offshoots.

The actions which comprised the forest work with Grotowski's staff seemed to be a kind of meditative stalking. The object of the hunt was not game for killing and eating, as it might have been for a shaman. The object was the self/other nexus. The goal was to become and encounter the subject. We hunted our original selves, although we ran after deer and were sought out in the night by the large birds and fowl. Self-hunting could easily have become narcissistic had not introversion and interpersonal contact been so effectively discouraged. The self for which one hunted was not "unto itself," nor within, but rather between persons and the environment. We hunted selves which were not turned in on, or blocked by, ourselves. The forest was not a ruse, not a hideout so people could have feelings or touch bodies. So Grotowski's phrase, "work on oneself," can be misleading and easily misinterpreted, especially by popular-therapy oriented North Americans. "Work as oneself" is better.

The hunting was symbolic insofar as no animals were killed, but quite concrete inasmuch as one's social self was drastically curtailed, and one's body, pushed to its limits and beyond. Perhaps another way to put the matter is to say that we were taught to hunt for an action—for the proper "verb" and "adverb." In shamanism one hunts for an animal or power. In Poland we hunted for the best way to hunt. The Theater of Sources was a meta-hunt, the object of which was to de-objectify our world. It was a hunt for a way of moving which allowed earth, sky, foliage, animals, and "the other" to appear as subjects. The effect of the explorations was centering, but not centripetal. We found ourselves connected and balanced even as we tripped and fell to the forest floor. But we also found that we were not the center of either social or cosmic attention. This point is regularly missed by those who hear phrases like "Song of Myself" or "working on myself," but do not actually participate in the actions led by Grotowski and his collaborators. I understand the misapprehensions that lead to comments such as, "Grotowski has crawled into his own navel and can no longer find his way out," but I cannot emphasize strongly enough that the Theater of Sources was not introverted or narcissistic.

We hunted anima, spirit. I do not mean anima in the Jungian sense of the feminine side of a human being, but in the etymological sense of an animating surge which is our own and yet flows through us, from among and around us. Describing the ethos of the hunting this way suggests both the continuity and difference between shamanism and

Grotowski's project. Shamanic animism finds the world already alive; whereas, the project took place at a time in our history when our bodies have become puppetlike and mechanistic, reflecting a secularized, industrialized environment. The animistic worldview finds anima unavoidable; it is "out there," pressing hard to come "in here." Whereas, a modern worldview can barely locate anima at all. In the popular view, spirit is "in here," in the privacy of feeling and ego. But in the form pursued by the Theater of Sources, anima is neither inside nor out. So things must be brought to life by doing the actions. The life of the forest, our bodies, and cultures must be activated, animated. This is the meaning of Grotowski's term "active culture."

WORK WITH THE HAITIAN COMMUNITY

In retrospect, I interpreted my explorations with Grotowski's staff as preparation for participation with the Haitians. While doing them, however, I did not view them as preparatory. I simply did them. The sequences of events, which differed for each participant, strongly affected people's experiences and interpretations, as well as their evaluations and capacities to integrate what occurred.

Grotowski's work is clearly phasic. To move from doing performances in which the action is not simulated but is actual self-revelation, to bringing part of a community of Haitians to Poland, is a significant change. Grotowski studies under them, with them, and alongside them. The "Laboratorium" really is a laboratory; the term is not a euphemism. But there are no specimens in it. Or, if there are, Grotowski, like the Haitians and the invited participants, is one of them. The study of others is a phase of self-study. Self-study is a phase of the study of others. This attitude by-passes the dualism that segregates the view of orthodox liturgics ("This work is only for us") from that of conventional anthropology ("This work is only theirs").

However, the attitude is not syncretistic. Insisting on this is important. Shamanism is commonly syncretistic. But Grotowski is not borrowing from shamans so much as trying to locate the sources before the borrowing begins. The intention to borrow, like the one to invent, ritual is self-defeating. And it differs considerably from the view that ritual can only be creatively discovered as we enter the ways of others in order to better find our own. What transpires in the Theater of Sources is genuine ritual, though it is ritual experiment rather than ritual tradition. This, I think, is a truly post-modern form of ritual—dependent as it is on possibilities for travel, study, cultural interchange, and leisure.

I am tempted to speak of the Haitian work as "ritual contact," because of its cross-cultural emphasis, or as "initiation," because it was marked by a ritual beginning in which neophytes made their way toward the poteau mitan, (central pole or tree). However, I think the neologism, "sourcing," or "greeting the sources," expresses the event better, since it suggests an action from or toward an originative zone—an action in which contact is made across a chasm, in this case a religio-cultural one.

We were not initiated into Voodoo religion, which is a creative cultural synthesis of Yoruba, Christian, and Arawak symbols. No one taught us sorcery. Nor was debased Voodoo theatrically performed for us, as is sometimes the case at night clubs in Port-au-Prince. Nor did we observe Voodoo possession rites for the purpose of documenting them in scholarly monographs or imitating them in theaters.

I do not want to describe the details of our explorations with the Haitians, but to indicate what conditions were present that facilitated the emergence of ritual attitudes.

First, the environment differed significantly from that of either the ritual initiators or the ritual respondents. We were not in Haiti and not in a European or North American, urban setting. A number of people remarked how odd it was to consider Haitians and Voodoo in Poland. But this was precisely the point: to overcome the usual indigenous/outsider split. Prior to bringing the group to Poland, Grotowski had worked with them for extended periods in Haiti. And the move, which was, of course, temporary for the Haitians, was not arbitrary. They were not in Poland as part of a cultural zoo or ritual circus.

Even though the very old and very young stayed behind in Haiti, a significant portion of the community came; so it clearly was part of a society, not merely an assembly of individuals from the same country. There were both dislocation and solidarity. Most of the invited participants were dislocated linguistically and geographically, but we shared many of the same values that permeate Western, urban, literate, mobile, post-industrial societies. The Haitians, Grotowski, and part of his international staff lived in a barn and shanties an hour or so away from Wroclaw, Poland. The Indians, the rest of the international staff, and the invited participants usually stayed in two barns a few miles away from the first one. Most of the work took place in what Grotowski has called "the forest womb." Even though the Haitians were more native to forests than those in the invited group, much of the ritual contact with them was indoors, in a barn that they had been allowed to convert into a sacred place. So they were literally removed from their own soil, but we were put in the symbolic position of walking on their holy ground.

A second condition for ritual re-sourcing was learning to see without looking. The Theater of Sources Project was able, to a surprising degree, to avoid the interpersonal highs and nostalgia for communitas that one has learned to associate with encounters and retreats in the North American human potential movement. The success in doing so depended on being taught to keep our eyes open, usually toward the horizon, often in a circular pattern, and typically not focused on any one object such as a flower or rock. When we worked with the Haitians, we knew what was meant when they asked us to participate in a ritual by "seeing without looking, hearing without overhearing." If at first we thought this was for their benefit—they did not want us staring or analyzing—we later found it was also for ours. We were able to find, without embarassment, our own ways of knowing what was going on. I say "knowing" rather than "explaining," because our way of understanding arose in the Hebraic sense of knowing, which connotes bodily engagement.

We do not recognize, I discovered, how much we paralyze ourselves by making eye contact too readily. Being prohibited from observing, we found that we saw more. We had to see with organs other than our eyes. Learning to do so is as useful for interpreting a ritual as for running in a pitch black, foggy Polish forest.

A third condition was that of being relieved from the burdens of having to believe, explain, or perform. The Haitians did not have to perform rituals for us. We were neither tourists, anthropologists, nor a theater audience with tickets. Nor were we Voodoo initiates. These are the usual role definitions for seeing a ritual. No one was asked or expected to believe in the things he or she did. Belief was an irrelevant consideration. And going native was impossible. We just did what we did—sang, danced, painted, hummed, shouted, imagined, got tired, jumped, and a hundred other nameless actions. We were asked not to come with a view to profiting from, or explaining, what occurred. Although I am sure a myriad of mixed motives characterized our group, we were invited to test and try only for ourselves. In short, the tone was experimental. We were encouraged to enter tentatively—with a questing, questioning attitude. The subjunctive mood of the event was acknowledged, even made central, but without any sense that what we were doing was imitation of something better or more real. In effect, what transpired was ritual modification for the more traditional participants and the incubation of a ritual sensibility for the more secularized ones.

A fourth condition was gestural concentration. An axiom of much contemporary liturgics and social anthropology is that one should, as a prerequisite, know the language of the ritual, for example, the Latin of a pre-Vatican II Mass or the Creole of Voodoo, presumably for the purpose of knowing what the various gestures, postures, objects, and actions mean. There are occasions like this one, however, when not knowing the verbal language is useful. Not knowing is the prerequisite for knowing in another way. Learning the exegetical meaning (Turner, 1967:50-54) of a symbol before internalizing the orectic, or felt, meaning can lead to reification and false objectivism.

We learned to sing songs we did not verbally understand; we danced dances on a rug sewn with spirits most participants could not name. Our voices and limbs would never have learned so well, if we had known the meanings of our gestures too soon, because we would not have attended in such a concentrated way to non-verbal channels of communication.

A fifth condition was cultivated receptivity. Our ideologies, like our technology, are strongly activistic, and therefore in cross-cultural contexts, often imperialistic. The Haitians gesturally followed us. Even though they were teachers and we, learners, their way of instructing included following and responding to us. This was most obvious in singing, dancing, greeting, and departing. I have not known such powerfully transformative tracking of the vectors of one's movements except among Aikido masters.

I have characterized the Haitian experiment as re-sourcing, or greeting the sources. Since only a few intense days were spent together, considering the event an initiation rite would be claiming too much. So even though there were other ritual elements, such as meditative waiting, ritual painting and burning of paintings, singing, dancing, veneration of the sun, and other actions for which I have no names, the overall character of what we did is best interpreted as a ritual introduction to, or greeting of, the sources.

Greeting and departing rites were prominent, deeply moving, never routinized. The Haitians found a new greeting for every person, on each occasion of meeting. Each action of greeting seemed attuned to the specific person and level of intimacy present at the moment. Warmth, joy, and lingering were typical; but laughter, irritation, and suspicion were permitted. One did not merely repeat a convention of greeting such as handshaking or hugging, but searched anew for the source of greeting. A simple discovery made in the greeting rite by many non-Haitians—one with immense ramifications—was how flexible and hard the Haitians' bodies were, and how soft and inflexible ours were.

I take greeting as a model for the whole of the event, because in it no one was able to forget his or her own culture or ignore the others'. We and they were expected to discover a mutual greeting which neither had brought to the ritual interface. We could not retreat to gestural cliché, imitate, demand imitation, or deny that we bore our cultures in the very marrow of our bones. We were thrown back on our cultural resources, and yet had to find new resources among ourselves.

Preparing for ritual contact demands training in bodily flexibility and in doing nothing. A crucial element in many rituals, not just Voodoo, is diffusion of attention, intention, and action. Such times are not the occasion for boredom, preoccupation, or planning—the three ways that people of Euro-American cultures typically respond. Ritual is misunderstood if defined as activity, especially if activity is restricted to its overtly active or intentional forms. Some of the most important ritual gestures are unintentional and receptive, rather than active, in tone. The cessation of an action has as much meaning as the initiation or sustaining of one. Monotony and repetition—so rejected by the Westernized, urbanized, and theatricalized sensibility—are necessary conditions for receiving a gesture, which is the most fruitful way ritual symbols emerge from their sources.

A final condition was a sense of the sources as both unitary and plural, both concrete and transcendent. The Haitian group was called Saint Soleil. For it, the sun was a concrete manifestation of the unitary sacred. The many figures on the rug were symbolic embodiments of sacred plurality. No choice between monotheism and polytheism would have been necessary had we spoken of the matter. All that was necessary when the windows were opened during a particularly dramatic sunset, was to be open to sun-being. Questions whether the sun is god, whether we are divine, whether the sacred is scattered or together, were of little importance. The lack of discussion of them had little to do with language differences, but was a function of an ethic of silence so ritual re-sourcing could proceed. The source of cohesion between us and the Haitians was action, not theology. Of course, we did not constitute either a tradition or a society. At most we were a nascent community-event, so reflection and words were not so necessary. But the experiment did demonstrate that much verbal, interpretive work is unnecessary when a ritual greeting of the sources is made the ground of meeting.

WORK WITH THE INDIAN GROUP

The people from India were in the process of becoming a group in Poland. Unlike the Haitians, they were not part of an already constituted community. Often they participated in the same way as we invited participants, though some of them had previously gone through the Theater of Sources Project. They also served as a support group for a young Baul from Bengal. The only directed work done with him was our sitting, spines erect, listening to his music, and watching his dance. In addition, the Baul was a source of spontaneous outburst, affection, and humor—all qualities missing from the directed, structured phases of the project. He was a ritual clown, talking when silence was the rule, hugging when interpersonal gestures were being discouraged, moaning about the food when we were busy learning austerity, and refusing to run in the forest because doing so was too hard. He gave voice and body to the desires we had to suspend. He inverted the extraordinary reality created in Poland, but the "ordinariness" he performed—and "performed" in this case is the right word—was itself astoundingly holy, vulnerable, and comical. His combination of virtuoso religious performance and deviance from the project ethic kept participants from taking the explorations with the unbearable, brooding seriousness which has sometimes been associated with the Polish Lab.

Before and after the project the Indians were regularly interacting with invited participants—something neither the Haitians nor Grotowski's international staff did. So on the streets, in the trains, at the zoo, and in the restaurants they were a threshold group, filling the interstices of the project's structure and performing an important bridging and communication function. They were ferrymen, crossing rivers toward both shores: East and West, village and city, personal and political, highly educated and relatively uneducated, mystical and secular, leaders and followers, spontaneous joy and meditative quiet. Their informal work was utterly necessary for making the transition from the forest womb into the restive, bus- and train-filled streets of Polish cities.

But from there toward home, each person walked, rode, or flew alone.

CHAPTER 12

RITUALIZING AT ACTOR'S LAB

Actor's Lab is a professional research and performance ensemble in Toronto, Ontario, Canada. Besides its administrative and fund raising tasks, the Lab conducts five kinds of activities: (1) public performances; (2) continual group and personal research, usually referred to as "the work," specific instances of which are called "studies"; (3) periodic pararitualistic events called "Public Exploration Projects" (PEP's); (4) teaching classes and workshops on movement and rhythm; and (5) occasional conferences, referred to as "New Directions in the Performing Arts," for actors and friends of theater. In this chapter I will consider the first three activities.

Actor's Lab was founded in 1971 on the campus of McMaster Universtiy by Richard Nieoczym, who was at that time a student of religious studies with strong interests in theater, particularly that of Jerzy Grotowski and the Polish Theater Laboratory, and philosophy, especially the works of Nietzsche. Shortly after its inception, the Lab left the university to pursue full-time performance and research into theatrical and paratheatrical processes.

Performances by the Lab are not thematically Canadian, though some of its playwrights and most of its members are Canadians. Though some might refer to the Lab's productions as "impressionistic," "experimental," or "avant-garde," I think two other terms, understood correctly, are more descriptive: "archetypalist" and "ritualized." As suggested by its earlier name, "Le Theater de l'Homme," the Lab tries to achieve a theater of essential humanity; so its themes, gestures, settings, and rhythms are typically elemental and non-narrative with strong emphasis on shadow, silence, and a flowing form of movement that audiences sometimes regard as dancelike. Lab theater reflects many of the ideas and images found in the writings of C.G. Jung and Mircea Eliade; hence, its plays are often relatively unconcerned with specific times and places. Instead, they are set in "the space" and in no particular historical period except the "eternal now." Symbol, myth, and ritual pervade the stylized bodily flow and incantatory use of language typical of Lab productions, creating a pervasive ethos of mystery and "otherness." For this reason, comparisons and contrasts with shamanic performance, the ritualized theaters of Asia, and ancient Greek ritual-drama are more fruitful than approaches to the Lab's work by way of the history of literary theater. Methods grounded in phenomenology of religion, symbolic anthropology, and dramatistic sociology are more apt than those based on aesthetics and drama criticism.

Victor Turner, whose work I discussed in the preceding chapter, has greatly enlarged Van Gennep's original concept of liminality. In the light of this notion, I will comment on some lines and actions from the play "Blood Wedding" by Garcia Lorca as adapted and performed by Actor's Lab. The play is a highly ritualized ensemble production with strong liminoid overtones. In my opinion, it was the best of the performances I saw during my fieldwork at the Lab: "Hasid," "Ah, My Brother" (later called "The Pact"), and "The Jewish Wife." Even if others would not share my judgment, "Blood Wedding" is still the most useful example to consider, because it involved all the members of the Lab and therefore most fully reflected their collective ethos.

My fieldwork with the Lab in 1976-1977 concretized as much of Turner as my consultation and study with him helped conceptualize the Lab. Each could be construed an implicit appropriation, critique, and extension of the other, and I might be considered the "field" upon which his words and their actions met. The "field," from the point of view of ritual studies, is not merely a place where I go to observe an action. A field is an arena where the process of symbol-conflict arises—where there is a meeting between a doer-as-observer and a doer-as-actor. To this end, then, I want to "read toward" each other the following excerpts, the first from the script of "Blood Wedding," the second from Turner's THE RITUAL PROCESS:

Down he went to the river, oh, down he went down!   And his blood was running, oh, more than the water.   Carnation, sleep, and dream, the horse won't drink from the stream.   My rose, asleep now lie, the horse is starting to cry.   Lullaby, my baby. . . (Nieoczym, 1977).

The attributes of liminality or of liminal personae ("threshold people") are necessarily ambiguous, since this condition and these persons elude or slip through the network of classifications that normally locate states and positions in cultural space.   Liminal entities are neither here nor there; they are betwixt and between the positions assigned by law, custom, convention, and ceremonial.   As such, their ambiguous and indeterminate attributes are expressed by a rich   variety of symbols in the many societies that ritulize social and cultural transitions. Thus, liminality is frequently likened to death, to being in the womb, to invisibility, to darkness, to bisexuality, to the wilderness, and to an eclipse of the sun or the moon.   Liminal entities, such as neophytes in initiation or puberty rites, may be represented as possessing nothing.   They may be disguised as monsters, wear only a strip of clothing, or even go naked, to demonstrate that as liminal beings they have no status, property, insignia, secular clothing indicating rank or role, position in a kinship system—in short, nothing that may distinguish them from their fellow neophytes or initiands.   Their behavior is normally passive or humble; they must obey their instructors implicitly, and accept arbitrary punishment without complaint.   It is as though they are being reduced or ground down to a uniform condition to be fashioned anew and endowed with additional powers to enable them to cope with their new station in life. Among themselves, neophytes tend to develop an intense comradeship and egalitarianism. Secular distinctions of rank and status disappear or are homogenized (Turner, 1969a:95).

In "Blood Wedding" a bride abandons her groom on the day of their wedding to be with a previous, but now married, lover. The two men eventually meet in a forest where they kill one another, leaving behind the wife, the bride, and the groom's mother. The plot is simple enough; it could be done as a soap opera. But as the Lab performs it, the play is not only stylized, mysterious, and symbolic, it is a liminoid event suspended across the threshold between ritual and theater. Audiences sense that they are outsiders, voyeurs. Some wish to be insiders or to flee. They are both repulsed and fascinated by the events that transpire. They wonder what myths and mysteries might initiate them into the Lab's gnosis ("secret knowledge"). Others resent the implied claim of superiority.

The lines I quoted are incanted by the wife while she is locked in an embrace and death-grasp with the village idiot, but the words are addressed to her husband and child, so the words do not reflect the action; they contradict it in important ways. The words are inverted by the action. There is what I call a "channel contradiction" between word and deed—a characteristic of Lab productions.

The idiot, the only character not in Lorca's text, but added to the script by the Lab's director, is, I think, the key to understanding the play, and even the Lab itself. The idiot is a "liminar," a "threshold person," to use Turner's terms. As the Latin etymology suggests, liminality is the process of crossing the threshold; it is a moment of boundary-crossing. The idiot of the play is also the on-stage stage-manager and boundary-crosser. He snuffs out candles, turns on moonlight and daylight, and becomes a surrogate for other characters, "going with" them, in whatever way suits their needs. He is an on-stage servant. Yet he is a soul-guide, seer of all actions, perpetual outsider, and tempter. He alone passes with immunity through the winglike nets of death that appear onstage.

An interpreter looks vainly in the working script for lines or stage directions relating to the idiot. He embodies the non-literary ethos of the Lab's work. So an interpreter preoccupied with words and written texts will err fundamentally in trying to understand the play or the group that produced it.

When Turner develops a series of binary distinctions contrasting liminality and the status system, he lists the following liminal traits, all of which are concentrated in the Lab's idiot, and most of which typify the processes and values extolled in the Lab's form of ritual exploration, which they call "the work": silence, foolishness, simplicity, acceptance of pain and suffering, disregard for conventional appearance, no wealth-based distinctions, unselfishness, nakedness or uniformity of clothing, minimization of sex distinctions, absence of status and property, totality, transition, and communitas (1969a:106-107).

COMMUNITAS IN A WEDDING CELEBRATION

"Communitas"(as I have said in Chapter 9) is the word Turner uses to designate the social "anti-structure" generated by liminal processes. The concept reflects quite accurately the social dynamics of Lab members during the work process, which I will discuss later. In Turner's view, communitas may take any of three forms: spontaneous, ideological, or normative, depending on the degree of structuring which has occurred (1978:252).

The scene in the play which most clearly reflects communitas is the one depicting a pre-nuptial celebration. This celebration is full of suggestive dance, music, laughter, and role-reversal. The villagers play with their socially assigned statuses. Men dance with men. The old mother appears as a young girl. The idiot, normally of no sexual consequence, teases the women by looking up their skirts. Enemies appear as friends. This is characteristic of Turner's "normative communitas," or what Blake calls "the winged moment as it flies," or Buber, "I-Thou relation." The bride during this celebration is pure and white, but in the concluding scene of the performance her dress is bloodstained; her "flower" is crushed. Her wedding gown has become a death-wrapping; she is the bride of death, and the idiot is the one who leads her offstage, to "the other side." In Turnerian language, the bride and her lover, Leonardo, had been involved in "spontaneous communitas" during their first affair, which has taken place before the play begins. When Leonardo, who is now married to someone else, runs off with the bride, they are in pursuit of "ideological communitas"; they pit themselves against the community and the status system and refuse the "normative communitas" of the wedding ceremony itself.

In Turner's view, the liminal period of a rite of passage is akin to death. A sense of ending seems to lie at the base of communitas. In the case of "Blood Wedding," it prevents the social-structural outcome of a wedding, namely, marriage. Marriage is homologous with property and social structure, Turner suggests (1969a:58). Therefore, it is a state opposed to the liminal process. So death is not only the dramatically and poetically proper ending of the play, it is a conclusion sociologically consistent with the ideological liminality and communitas of the Lab itself. Lab members are able to perceive the dialectical identity and opposition of ecstasy and death. What they have immense difficulty handling is aging, marriage, ordinariness--what Turner labels "the status system." So the Lab enters the lion's den when it takes on the performance of a play which is a marriage rite, but it does not take the risk of being gobbled up by marriage. Rather, marriage itself is put to death in the performance. What Lab people seem to want instead of marriage in the social system is a process of relationships akin to gambolling and dance.

The marriage is dramatically and ritually destroyed before it can be consummated or routinized. In the play, as in the Lab itself, no one is fully married in the socio-legal sense. In the play there are an idiot, a widow, her son (the groom), a faithless bride, an unfaithful husband (Leonardo), and his wife, (who is also Death and whose "child" is a knife). During my fieldstudy people sometimes developed long-term relationships and even assumed the responsibilities of child-bearing, but for none of them had the final, legal ritual been performed. Turner is right: marriage is the ritual symbol of the statuses of a social-structural state.

I am doing what some might consider a methodologically suspect, if not dangerous, thing. I am taking the interactions of the performance as a reflection of the sociology of the Lab itself. Why I do so will be clearer when I explain later how the Lab works toward performances.

FROM TEXT TO PERFORMANCE

"Blood Wedding" was written in 1933 by the Spaniard Frederico Garcia Lorca. The Lab's production of 1978 is an ensemble creation which differs radically from the written text. The director becomes virtual playwright. His working script eliminates approximately two-thirds of the lines of the play. Only one verbal addition has been made: a monologue from an ancient text. The basic modifications occur by elimination and re-ordering. A rudimentary plotline is still visible, though not central. Long sections of the performance consist of silent, highly stylized movement. Lighting is largely by candles or a single bulb, and shadows are so prominent that an audience is more likely to see the actors as embodiments of the dark figures on the walls and ceilings, than to treat the shadows as "reflections" of the human characters.

The play was chosen by the director specifically because of its links with archetypal themes which had emerged from previous performances and private, exploratory work based on the individual needs of Lab members. The personal goals and quests of Lab people were the central considerations in choosing the play and assigning roles. This is an important fact, since it inverts the priorities of the popular stage, which considers first the desires of the audience, the intentions of the playwright, or the form of the play itself. "Blood Wedding" was a vehicle for exploring and communicating themes already manifest in the private, non-performative context of the work: marriage, death, fidelity, motherhood, sonship, darkness, foolishness, joy, blood, violence.

Lab productions are often publicized as "studies" or "works in progress." "Blood Wedding" is a series of studies or scenes with more narrative and chronological continuity than most Lab productions. A frequent criticism of their performances is that they lack over-arching conception and narrative development. The Lab's usual response is that they are trying to do something deeper than tell a story or dramatize an idea; they are trying to tap the unconscious.

I have suggested in SYMBOL AND CONQUEST that archetypally inclined, ritual communities appeal to natural, rather than historical, symbols and that outsiders typically view them as socially gnostic, disembodied from the locality. Hence, such communities often feel themselves relatively homeless, even when they own land and a place. The community whose space can be anywhere, because of the universalism of its archetypes, sometimes finds that its space is nowhere. The Lab, like Liturgy in Santa Fe (Grimes, 1976:31), an archetypalist-Catholic group, has a pronounced tendency to choose the outdoors as a performative setting. Even when performing indoors, trees, rocks, weeds, and flowers are centrally present. Lorca sets much of "Blood Wedding" indoors; the Lab resets much of the action outdoors. Both Liturgy in Santa Fe and Actor's Lab were in the process of losing their respective quarters as I was studying their performances. This fact is as much effect as it is cause of their feeling that they are rooted not in a specific community, but in "nature" or "reality" itself.

Because of the way plays and parts are chosen and modified at the Lab, its members dislike being regarded as mere actors. A Lab person seldom dissociates him- or herself from some action by claiming that a deed or trait belongs to the character rather than to the person. What an audience sees is supposed to be a real action, not the semblance of one. The performer is not supposed to be hiding behind the mask of a character.

In her sociological study of the theater, Elizabeth Burns (1972:31-32) distinguishes on-stage ("authenticating") conventions from conventions which obtain between audience and performer ("rhetorical" ones). I suggest adding a third category: pre- and post-performance conventions, or what one might call "working" conventions. Since there is so little disjunction between working and performing conventions in the Lab, I maintain that a sociology of the play "Blood Wedding" is a sociology of significant aspects of Actor's Lab. The play reflects not just the characters (Leonardo, idiot, mother, groom, wife, and bride), but the interactions of the working members of the Lab.

For Lab people, neither the work nor performance is supposed to be a mere theatrical routine. On the contrary, they often speak of their being "addicted" to it or "hooked" on it. They are religiously committed to it. Routine is more characteristic of other Lab activities such as administration. The ritual dimensions of the Lab, in addition to being the means by which charisma is routinized, are also the matrices of flow, new insight, and innovation (see Turner, 1974a:248).   Lab repetition has the character of a search, but, unlike Eliade's archetypal deed, a Lab work is not supposed to reach backwards to a primordial, founding action which it attempts to imitate and thereby re-present. In fact, to imitate an action, even one's own from some previous occasion, is rejected at the Lab, despite their nostalgia for the time when an action first emerged.

One of the most frequent sources of ambivalence is the emergence of a pattern; it can indicate either that the act is stereotyped, pretended, and not real, or that it has tapped an unconscious source of power. If an action can be identified as one learned from drama school, traditional ritual, martial arts, dance, or even other Grotowski-inspired groups, it is rejected. The Lab cultivates a very distinct style, but also searches out and destroys style with vigor. I call this attitude a "gestural 'Protestant' principle." Processual flow is sought by a continual protest ("Not this, not this") and repeated adjuration ("Go further--there must be more").

A Jewish poet, previously in residence at the Lab, once suggested (in view of the long hours, emphasis on exertion, and value placed on work) that the Lab was "Calvinistic." I agree and would extend his insight further by suggesting that many of the principles of the Protestant work ethic hold, with the important qualification that they hold ritually, but not morally or economically. When this kind of theater errs, performance becomes "aesthetic athleticism," physical virtuosity on stage. Or it becomes self-indulgent and narcissistic. Audiences are sometimes intimidated by the sheer energy and physicality of Lab productions. As in the Calvinist ethic, one can never rest assured of salvation, which at the Lab would take the form of authentic, graceful, unpretended action. "It" occurs or "works" semi-independently of a person's deeds; yet one must be in a constant state of readiness to respond and "go with what emerges." People do not earn anything in this manner, but they do allow power to demonstrate itself through their actions.

A thorny issue at the Lab is how to mediate the tension between traditional and creative modes of ritual-dramatic performance. The issue takes the form of a question whether truly authentic enactment can be created or whether it must be received from some other source. The Lab must create ritualized structures, if it is have a form for encountering "It." The group is not part of some "great tradition" that provides it with a set of canonical rites. But "create" has the sense of "work while waiting upon." I can imagine a Lab person easily understanding the religious disclaimer (and covert claim), "Of myself I can do nothing." Lab people are dependent upon "It" and upon one another. Yet, when asked what is being worked on, they are likely to say, "On ourselves." "Self" is usually understood in two ways: "body" and "source of connectedness with all things."

THE RITUAL IDIOT

I return now to the idiot, whom I earlier suggested was the key to understanding ritualizing in Actor's Lab and whom I take to be the symbol for its way of handling the interface between tradition and creativity. The fool, with his various rites of celebration and status-reversal, is, as Turner notes (1969a:110), structurally marginal. He has no socially constituted, and therefore no socially inflated, self. In the play the idiot can enter any action because he is an idiot and can be safely ignored. Yet he frames every action by signalling, taunting, and tempting with his only "voice," a small bamboo flute, or by lighting and extinguishing candles. His actions are never "real" in the sense that those of the other characters are; his deeds are meta-real. They are the grounds of other people's actions. The ground of action is, as Aristotle might have said, both the "original cause" and "final cause" of the action.

Because the idiot is the only character in the play without a commitment (for which marriage is the ritual symbol), he alone can enter death with immunity. He is already socially and intellectually dead. He alone is free, in a way the husband never is, to allow himself to be completely dominated by Leonardo's wife during the village scene. The idiot uses his brains, his sexuality, and his freedom from commitments in the same symbolic mode that Lab members want. They are in pursuit of a meta-reality—a liminoid reality on the creative boundary of society. We see the Leonardo's wife do with the idiot what she wishes to do with her husband. Leonardo, unlike the sexless idiot, must always fear emasculation; so he incessantly prances around the floor like a stud horse needing to be broken. He cannot escape his social status as a male. He fights the marriage-status system, but loses as surely as the groom, who aspires to join the very system that Leonardo would leave. The idiot is the only male left at the end of the performance (except the director, who is offstage and who is thereby the idiot of idiots). Because the idiot is a liminar, a person categorically anomolous, one who falls between the cracks of the social grid, he survives, sees, and knows. In a later version of the play the director himself did, in fact, take this role.

The idiot is my symbol for the ethos of the Lab's ritualizing and Turner's theorizing, because he crystallizes their way of dealing with tradition and creativity. The idiot's solution is simple—but only in the sense that a clown is simple. The idiot handles tradition by appropriating it upside down. He inverts it and thereby renews it. The idiot so radically submits that, as the Taoists put it, he overcomes from underneath.

Turner is an academic fool. He has stood on his head and told us that rituals are hot seedbeds of change; that rituals not only control process, they generate it; that rituals not only mark boundaries, they evoke phasic motion in a culture.

The Lab is a collective clown. It periodically starves, loses its building, and plays on some nights to almost non-existent audiences. The Lab finds its power by inverting the traditional mythic, ritualistic, dramatic, and symbolic resources of Western religious culture. It hopes its violation is reverent, because it is a means of appropriating and renewing Catholic, Protestant, and Jewish resources. "Ideological idiocy," if I may coin a phrase, is a strategy for mediating the dualism of our existence, of which "creative vs. traditional" is only one manifestation. Ideological idiocy is a ritual strategy for tricking meaning out of opaque and solidified cultural forms. It is no accident that shamanism is a religio-artistic model for much of the Lab's activity. Shamans are self-cultivated idiots who, by giving themselves totally to performing symbolic gestures which neither they nor their cultures can currently or fully believe, re-open the possibility of participation in ritual. Their stage magic can evoke a world which is magic in the sense of "wonder-evoking."

Religio-artistic performances are the rituals of idiocy. Performers at the Lab do not believe in any traditional sense; but neither do they disbelieve in a modern, academic way. Liminars generate rituals. The views of Jung, Tillich, and Eliade notwithstanding, rituals can be created, but the one who creates them must also stand outside them. Only the others, those in the ritual-social system, believe or disbelieve. Marriages belong to believers, funerary rites to fools. The idiot "believes" in the process, but he must constantly kill off the product as it hardens into a form. He must opt for "art-ing" and "god-ing" (to use Leroi Jones' terms) over artifacts and gods. The ideological idiot is a ritual guardian and director who is beyond belief and unbelief; he just turns the lights on and off for the participants.

The fool is not unintellectual; he is anti-intellectual. The Lab's rhetoric is anti-intellectual; yet the Lab depends on the university for its archetypalist religiosity as surely as Turner's liminality depends upon the status system. The fool is ritually a knower and enforcer, but he plays his role in the mood of a "contrary," to use a Sioux and Blakean term.

Part of the Lab's ideological frame of reference is archetypalism, largely that of Jung. Turner's liminal/status system distinction is a binary typology. Yet both the performers and the anthropologist are ideologically committed to processualism, change-making, flow, organic metaphors, and other Heraclitan devices. The work of both Turner and the Lab blossomed during the early 60's and late 70's. One goal of their work was to reconcile the statics of typology with the dynamics of social change.

A typology should be used only as a strategic simplification. The ideological idiot simplifies things as a strategy for mobilizing power. His power arises from his being more deeply conserving, more fully traditional, than the status system itself. Hence the tool for change-making is ritual, a notoriously conservative cultural form.

The idiot's simplicity is actually duplicitous, yet his is a holy foolishness. He shares the dualism of his age and culture, but mitigates it by a deliberate act of unknowing. He chooses simplicity of mind. The difference between ideological idiocy and insanity is that in the former, one takes moral responsibility for assuming the role which he plays and is.

Post-modern humanity has no chance of entering a symbolic, religious mode in a mood of primal naïveté. We can only find meaning in traditional religio-dramatic scripts by a "trick" of interpretation or a Blakean "higher innocence." This mode of consciousness is virtual, or subjunctive, belief, as Turner suggests. In modern, industrial society this trick no longer occurs in the liminal phase of a traditional rite of passage, but in the liminoid rites of religio-aesthetic performances like those of the Lab, and in the academic rites of fooling around in Turnerian fashion with words as if they were playthings.

THE WORK OF ACTOR'S LAB

"The work" is the least accessible aspect of the Lab; yet it is the generative matrix of performances, workshops, movement training, and PEP's. Physical exercises, sometimes done to music, are the usual way of preparing to do the work. The exercises are typically circular and flowing, and the order in which they are done may seem random, since individuals pursue whichever ones they choose, at their own pace. I noticed a tendency for people to begin with head and limbs and work toward the trunk, and a penchant for alternating rotations with dancing, jumping, or running. Sometimes gymnastic or yogic fragments appear, but so do individually or collectively discovered elements. The Lab's exercises avoid systematization, encourage the finding of one's own limits and rhythms, and alternate   between individual and collective phases.

"The space," wherever it may be, has a mystique for Lab people, but not because it is architecturally special. The Lab prefers to work in an empty space, the doors and windows of which can be secured from curious eyes. It uses no stage, and its most important architectural feature is a four-inch high wooden platform covering most of the floor and serving as an ever-present drum upon which bare feet can find their rhythms.

The Lab seems to prefer a space which is not fully lit, so the harsh light of clarity will not obliterate fragile, unconsciously motivated actions. Some Lab people refer to their space as a "womb." The metaphor is apt, because the work is replete with perinatal postures and gestures. The space is "bracketed." It is set off, "sacred" in the etymological sense. The very blankness of the Lab's preferred settings gives the space the quality of a New England Puritan church. But the way of lighting the space often projects upon this starkness the labyrinthine qualities of Plato's allegorical cave or a European cathedral. The space is chosen not for its ability to direct the imagination, but for its capacity to receive the projections of participants.

Lab people sometimes use the term "space" metaphorically, as for example, when they say, "Find your own space." This space is not a spot in a room, but a sense of one's body as flexible and radiating outward.

Despite the Lab's collective ethos, which is part of its ritualizing sensibility, a strong individualism, privatism, and ownership ethic pervades the work. So often members speak of "their own bodies," "their own rhythms," and "their own songs."

The basic format for doing the work is simple. One or more persons enter a space (usually indoors, though sometimes during PEP's, out of doors) and begin to move expectantly, while one or more others watch. There is no script; no one is supposed to be acting or performing; so this activity is not improvisational theater. Action, not acting, is the goal; the work has no intrinsic connection to theater, though it can serve theater, just as it can serve religion, education, or therapy. Doing something in front of others is not only the theatrical situation, it is the human situation.

The basic attitude with which Lab people watch is, "Let's see what emerges." The basic attitude with which people do the work is, "Let's attend to and follow the rhythms and impulses encountered in the space." One can speak of this as "unstructured," because in comparison to usual activities, theatrical or otherwise, it is. But a structure often appears. I suspect that one always does, but Lab people sometimes regard a series of movements as formless and chaotic, as having no structure. However, I assumed that such movements did have structure, even though neither they nor I were able to perceive it at the moment. After seeing or doing the work, I frequently had the experience of finding retrospectively a pattern in the actions.

In open work there is structuring, though not pre-structuring. Occasionally, people at the Lab pre-direct a work session, and they then speak of a "study." In a study I might, for example, enter the space after placing something in it, say, a stump or chain. Or I might enter it with what the Lab calls a "metaphor." A metaphor is a word, concept, or phrase with which one works to become fully identified, but about which he or she does not think during the work session. Working with something is similar to the way a Zen Buddhist sits with a koan. The goal is to get rid of the object as something "out there," as something thought about or imitated. The intention is to become fully unified with whatever is there—whether it is merely the empty space and floor or some object chosen from one's own waking or dream life.

What occurs in the work is a form of "divination" (my term). Of the divining process, Rudolf Otto says, "It is not concerned at all with the way in which a phenomenon—be it event, person, or thing—came into existence, but with what it means, that is, with its significance as a 'sign' of the holy" (1958:145). People at the Lab do not read bones or cards to fortell the future, but want to "read" the body as a presence portending the path one should follow in exploring the unconscious. Whether the object of divination is one's body, a space, or an object, the intention of working with it is to find a "presence" in both the religious and dramatic sense of the word.

THE WORK ETHIC

The work is not, then, an imitation of an action; it does not fit an Aristotelean or classical notion of theater. The work is action in search of simplicity and immediacy. Or at least it ought to be. This "ought," I think, is the heart of the Lab "ethic": I ought to be there in the space. I ought to be identified with my own actions. I ought not be imitating or merely repeating exercises I learned in church, theater school, or physical education classes. I ought not even imitate myself by trying to duplicate some action I have imagined or accomplished authentically before. The basic double-bind that arises before each performance is that one must repeat the sequence of actions dictated by the working script, but must not imitate.

Mircea Eliade (1961) understands ritual to be a return to the origin. In a ritual performance, argues Eliade, one imitates, and thereby renews and re-effects, the founding, paradigmatic action of the gods or heroes. Every ritual action is a reinstatement and re-actualization of the original action; every ritual act is a repetition. The Lab's work is ritualized in one of these senses but not in another. The work is an effort to return to the origin, the matrix, of all personal and social action, but it is not aimed at repeating any specific content or structure. So in this respect, the work is pararitualistic. Its aim is ritualizing (a liminoid process) not rituals (a function of the status system). society at large.

Since Lab people are searching for an action without a name, their language often sounds mystical or esoteric, despite their efforts to find a more publically accessible rhetoric. Typically, they watch one another's work in silence. After it is finished, a few comments are made, but these are tentative, even hesitant; though after seeing a person work several times, Lab people can become unusually assertive that they know what the person needs to do, or, more often, stop doing.

Describing the principles of the work is easier than describing a specific instance of it. How does one describe "an action without a name"? How does one give a name to a newly emerging action? Describing a piece of work is a very interpretive action—far more so than describing an object—because we lack the eye, vocabulary, and sensibility for describing bodily and kinesthetic processes. Ours is an objectifying language, and we have a severely limited vocabulary for describing motions and actions.

The work, one might say, is "a fantasy of the body." I do not mean that one ought to fantasize during the work; one ought not. I mean that in doing the work I cut myself as free as I can from the usual way of putting gestures and motions together. I let my body go. I allow it to find its own way. When such a moment occurs, body, soul, mind, spirit (and whatever else there is to human beings) come together; there are no parts, only an organically integrated whole. So one must not be confused by the dualistic sounding rhetoric that Lab people sometimes use, for example, "working on my body." I work on my body only to find a way of "working as my body" (my term).

Doing the work has one element that some might consider specifically theatrical. The actions of the work are quite real, as real as anything in ordinary social interaction; however, some actions, especially those involving sexuality and aggression, have, what one might call, "brackets" around them. They become symbolic or sublimated. Where the line is drawn varies, however, because people do sometimes get hurt or touched. If there are no explicit ought's concerning the content of the work, what is surprising to me is not that sensual and aggressive motifs arise, but that they are so seldom acted out literally. Working through blockages concerning aggression or sexuality does not seem to demand an actual consummation, that is stripping, love-making, hitting, or hurting. Consummation becomes "working through," and usually it can be accomplished by giving oneself permission to let the impulse arise in symbolic form, hence the strong ritual atmosphere. Allowing it to surface tends to socialize and integrate the impulse, though I do not think this is always the case. Whether the bracketing and symbolizing are motivated by ethical considerations or theatrical ones is not easy to say. I suspect the motivations are ethical and psychological. After all, one does not always know to what extent some emerging sexual or aggressive action may directly implicate and involve others. The Lab usually—and wisely—protects itself by substituting objects for persons when clear dangers arise for others.

These problems are basic to most studies: (1) coping with the pressure and support of being watched; (2) knowing what to do with images and words that spontaneously arise; (3) learning to respond rather than imitate, push, or plan; (4) distinguishing intuitive connections from arbitrary, willed, intellectualized, or socially expected ones; (5) avoiding the conflation of verbal metaphors and interpretations used afterwards to describe the work with those encountered during the work; (6) weighing one's own associations against those of the director and other observers; (7) knowing whether to screen out or include pre- and post-work intentions (to perform, to write, to find "It," to know oneself, and so on).

The work, when "It works," generates a sense of wonder and awe among participants. This "It" is elusive, powerful, fragile, and highly valued. And one needs to be in a specially tuned state of body-mind to encounter it. The hermeneutics of religious language are useful in interpreting a study. One never has a sense of finality about the meaning of an action, because the ones that "work" are ineffable. Lab people do not seem to value the recognizable, the repeated, or the re-emergent as they do actions which are breakthroughs. This one element of their ethic is quite anti-ritualistic and is a post-modern theatrical-artistic value rather than a traditionally religious one.

Nevertheless, I maintain that the work is a ritualized activity. The Lab has nothing to do with occult or sectarian religion, nor has it any creedal formulation, theology, mythology, or cosmology. But its pursuit of immediacy and identification with flow and mystery make its research ethic unmistakably akin to ritual.

The distinction I am making between a ritual ethic and a ritual aesthetic is important. The Lab does not merely employ ritual symbols in plays nor simply imitate ancient rituals to entertain or edify audiences. Rather, it tries to find the gestures which actually connect to   the actors' values. So "acting" does not mean "pretending" so much as "doing." Like all ethics, this one is aspired to, not always achieved. In a given study or performance, I may well find that I am simulating, rather than doing, my own actions or feelings.

An ethic is a set of standards or ideal images to which a group aspires. The Lab has no name for its ritual ethic, but some members draw their heroic imagery from shamanism, a religio-dramatic phenomenon of growing interest to contemporary theater (see Chapter 15). Although shamanic imagery emerges within the work in the form of recurring motifs such as flying, dismembering, dancing, and animal-like sounds or movements, there is little of shamanism in the structure of the work. The Lab has no initiation rites, and it regularly uses terms such as "process," "intuition," "response," "emerging," "energy," "clean," "clear," and "decisive" to convey its ethic—almost never words such as "possession," "tutelary spirit," "healing," "exoricism," "magic," or "demon." So its "shamanism" takes the form of a demythologized, strictly contained ritual motif. Most of what is distinct about shamanism—dissimulation and trickery in the service of healing, trance, stories of ascending or descending to other worlds, ventriloquism, spirit languages, use of psychotropic plants, magical divination, and mediumistic communication—are all missing from the Lab's work. The major sense of kinship with the shaman arises, I think, from the Lab's liminal social position, its effort to avoid aestheticism, its desire for power, and its penchant for archetypal symbols.

Fidelity in doing the work means primarily being true to one's own body, feelings and rhythms, not to a secret wisdom imparted at initiation nor to a tradition of practices and symbols. So what I call "the myth of the Heraclitan body," is more determinative of Lab aspirations than are the actions of shamanism: flight, metamorphosis, curse, and trance. The Lab's goal is more akin to Gestalt therapy or Zen practice than to shamanism, because its repeated emphasis is upon the emerging, the flowing, and the present. The surest way to violate the Lab's "work ethic" is to be "out of oneself" or not fully present in this space at this time—something shamans regularly attempt to do.

"Thinking," "being in one's head," "interpreting," "augmenting," "being blocked," "fantasizing," "acting," and "hesitating" are words which constitute the cardinal sins of the work. They all amount to the same thing—dualism, a split in consciousness, or a split between persons, which results in an indecisive, unclear action. An action not fully done because I am not fully present generates illusion (Zen), leaves an unfinished gestalt (Gestalt therapy), or does not work (Actor's Lab). A failure of bodily respond-ability implies a breach of respons-ibility.

When I enter the work floor with someone else, my fundamental responsibility is to find some form of action by which to mediate the dualism between my rhythms and another's. I am, in Lab language, to "go with" the other presence but to avoid imitating, merely submitting, or merely overpowering. The goal is to sustain an interaction until it dies a non-arbitrary death. If the director asks for a study to be repeated, as sometimes is the case, the goal may be either psychosocial (to allow "It to emerge") or theatrical (to find a usable dramatic form).

An authentic "going with," because I am avoiding both introspection and the heteronomy of imitating the other or acting for the sake of a spectator, is a fully embodied response. All Lab action is supposed to be the result of fully contacting oneself and openly meeting the other. Such an action is not to linger or oscillate between these two poles of inner- or outer-directedness. Of the best studies one can only say that the process (the mysterious "It") occurred. The goal is to develop a person whose making of ethical, social, and aesthetic judgments is not a separate step from the process of interaction itself. Simplicity and spontaneity are the sought-after virtues of such an ethic. This kind of theater is one which happens before others, without being for others.

Since studies employing objects typically search for "the presence" of a thing, the ritual ethic of handling shawls, stumps, shoes, knives, or rocks is the same as when working with a person. One might call this the "animistic" dimension of the work. Treating things as persons or powers is one of the most consistent characteristics of Lab productions and studies. Such an attitude approaches shamanic reverence for talismans, the main difference being the introspection that accompanies many studies despite intentions to the contrary. The Lab's sense of objects is iconic. By projecting my feelings onto, say, a piece of black cloth, I also "animate" it with a resonance that generates a sense of mystery when others see the dead, inanimate thing come to life. Though a Lab production would probably never use traditional puppetry (because puppets imitate humans and talk too much), objects in studies and performances are sometimes more alive than their animator-actors. Performers seem to follow them, and not vice-versa; so the performers may seem "possessed" when their animations of an object become truly transparent.

Projecting onto "It," others, and objects in studies can confuse or clarify choices in unclear circumstances, just as the shaman's divination, for example, minimizes anxiety and randomizes a tribal choice of which land to hunt or farm. In a study I both find and make a meaning. A good choice in a study is "clear." It lends a sense of cohesion and meaning to the flux, making it "flow." A set of connected choices and actions is the Lab's implied definition of meaning. There is no meaning/function dualism. Meaning is a connected web of functions, and the intuitive source of connectedness is non-manipulable, in their view.

The ritual ethic of doing the work is coupled with a hermeneutic for seeing, interpreting, and directing it. The director sees virtually all of the work done by Lab members. They see fragments of one another's work and, occasionally, some of his. Work is not done in solitude for several reasons: (1) one obtains "energy" from being seen, (2) one is less likely to become self-indulgent in the presence of others, and (3) one needs to learn how to act authentically in spite of being watched. I say "in spite of," because those doing the work seldom respond directly to someone who is watching. Eye contact with viewers is avoided, and witnesses usually remain quiet and unobtrusive. Eye contact is reserved for occasions when someone doing the work wants to invite a witness to join him or her.

DIVINING AND SEEING THE WORK

Those who do the work, I suggest, are "diviners." Those who watch it one might call "seers" (both are my terms). The two roles demand one another. Diviners physically and kinesthetically interpret bodies, spaces, and objects. Seers verbally interpret diviners. An action done alone is not, in the Lab view, the same as one done before those who see, because great vulnerability and pressure accompany being seen. On one level, a seer may know more about the meaning of an action than a diviner does; so active collaboration, trust, and suspension of judgement must occur if the work is to succeed.

The one who does the work is supposed to be its primary interpreter. The director's role is to push me into areas I resist and to encourage me to search myself for the meanings of an action. Direction takes a paradoxical form. The director often says "I do not know what you need." Yet he also claims superior intuitive knowledge and gives imperative directions which declare, "You need to do this."

The overall tone of the directing, however, is one of trial and error. Studies are seldom interrupted by the director's "Stop!" and the predominant viewing ethic is one of non-judgmental attentiveness. The director's priority is first to enable members to find what they want. Only much later, does the goal become that of galvanizing what emerges into a production. What is to be discovered precedes what is to be constructed.

Studies are understood by Lab people to have a life of their own, semi-independent of the wishes and intentions of the individual participants. This life, like that of a person, is to be respected, followed, and not violated by arbitrary withdrawal or deliberate manipulation. Therefore, studies vary considerably in length and intensity, though thirty to forty minutes is about average. Seldom is a study stopped by the director, though it can be, if he feels that the duration of an interaction is being extended beyond its natural life, trifled with, or completely missed.

Often people cannot remember what they do in the work, or if they do, they cannot describe it. And if they can both remember and describe it, they sometimes cannot interpret it; so the hermeneutics of the work resemble those of dream interpretation. Often no one comments on them, sometimes for fear of naming the actions too soon and thereby destroying them, at other times, simply because no one knows what to say. Those who watch are supposed to do so without judgment, but not without interpretation. Sometimes, therefore, interpretations are offered, and they tend to be couched in the language of myth, ritual, and archetype, which itself engenders an aura of the primordial and essential, even when a study seems to fail.

During the early phases of a person's work, vagueness is, it seems to me, cultivated. When the process succeeds, this vagueness gives way to mystery in performance. Mystery, unlike vagueness, is not incompatible with precision.

The most anti-ritualistic aspect of the Lab's work is its suspicion of formulas. Yet, their "work ethic" and "seeing hermeneutic" are themselves formulas. The preparatory exercises, which are intended to attack the routinization of the body, constitute a counter-routine. A counter-routine is still a routine, even though it is preceded by a minus sign. So, not suprisingly, a definite, describable Lab style comes out of the work. Flow always becomes structure, and archetype always decays into stereotype. This process is, of course, not unique to Actor's Lab. To the   question, "Why do the same patterns and gestures keep emerging?" Lab people usually reply in one of two ways. Either they suggest that it is because they are lazy and have not broken through their own resistances and clichés, or they imply that they have contacted "It," the primordial rhythm which surges through all things. Another possibility, however, is that Lab members unconsciously absorb aspects of one another's patterns until a collective style of movement develops. If people who share basic values and personality needs move together randomly for long enough, they are bound to generate a collective style. Unless the body remembers, no group coherence is possible.

A distinctive feature of the Lab's ritual-ethic is its "kinesic congruence" (Schechner, 1977:105), its collective gestural and kinesthetic style. Words are particularly innocuous to convey it; film is needed. Nevertheless, some of its features are a wavelike circularity, birdlike or serpentine writhing, radiation of energy from central trunk outwards toward head and limbs, avoidance of localized or isolated movements, centering in the lower abdomen and pelvic region, decisive starts and suspended stops, spewed and relatively uninflected barrages of language alternating with unvarnished silence. Other supportive, but non-kinesic, characteristics of the Lab style are its use of candles and shadows, simple musical sounds employing simple instruments, minimal costume, no make-up, small audiences, mythological themes, and roles which pay first allegiance to actor needs and values rather than the characteriztions of playwrights or demands of a text. This ethical, rather than aesthetic, approach to roles is the factor which leads directly to the non-theatrical, ritual explorations of a PEP.

The Lab's distaste for the repeatable and structural produces the feeling that nothing is ever finished, or for that matter, finishable. Incompleteness is characteristic of the work and the performances. (which are usually called "works in progress"). This can mean that the carrot is always an inch away from the donkey's mouth. One is perpetually prepared for a momentous culmination which may never arrive. It can also mean one never fully leaves the Lab after having been a member of it.

On the other hand, this "Protestant" ethic, which protests, "Not yet, not this," is a way of recognizing that every gesture or form has a lifespan which is easily, but perilously, ignored. An action performed attentively and with presence this time becomes an idol or a lie next time.

One result of the Lab's view of process and structure is a tendency to equate a gestural lie with a traditional, or repeated, gesture. It operates on what Paul Ricoeur (1976a) calls a "hermeneutic of suspicion." Even after searching for the right gesture, it checks and re-searches. Lab publicity materials say they are engaged in "theater research." "Research" in this instance designates no scientific or systematic procedure. The term applies not to some specific form or forumula, but to this repeated self-investigation for insuring that one is not indulging in habit, lying, or taking the easy way out. The "good" gesture—and I intentionally choose moral language—is one which is sufficent for the moment. But what was sufficient a moment ago is not sufficient now; so one must always be suspicious of actions that have worked before.

Since the Lab calls its form of actor training and personal research "the work," a word about working and playing is in order. At the Lab considerable tension exists between doing the work and performing plays. I recall a rehearsal in which the director chided the members for losing their spirit of playfulness as they shifted from the work toward performance. The shift had nothing to do with a transition from a mood of lightness to one of heaviness, but rather, with a move from private exploration to public repetition. The work is seldom humorous; occasionally it is joyful. Usually, it is heavy. Robert Neale (1969:9) defines work as action aimed at resolving the conflict between our needs to discharge energy and to design experience; play is any action expressing a harmony between these two needs. In the work discharge dominates; in performance, design does. So the most likely times for play, in Neale's sense, is late in a study or early in a run of performances. I think that, if forced to choose between the work or performance, most Lab people would choose the work. Another characteristic of play is that it is valued in itself; it is not a means. This is why Neale eventually identifies ritual celebration as the fullest form of play. The dramatic side of the Lab's work necessites using "It," while the ritualistic side calls simply for doing "It." The problem with which the Lab continues to struggle is how to live in the interstices between dramatic productivity (work) and ritual search for the sacred sources of action (play).

PUBLIC EXPLORATION PROJECTS

A Public Exploration Project (PEP) is a pararitualistic event drawing on religious and dramatic resources. PEP's, with names such as "Night of Vigil" or "Night of Wanderings," can last from a few hours to several days. Usually, they last at least overnight. At the end of my first project I was in culture shock. When this way of describing my state occurred to me, I thought it a hyperbole. Now I do not. I have decided that a PEP is a temporary community, a subculture appearing as an event. An event is more ephemeral than the network of structures we call a "culture," but the event in which I participated jolted my connections with stable social institutions. So I had no choice but to reconceive the assumption, which I had carried to much of my scholarly work in religious studies and anthropology, that culture is a configuration largely of language, thought, and art. I became certain that culture also resides quite literally in the bones, in our patterns of moving, breathing, walking, and so on. Two weeks of radically altered ways of moving precipitated for me new ways of thinking, speaking, and being with others. After the event I found that I was having almost translatable physiological and kinetic responses to ordinary events around me. Despite my reservations about it, the PEP left a deep impression.

Several months later, during a seminar on ritual at the New Theater Festival in Baltimore (June 1978), a vigorous discussion developed. The most debated issue was whether, as Richard Schechner contended, experiences in paratheatrical events, such as those conducted by the Polish and Canadian Theater Labs, could be integrated into either the ordinary lives or theatrical work of the participants. I recalled that, anticipating the end of the PEP, several participants broke silence to raise this very issue. They wanted to know how anyone could be satisfied with the "real" world after the intensity of the new one generated during the exploration. To illustrate the seriousness of the debate about the integration of ritual-like events, I will describe the Lab's first major PEP in 1976.

The polarities between which the PEP swung were ecstatic transport in a closed space and loosely structured ambling through the public streets of a heavily industralized, urban city, Hamilton, Ontario. On the one hand, at least two participants, enabled to "fly" and brought down by others, entered what can only be called a trance-dance. And on the other, the entire group took a long, rambling walk at dawn across the city. Most of the activities were somewhere between these poles of intensity and diffusion, but whether intermediate activities can actually form a bridge is a question raised by Schechner and explored by members of the Lab. How can we integrate ordinary walking and shaman-like "flying"?

Various ways of naming the goal of the PEP were mentioned by Lab members, among them, "getting rid of baggage," "authentic interaction," "finding 'It.'" Most of these terms, however, were excessively ideological or already clichéd. They obscured the exploratory tenor of the PEP, as well as the Lab's own tentativeness about what it was doing. The PEP was an experiment, and, as always in experiments, the experimenters were often uncertain both about what they wanted and unclear about the criteria for judging the results. The goal was to do the work with a large group of strangers.

Some participants spoke of the PEP as "unstructured." But a more careful scrutiny revealed that structuring was constantly occurring. Several principles engendered the basic ethos of the PEP: (1) Much of the work was done in silence and with minimal or no introduction. Actions were not framed for the strangers by being named "performance," "workshop," "ritual," or "therapy." (2) Work continued around the clock with minimal time for sleeping, eating, being alone, and talking. (3) Leadership, except during exercises, was covert; effort was made only near the end to share leadership with participants. (4) Discussion of the event itself was forbidden both during and shortly after the PEP. (5) Physical and psychological demands were heavy; role-oriented expectations and socializing were light. (6) Acting, pretending, and stylization, as well as mindlessness, laziness, and introversion were gesturally, and sometimes verbally, discouraged. Attentive presence was cultivated.

Calling the PEP a "paratheatrical" event has limited usefulness, because it construes such an event only in terms of its deviation from theater. And in recent usage it has been associated specifically with the post-poor theater phase of Grotowski's experiments. I usually speak of the PEP's conducted by Actor's Lab as "pararitualistic" partly because of the ritual studies interests that I brought to my participant-observer study of its work, and because I am convinced that the Lab's aspirations toward shamanism have implications for religion as surely as they do for theater. When "It works," the language, logic, and gestures of Lab members are clearly recognizable in terms of what religionists call "mysticism." Mysticism does not denote obscurantism or secrecy, but rather a disciplined, bodily identification of the self with the sources of energy in the cosmos. Mysticism is the search for simplicity and immediacy of access to power.

The first meeting of the PEP was a gathering of approximately forty people in a closed space "for the purpose of going beyond acting." The first movements of the evening came not from Lab members, but from the guests, who presumably felt that singing, dancing, or talking could catalyze some action. The Lab responded only by listening and watching. Some participants did not know for quite a time who were Lab members and who were "the public." So mystification of leadership was felt from the very beginning of the event. A group dynamic, consisting of guessing who the leaders were and fantasizing about their secret purposes, set in early.

In the face of an unnamed interaction among strangers who meet and, for a moment, go with one another without anticipation or regret, the dominant tone is one of mystery, awe, and fullness. But mystery need not become mystification. Mystery happens when an opening, a revelation, occurs between people who meet with minimal pretense, but mystification arises when those in positions of power hide their own processes and uncertainties behind the trappings of elusively maintained separations. Both mystery and mystification were strong in the PEP, though only the former was intended by the Lab.

After the opening session, participants soon learned who were Lab members by observing eye contact and rhythm patterns. While Lab people were identifying, and implicitly criticizing, actions borrowed from other body-mind training sources, the participants were identifying, and beginning to imitate, the Lab's own style of moving and interacting. Enough whispering took place during breaks that participants began to collude in a concerted search for the hidden criteria by which they imagined they would be judged worthy of inclusion in the later phases of the event. The assumption was that initiation was dependent upon competition to be judged by criteria known only to the Lab members. As a matter of fact, Lab people decided during the PEP not to make such a selection but to proceed by attrition. However, for a long time participants did not know this. So in trying to please some unknown, largely fantasized, attentively watching Lab members, the process called by Philip Slater (1966:17) "deification as an antidote to deprivation" set in. The Lab ensemble, because it wanted to facilitate, observe, and go with the initiatives of others, was experienced as an absent, but all-seeing, overlord (deus absconditus). It was sometimes experienced as the ultimate audience before whom participants tried to do-without-acting and whose will was to be discovered only by risk, trial, and error.

Implicitly, the PEP was a nascent subculture, a temporary "total institution." As in monasteries, prisons, religious retreats, and groups of tribal initiates, the PEP greatly reduced people's access to food, sleep, and social amenities in order to generate a simpler form of community. The lifestyle of this temporary community was typified by the symbolic poverty of simple food, the chastity inspired by lack of sleep, obedience to the group ethic, and verbal silence—a familiar ethos to students of monastic rites. As a result, actions began to be hyperkenetic, hungrily aggressive, gesturally erotic, occasionally rebellious, and musically noisy.

Several different kinds of events occurred: (1) preparatory exercises indoors and outdoors, for example, leapfrogging, galloping, gambolling, and the Lab's adaptation of Grotowski's plastiques; (2)

entering and interacting in an open space--alone, in pairs, in small groups, as a whole group; (3) provoked interactions, for instance, Lab people using musical instruments, soil, water, wood, or candles to create settings for actions and overtly animating (inspiring, instigating, leading) participants to find their own rhythms and spaces; (4) working bodily with metaphors such as "The river is my source and my sister."

Most of the events of the PEP required a dialectical split of attention and energy. In one, for example, we were asked to explore our own rhythms using simple instruments such as bells, drums, and blocks, but to "go with the flow" emerging from first one sub-group then another. In another instance, we entered a preparatory space, created rhythmic movement, and then carried it to another space, allowing what we encountered in the second one to modify the way of moving we had begun in the first. Lab members hoped to prevent escape into the duplicities of mere interiority of solipsistic fantasies. Musically, bodily, and socially, the PEP pressed people to discover some "third rhythm" (my term), which was the dialectical outcome of an interplay between the rhythms of two or more participants.

The problem of finding this third rhythm (or "narrow pass," as the shamans call it), in terms of which two persons can go with one another, is a microcosm of the integration problem raised by Schechner and some PEP participants. How a big male and a small female, or more acutely, a large woman and a tiny man, can learn to follow their own aggression in wrestling and tumbling without destroying the interaction, or how a slow runner can handle bad feelings alongside a fast one, without lapsing into competition or giving up, is precisely the same as the one of integrating the cultural rhythms of the "real" world and those of a temporary subculture such as the PEP. So the PEP did not overcome the problem; it miniaturized, and thereby incarnated, it.

Group work during the Lab's PEP was elemental. Noticeably absent were theater games contrived to pick at psychological sores--a bane that haunts the edges of much theater. Alongside what one reads of workshops and actor training in books like Schechner's ENVIRONMENTAL THEATER, the PEP was utterly cautious and full of decorum. I suspect this might have changed had the Lab pursued its original plan to relocate the final phase to a wilderness area of Northern Ontario. Such a shift might have romanticized the PEP by removing it from the harsh urban sounds and smells of Hamilton.

The PEP had no necessary connection with theater, though most of its participants were interested in just that; so they brought with them expectations appropriate to workshops. Playing could occur with approval, but not pretending to play. The PEP was a critique of mimesis as a matrix for theater, and it was also an implicit claim that "interaction ritual," to use Goffman's term, is a better foundation.

Because of the strongly ritualized, heavily archetypal style of productions by Actor's Lab, some invited participants assumed its paratheatrical work would be at best cultic, or at worst, occult. The PEP was neither. Despite the kinship of a PEP to an initiation rite, no secret gnosis was transmitted, though comments about the work and life-directions of participants were offered. And the injunctions to silence after the event tended to reinforce participants' suspicions that there was superior wisdom, when, in fact, there was none. The PEP, it must be said, did engender an expectation of further community, a formal initiation, or conclusion which would allow the neophytes to peer behind the curtains, the strings of which were controlled by Lab people. The PEP was experienced by some participants as an incomplete initiation for at least two reasons. First, no ongoing structure after the PEP was available for them. And second, inititaion could not be into either the Lab itself or the larger society. The Lab could hardly support thirty or forty new members, and its disdain for the consumer-oriented values of modern urban society, which it viewed as the source of blockage to meeting and flowing, prohibited its taking Main Street, Hamilton, as the proper destination for its newly flexible and sensitized "public." So a "Public" Exploration Project does not necessarily produce better citizens any more than it ordains priests of a new order of holy actors. Perhaps, as David Rosenfield (see Nieoczym, 1974) suggested, the Lab has more "pedestrian" concerns. The PEP allowed people to re-walk, a form of re-search. To return to the origin of walking can both feed and upset traditional theatrical, political, or religious institutions. Learning just to walk, as a Zen Buddhist pursues "just sitting," is at once a startlingly simple and terrifyingly difficult task, because we must first be untrained.

A primary value of the Lab's PEP's, then, was its reducing our ways of moving to more elemental forms. The PEP engendered a transient subculture with a curiously simple, shared value, walking. I consider walking the most honest gesture in the PEP, because even the flying of ecstasy took a perambulatory form. Human birds necessarily have feet.

A CRITIQUE OF RITUALIZING THEATER

While at the Lab, and for some time after, I considered it inappropriate to offer a public critique of its work. I did not want my function confused with that of theater critics who saw it as their task to recommend and condemn plays. I also refrained from making public judgments that would reflect on specific personalities. Furthermore, funding agencies were likely to exploit my comments in their deliberations whether to give arts grants to the Lab, and the

Lab was likely quote my evaluations as selectively as artists always do when preparing publicity materials. All this is unfortunate but understandable.

My intention in doing the fieldstudy was to locate basic processes and describe abiding patterns at the Lab, so I could better understand the connections between theater and ritual. Any criticism, I felt, was only as valid as its comprehension of these processes and patterns, which journalistic theater critics frequently misunderstood. Eventually, however, any fieldstudy arrives at a point where judgment is implicit, if not unavoidable, and the ethics of a fieldworker join or clash with those of practitioners. My fundamental sympathy with both the Polish and Canadian Labs is, I suspect, obvious enough. I have, after all, incorporated much of what I learned from them into my own research and teaching.

The Actor's Lab of the present is not identical with the one of 1976-1977. Major changes include its moving from Hamilton to Toronto and its allowing people to do the work without being in performances and vice-versa. People at the Lab, I suspect, feel more strongly than I that they have changed significantly in the past few years. So our views of the validity of my critique probably differ. Judging from recent (1981) performances of "The Passion and the Vigil," "Momo," and "Etudes," I think my comments are still applicable. In any case, ritual criticism is essential to the way I have proposed to study ritual. The critical task cannot be avoided. By holding such a view, I am more akin to theologians than anthropologists. The preceding discussion of a performance, the work, and then a PEP were largely about the way successful examples worked. The following comments are attempts to say how this kind of theater ("ritualizing theater") can fail:

(1) Ritualizing theater can view itself as beyond criticism. The Lab exists in a vacuum in Canada. With perhaps one exception, it is the only theater of its kind; so it can too easily claim to be the best of its kind. Comparisons with conventional stage theater are inappropriate, but comparisons with Grotowski's Lab are pretentious. And comparisons with religious groups are only partially apt. In the absence of good criticism, that is, criticism which is relevant and sympathetic, but also pointed, ritual theater sometimes becomes cynical or inflated about critical evaluation.

(2) Actor's Lab sometimes unwittingly fosters contempt for performance, characterization, and narrative, as well as other aesthetic forms, and yet it continues to use them. In other words, ritualizing theater is not always justified in rejecting criticism based on conventional theatrical standards. Sloppy diction, for instance, is inexcusible by either set of standards.

(3) The Lab has a disdain for the work of playwrights and an underlying disrespect for language. Lab members would not say this,

but it is implied, I think, in their performances. The Lab replaces scripts with lesser quality verbal collages which sometimes do not work either as communication or chant. Not every moan is an articulate outcry. Voice, it is said, is essential, but language perhaps is not. My objection is not to this claim but to the assumption that voice criticism is also inappropriate.

(4) The claim that ritualizing performances "appeal directly to the unconscious" and by-pass rational-analytical defenses may be true. But how would we know if Lab performances failed to touch the unconscious? And even if they did affect an audience below the threshold of consciousness, therapeutic standards should apply. Breaking down defenses may be destructive to personality. There is no virtue in blasting open the unconscious unless we have the wisdom and structures to cope with the results. The work, if abused, becomes an endless wallowing in one's own psyche. Catharsis during crisis is one thing; catharsis as a way of life is another.

(5) During the work one easily "bonds" with the director, regarding him first as father or messiah and later as the devil. The work is supposed to dissolve role-playing in theater, but it reinforces these religio-social roles in order to achieve the goal. In any nascent state the "newborn" fixates on whoever provides an attentive gaze. A director can willfully or unwittingly exploit this bond and quickly become a self-acclaimed master. The neophyte develops correspondingly inhuman expectations of this primary witness. One can see this bonding dynamic operating even as people try to leave the Lab. Frequently, they return again, feeling mysteriously drawn back.

(6) Audiences witnessing a ritualized performance sometimes desire to join it. On the other hand, they just as often feel the performance is contemptuous of them, since it seems to make little effort to communicate. If performers discover something for the first time, they may come too feel they were the first ones to discover it. Consequently, they can be condescending toward the uninitiated.

(7) If we claim to be revealing ourselves, not just acting, we often overlook the subtle shift into performing our honesty or passion. Risk, stripping away, and self-exposure have their own ways of becoming means of hiding. And even the Lab, which would peel away masks and push through every barrier, is not immune. Except during very rare moments, thinking one is free of performance is an illusion.

(8) Ritualizing work can lead to the cultivation of falsely extreme emotions. Writhing and wailing are not the only, or even the most effective, ways of tapping "It." Reality is no more real at the depths or on the outer limits than it is in the middle of ordinary life.

(9) The Lab's continuing preoccupation in performance with darkness, violence, sexuality, and insanity can undermine its own emphasis on process. The Lab's gestural style continues to be

surprisingly uniform. The thematic and gestural qualities of its plays seem to have evolved very little since their inception. The Lab's emphasis on flow may have produced its opposite: thematic and gestural fixation. And its stress on unlearning techniques may have become a technique. An atmosphere which fosters the synchronizing of bodily rhythms can just as well engender collective, kinesic contamination.

(10) In my estimation, the Lab is torn between understanding itself as a group of likeminded professionals and being a religious community. This position in society is one of the reasons for its creativity; the resulting ambivalence is also a crack in its foundation. It leaves individual Lab members fundamentally isolated in a privatistic society and yet elicits from them moments of intense communion. The shift back and forth between the two kinds of social life traps them psychologically and vocationally. Despite this, the Lab continues to ride with considerable commitment between the horns of the dilemma.

CHAPTER 13

TWO PUBLIC CELEBRATIONS

Public ritual is identical with neither civil religion (Bellah, 1974) nor secular ritual (Moore, Myerhoff, 1977), since it may involve symbols less official, more regional, or more ethnic than the former and more sacred or ecclesiastical than the latter. "Public ritual" (Grimes, 1976:43) is a broader category capable of including most examples of civil and secular ritual. Public ritual is distinguished by its interstitial position on the threshold between open and closed groups—by its aim to tend the gate which swings in toward those who are ritual initiators and outward toward ritual strangers.

Two contrasting examples of public ritual are the Fiesta of Santa Fe, New Mexico, described in Chapter 2, and the Public Exploration Projects, described in the previous chapter. The fiesta, held annually since 1712 for several days in November, is a citywide celebration, attended by tourists, who typically outnumber the population of the city of Santa Fe. It is a collage of parades, pageantry, processions, plays, proclamations, raffles, Masses, dancing, singing, melodrama, drinking, crownings, knightings, fashion shows, competitions, art displays, fighting, blessings, ambling, and sales. Although the fiesta has moments of symbolic inversion (Babcock, 1978:13-33) and spontaneous communitas (Turner, 1969a:132), its dominant ethos is better described as ritual "superstructuring." Government and tourism, the city's dominant industries, provide civil and economic symbols which pervade the fiesta but do not determine its ideological center. Ethnic, civic, and ecclesiastical symbols such as the De Vargas figure, the fiesta queen, and the Marian statue La

Conquistadora, are the core symbols. The fiesta occurs in a tri-ethnic city inhabited largely by Hispano Catholics, Anglo Protestants, and some indigenous people, particularly Pueblos, Navahos, and a few Apaches. The historical roots of the fiesta lie in the mythico-historical story of the Virgin's inspiring Don Diego de Vargas to reconquer without bloodshed in 1692 the village of Santa Fe after the Tano people had driven the Spaniards back to El Paso in 1680.

Public celebrations which differ from the fiesta in all but the most essential respects are the Public Exploration Projects. Whereas the fiesta revels in regionalism, ethnicity, history, and civic display, the PEP's are marked by ideological universalism, ahistoricism, natural settings, and open or sequestered spaces. Lab people want to initiate the public into its explorations, while fiesta organizers want to introduce fiesta spirit into the public arena. Much hinges on this distinction between introducing and initiating. The Lab intends to create spaces and animate interactions so its half-dozen or so members can meet fully—without name, status, or pretence—strangers who are invited to the PEP's.

Although writing, directing, and acting at Actor's Lab are done by Canadians, its performances are not typically about Canadian or regional themes, despite the close connection of the PEP's and the Canadian bush of northern Ontario. The emphasis in performances and projects alike is on elemental symbols such as pieces of cloth, candles, stumps, water, earth, stone, and fire. While the geographical center of the fiesta is the central city plaza, the Lab often takes participants to natural settings, as the title of one of its projects, "Theater Wilderness," implies. PEP's can include, for example, silent walks, non-verbal sound, dancing, searching, waiting, stalking, resting, and so on. The tone is that of vision quest, rite of passage, and shamanlike attendance to embodied actions arising from the unconscious. PEP's have titles such as "Night of Vigil," "Night of Wanderings," and "Night of the Song of Myself."

Celebrations transpire in the ambience of varying kinds of ritual strategies. Two such strategies are the "superstructuring" and "deconstructing" of ordinary, interaction ritual (Goffman, 1967). Deconstruction is a mode of negation, of symbolic stripping. Superstructuring, on the other hand, is a form of symbolic amplification. If we take as a baseline the gestures, postures, rhythms, dress, and other symbols of everyday living, ritual deconstruction drops below the line of habitual decorum before it rises in dialectical fashion to the immediacy of celebration. Superstructuring, on the other hand, ascends positively by augmenting everyday life to produce a ritual hyperbole.

Since we usually think that celebration is a collective way of ritually ascending, we often are blind to the underbelly of festivity, even though demons, devils, and monsters may blatantly haunt public celebrations in masked costume. We are apt to overlook the downward movement of festive rituals, since we think of them streotypically as consisting only of fun, happiness, sport, play, and extraversion. We imagine that celebration can arise only by amplifying or inverting the grey routine of humdrum, workaday ordinariness. We are also prone to treat as celebrations only those open to the general public; so we seldom think of celebrations as bringing in an invited public. When the word "celebration" is invoked, we conjure images of revelrous noise, floats, tall puppets, loud music, long speeches, much drinking, bawdy behavior, and gross masks. In short, we identify celebration with its expansive, superstructuring form.

But celebration is not necessarily upward- or outward-moving, nor positively related to everyday behavior. Celebration may be an inversion of such behavior, but regarding it as such does not answer the question whether a specific celebration turns ordinary action right side up or upside down. Superstructuring a celebration means magnifying and turning a culture's good, virtuous, proper side to public view. Deconstructing a celebration means turning the public view toward the under, down, dark, unstructured, or emergent side of culture.

Rituals are not only embedded in social processes, they also process actors, things, spaces, and times. Furthermore, they are in process; they develop and decline. So one should not too quickly summarize the essence of some type of ritual, say, celebration, without noting these three distinguishable kinds of ritually significant processes: the social processes surrounding ritual; the work of processing which a ritual does; and the process of change which a ritual undergoes. My concern here is to illustrate the work of ritual processing which the fiesta performs by superstructuring, and the PEP's, by deconstructing. Both the Fiesta Council and Actor's Lab engender not only ritual processes but related dramatic ones as well; so I will offer an interpretation of the fiesta's "Entrada Pageant," as well as elaborating what I have said about the Lab's production of "Blood Wedding." My processual interpretation employs a framework that I articulated more fully in Chapter 3; it distinguishes several moments or layers of any ritual: ritualization, decorum, ceremony, magic, liturgy, and celebration.

THE FIESTA AS RITUAL SUPERSTRUCTURE

The fiesta begins with a decorous phase. Decorum is a ritual mode of civility, politeness, and neighborliness most obvious in everyday, face-to-face interaction. Decorum is ritual in the sense of habitual hello's, goodbye's, and handshakes; also in the less visible sense of preconscious stylizations of gesture and social space. Many examples of it appear in the fiesta: variety shows, style shows, concerts, audiences with fiesta royalty, formal banquets, and indoor balls. Decorous actions are scattered throughout the festival but dominate the initial phase by providing the first major fiesta symbol, the fiesta queen. On the opening day of fiesta, her crowning and enthronement is the most ritually elevated daytime event. Even though it is coupled with the knighting of the De Vargas figure, the event is usually regarded as hers in the same way that weddings are felt to be in some special way the bride's.

The second major fiesta symbol to appear is Zozobra, a giant puppet of Old Man Gloom, who is burned atop a high hill after dark on the first day. The burning is a celebrative rite, which many regard as the popular beginning of the fiesta. Celebration is that kind of ritual moment which occurs toward the play end of the work/play continuum. Celebration is immediate, momentary, comparatively free of pragmatic goal-orientation; it is relatively expressive, "useless," and free of heavy ideology. For this reason specifically celebrative actions are often experienced by fiesta participants as pagan or profane.   Other fiesta activities which evoke a celebrative sensibility are carnival rides, parade clowns, street dancing, eating foods purchased at booths, a children's costume and pet parade, and an iconoclastic melodrama.

Fiesta participation is broadest in decorous and celebrative events. It is narrowest in the liturgical phases, epitomized by the Marian image La Conquistadora ("The Conqueress") and the solemn, pontifical, fiesta Mass, which is enacted in an Hispanic, mariachi idiom. Liturgical rites are those which constitute the intentional work of a people toward symbolizing ultimacy and transcending the naturally-socially constructed world. The liturgical layers of the Santa Fe Fiesta are ecclesiastical, specifically, Roman Catholic. Masses, publically displayed retablos ("flat paintings") of saints, and processions—particularly a candlelight procession to the Cross of the Martyrs (Franciscans killed in the native revolt of 1680)—bear the liturgical weight of the fiesta.

The fiesta's ritual strategy is to "superstructure" a link between Catholic liturgical and Hispanic ceremonial symbols. Ceremony consists of power negotiations in ritual form. Usually, it involves official, political, tribal, or ethnic groups.   Its ethos is rhetorical and imperative, which contrasts with the stylized friendliness of decorum. Ceremonial gestures are bids for authority, prestige, recognition, and control, usually on an intergroup level. The key ceremonial symbol of the fiesta is the Hispano male elected to play the role of Don Diego de Vargas in the "Entrada Pageant." This ceremonial drama provides the rationale for having a fiesta at all, and the determinative scene from the pageant is clearly of a negotiating tone:

De Vargas, with his soldiers and Franciscan priests, approaches the villa of Santa Fe on horseback. The year is 1692. The dramatic action is now occurring on soil not far from the spot on which the original entrada ("formal entrance") occurred two hundred years ago. The native people who drove the Spaniards out in 1680 still hold the city. When the Tano Indians (played by Hispanic actors, since native people in 1973 refused to play the parts) resist De Vargas' entry, he persists. The hero takes a gamble, requiring faith and guts, the narrator reminds us. He removes his armor and, under the guidance of La Conquistadora, the conquering Virgin, (and the symbolic head of genealogies for many modern descendants of conquistadors), he enters the city unprotected. With sheer boldness, friendly confidence, and daring faith he intimidates the natives into surrendering and complying with a ritual submission to the Spanish king and God. Then the play concludes by implying that the fiesta is the happy result of this conquest of violence itself. This declaration, I suggest, is a good example of civic magic, inasmuch as it treats symbols of harmony as causes of harmony. What is not dramatized in the pageant is De Vargas' Journal account of how he cut off the village's water supply and had to lead a bloody, second reconquest a year later.

Liturgical actions precede, follow, and permeate the pageant, marking it as the fiesta's ritual apex. The pageant is a dramatic superstructure, erected on ritual bedrock. The play amplifies the city's history, transforming it into a chartering tableau. It elevates a diachronic moment in Santa Fe's history into a synchronic paradigm for modeling the conditions under which festivity can occur. Everything occurring before and after this performance is in the wake made by De Vargas's definitive penetration into the spatial heart and soul of the city, the Santa Fe Plaza.

A comparatively unemphasized layer of ritual processes in the fiesta consists of action not deliberately structured and arising from primary psychobiological roots. "Ritualization" consists of gestures which some might regard as instinctive, mindless, accidental, irrelevant, or unconscious. Ritualization is pre-intentional symbolic action. It differs from celebration inasmuch as the latter is post-intentional, presupposing a suspension of work, goals, and deliberate action. Ritualization processes are difficult to disentangle from decorous and celebrative ones. Examples of actions in which ritualization clearly increases are: drinking, gorging, erotic behavior, fighting, smoking, browsing, joshing, and some of the moblike qualities which follow the burning of Zozobra, or spontaneous actions that arise in the children's parade. In these value and intention, as well as meaning, must be inferred from what seems to happen spontaneously or idiosyncratically, but nevertheless repetitively. Ritualization is cultivated during the fiesta mainly through over-eating and -drinking, though the decorum of fiesta-going requires that people complain about the excesses, hide the fighting, and turn an indulging eye away from erotic encounter. Ritualization is rife, but rhetorically treated as crude and unnecessary.

PEP'S AS RITUAL DECONSTRUCTION

If I interpret the PEP's in terms of the same ritual modes, their intentionality does not appear so expansive and upward. PEP's deconstruct ordinary behavior. Their object is to unravel or un-jam habitual ways of perceiving the world. Their goal is not liturgically buttressed ceremony, but ceremonially provoked ritualization. Ritualization, not ceremony, is the principle process; so their movement is one of deconstructing the chronology of history and the decorum of the larger society.

A project begins with ceremonial gestures which establish who is an insider and outsider, who is in authority, and what some of the rules are. People are invited to participate; sometimes they sign up and pay for their participation. With the shutting of the first door, the invited public begins a rapid, initiatory stripping away of gestural habits in order to approach transient communitas. People are told not to talk, especially about what is transpiring. Conversation is discouraged. Performing or actor training exercise is prohibited. And mystification of leadership, a sure sign of ceremonial process, is strong. People feel apprehensive, unsure, afraid, inhibited. Doors are closed, or cities are left behind. Lights are dimmed; explanations are withheld. Leaders are sometimes not explicitly identified; so participants privately speculate and covertly search for authority. People watch and listen expectantly, never quite knowing when they will eat, sleep, interact, or have free time. Sometimes they are told that the Lab will not teach any positive technique, but only help remove blocks and clichéd actions. The question informing the ceremonial phase is, What is the minimal structure, language, and leadership necessary for self, other person, and Otherness to emerge and meet?

Ceremonial rites facilitating such an exploration consist of Lab members' having covert meetings and discussions among themselves, setting up or choosing locations, subtly animating what seem open or undirected actions, providing objects for participants to work with, and sometimes overtly directing action. Part of the Lab's ceremonial agenda is to keep leadership in low profile to facilitate non-hierarchical interaction. But hierarchy is needed, of course, to enforce egalitarian processes; so the Lab maintains the status and prerogatives of directorship.

Ceremonial actions by Lab members aim to facilitate ritualization processes which arise from the untamed, uncultured depths. In its freest form Lab work is undirected action in an empty or open space in which one or more people go with whatever emerges from inside or among them. What emerges is a source of animating power, an undefined "It." "It" can connote the unconscious, the sacred, rhythm, or the unpremeditated.

Ritualization processes are, of course, hard to describe or isolate. They are better understood as a special quality of action rather than special actions. Outsiders might see them as animal-like, crazy, aimless, demonic, drifty, or even ridiculous. But insiders experience them as a flowing surge of animate energy, sometimes foggy, sometimes crystal clear, but always moving, literally and metaphorically. As soon as one can name a specific action by having worked through it, it is already leaving the zone of the work.

The object of every PEP is to help participants peel away bodily and emotional acculturation so this primordial sense of animate responsiveness to the internal and external environment can develop. So ritual criticism offered by Lab people takes the form of locating nameable or typed actions and urging participants to break through them to actions they cannot name. The resultant atmosphere can be mysteriously simple or astonishingly full of undertow.

Walking, dancing, and, occasionally, eating are typical celebratory rituals in Public Exploration Projects. Celebration in this context is mystified ordinariness. Lab members seem to feel that one reaches this kind of quietly powerful simplicity only by going through the chaos of ritualization and its attendant explosiveness. So celebrations are actional afterglow in the PEP's. When the ritualization work fails, the celebrative gestures have the aura of a hangover. When the ritualization-to-celebration bridging is successful, one celebrates with no special celebrative apparatus—no costumes, games, rides, or revelry—just the immediacy of attentive walking, eating, or some other ordinary action. Only if a final meal is served, does anything like extraordinary, corporate festivity arise.

When a PEP ends, Lab members must face their profession, performing. Other participants return to acting or some other job. Decorum is barely visible at the end of a project. A few names and addresses are exchanged. Politeness returns, leaving people feeling strangely false. Watches are put on; schedules are restored. Most participants experience considerable culture shock and dislocation; their own culture seems foreign. Its stylizations are too obvious. Leaving the bonding of communitas is a rite of separation and reincorporation. One is quite aware of "putting on" the face necessary just to walk down a sidewalk, make a phone call, catch a bus home, and try to eat a meal with one's family—all without being a stranger.

The difficulty faced by Lab members subsequent to ritualization work in PEP's or studies is how to value performing after searching for, and teaching, an attitude of non-performance. Sometimes they deny they are performing at all. They do not pretend to be someone else, they reveal themselves, they say. The intention to reveal rather than conceal is declared by both PEP participants and Lab members. The difficulty and desirability of doing so arises on both sidewalk and stage. So Lab performances are, I suggest, liturgical, not in the sense that they contain ecclesiastical rites, but in the sense that they are "good works," necessary but insufficient ways of remembering and anticipating moments of grace-giving breakthrough. Performances are structures for preserving moments of flowing ritualization, but the very act of preserving demands the reintroduction of theatrical decorum, no matter how intimately revealing a performance may be. The problem against which Lab people perpetually struggle is that preserved immediacy can itself easily become a musclebound habit, in which case archetype slips embarassingly into stereotype.

In my estimation, the richest example of a Lab play is its adaptation of Garcia Lorca's "Blood Wedding." It is a drama containing a ritual, as is the "Entrada Pageant." A scene which compares provocatively with De Vargas' entrance into the village of Santa Fe is the pre-nuptial village scene:

Dancing breaks out. The energy is high; the air is full of leaping. The costumes, elaborate by Lab standards, only minimally suggest Spain. This place could be Anyvillage, Anywhere. The groom and his competitor mockingly display their rivalry as if the display itself might stem the need for violence. Soon the village idiot, played in later versions by the Lab's artistic director, becomes the focus of attention. He seems both to determine the action and to be the toy with which others play. He is teased and tantalized. Sexuality and violence are played at, as if they have no power to disrupt the collective joy of the villagers. The determination to celebrate seems at once to preclude violence and to prepare and foreshadow it.

Audience members who see the performance often comment that they wish they could have joined the festivities at this moment. Such sentiments, of course, miss an essential point of the play, which is that participation in the wedding celebration implies complicity in the ritualized dance of mutual murder which climaxes the play, leaving in its aftermath tragically isolated women and two dead men wrapped arm in arm, virtual brothers in death.

THE LIFEBLOOD OF PUBLIC RITUAL

"Violence," says Rene Girard, "is the heart and secret soul of the sacred" (1977:31). Religion, he argues, consists of the ways we try to defend ourselves against the contamination of violence, which spreads with the dynamism of a plague. Ritual can be a means of substituting "good" or "pure" violence for this polluting kind. A sacrificial crisis occurs when these rites are neglected or break their containers so the distinction between contained and free-floating revenge disappears. In such a crisis "violent mimesis" (47) sets in, and the resemblances between combatants grow. Hero and villain look increasingly alike.

Girard tells the terrible half of an important truth. Public festivity can contain the lifeblood of a group, city, or culture, and if it does, such festivity simultaneously and symbolically makes of the many, one blood and spills symbolic blood in doing so. I will venture to say it: every celebration is in some sense an entrada and a blood wedding. Every attempt at public celebration is a paradox of tragic isolation and festive integration. Every celebration makes us symbolic kinspeople and enforces our separation. Every celebration is an inspired, bloodless reconquest and a bloody act of cutting off a waterflow.

Fiesta participants speak of the De Vargas figure and the fiesta queen as if they were symbolically husband and wife, even though no ritual marries them. Ethnicity is wed in sentiment to civicality. But this "marriage" is never ritually enacted, so the re-conquest continues to happen. And in "Blood Wedding" the wedding between bride and groom cannot be completed because of infidelity. Instead, rivals become brothers in blood.

Because "Blood Wedding" is constructed out of the psychosocial lives of Lab members, and the Entrada, out of the historico-civic lives of Santa Feans, neither drama is merely aesthetic or formalistic. Neither situation permits the luxury of speaking with impunity about making bonds or spilling "blood." Both dramas are active attempts to condense the dominant symbols and values of participants. The rituals and their attendant plays not only illustrate or reflect upon living situations, they also transform and, in uncanny ways, foreshadow what happens among the participants. The rituals work. Because they work, they are dangerous. But they work because they transpire in the danger zones of culture.

Celebration rises as a bubble in a cauldron of public ritual. Rituals are the lifeblood of culture. They circulate and keep in process what is immensely destructive if spilled in society at large and left exposed to dry. Rituals, like blood, must be contained and yet must flow; they signify death as surely as they signify life. They float on the surface of crisis and rift. What if the dark chaos unleashed by the Lab's ritualization work corrodes group integration, precipitates hasty or faithless marriages, or reduces directors to wordless idiots? What if the fiesta's ceremonial display of a bloodless, military reconquest only perpetuates an ongoing cultural reconquest? And what if those of us who witness and interpret celebrations are implicated by complicity and become voyeurs or parasites, unable either to face our own shedding of blood or to make ritual kin?

Celebratory moments are the most fragile in a ritual. Ritualization and ceremony are the most powerful or dangerous, and liturgy and decorum, the safest and most stable. Is it claiming too much to suggest that all ritual aspires to celebration? In the celebratory moment form and dynamic, spontaneity and structure, are not mutually opposing alternatives. Of course, not every ritual which aims to become celebratory should be called a celebration. The celebratory motive is "fictive" (Kliever, 1979) or ludic (Huizinga, 1955). It is a magnet for cultural creativity and ritual subjunctivity (Turner, 1979). In the very moment that Santa Feans "reconquer not Indians, but violence itself," they have created a ritual "fiction." Fiction is not the same as lying or wishful thinking, because a fiction draws culture into its wake. Its object is not merely to reflect the cultural status quo, but to transform it in a moment of specially concentrated time. Such a moment can quickly be dragged back into the social system or even co-opted by other ritual processes such as ceremonial ones. The Lab's aspiration "to meet without hiding or pretence," like the Fiesta Council's goal of conquering violence itself, is a creative ritual fiction--a form made not just to mirror the conflictive, violent social situations from which it is born, but also to deny aspects of those situations and emphasize others. Rituals and dramas can be either a substitute for, or prelude to, the actions they symbolize. Celebration is that ritual moment in which such enactments actually effect what they symbolize. They are not practice for some more real kind of action, say, pragmatic or economic action, nor are they sublimations for some remembered or more desirable action. In a celebratory moment the ritual action is a deed in which the symbols do not merely point, mean, or recall, but embody fully and concretely all that is necessary for the moment.

If celebration is understood in this way, it functions as a goal and criterion. So we need to judge to what extent fiestas, projects, and other public rituals are fictive deeds, not just the semblances of deeds. To do so we would have to decide whether the repetition of such ritual actions means that they have not quite accomplished what they signify. Classical psychoanalysis would have us regard ritual repetition as compulsive. But I propose another view. Even when rituals are culturally creative and for a moment accomplish what they signify, entropy is a fundamental law; therefore, whatever is achieved ritually begins to erode in the very moment of its success. Consequently, we repeatedly pay the high cost of spilled symbolic blood as we await receptively the moment in which a celebration can make of us one blood. A public celebration is a rope bridge of knotted symbols strung across an abyss. We make our crossings hoping the chasm will echo our festive sounds for a moment, as the bridge begins to sway from the rhythms of our dance.

CHAPTER 14

TEMPEST ON SNAKE ISLAND

One of the boldest examples of public ritual in recent times was "Tempest on Snake Island," held just off the Toronto shore in May, 1981. The event was under the direction of Welfare State International of England, in collaboration with residents of the Toronto Island communities and the Toronto Theatre Festival: Onstage '81.

Welfare State International (WSI), established in 1968 by John Fox, is a group based in Ulverston, England. Eleven of the group led the celebration./1/ Their activities have included namings, weddings, seasonal festivities, street music, mumming, puppetry, barn dances, sculpture gardens, and dramatic performances. They are both artists and makers of ritual whose art tends toward "epic cartoon style" and whose public ritual is a kind of "civic magic" or "nursery rhyme celebration."

The group prefers working outdoors with communities and neighborhoods to whom they teach their skills, thereby demystifying technique, and with whom they create environments in which a primal sense of mystery can arise. One of the outstanding features of their activities is the way they connect art with ritual. Aspects of their work might be compared to the large-scale, sacramental puppetry of Bread and Puppet Theater. Though Welfare State is sometimes regarded as a performance group, some of its members, including the director, began as painters, musicians, or sculptors. Accordingly, their celebrations are marked by an attunement to rhythm, space, and construction not ordinarily found in contemporary theater. They are not primarily concerned with plot, acting, or character development. They are not just interested in rendering religious themes (such as birth, re-birth, descent, death, or marriage) in aesthetic fashion, but in dissolving the barriers which isolate art into aestheticism and religion into sectarianism. Though the group evolved from the arts, not the church, they perform ritual functions once traditionally done by religious institutions. WSI has strong moral, ecological, and political concerns, but is not really guerilla theater. Its tone is humorous, gently ironic, and playful, not rhetorically revolutionary. No matter how religious or political its images, its face always sports a bulbous red nose.

When Welfare State International was invited to participate in the Toronto Theatre Festival, it sent two people on reconnaisance to locate a social and physical environment for the event. They chose to work with the Toronto Island Community. The fifteen Toronto islands—the main ones being connected by walkways and bridges—are a ten-minute ferry ride from downtown Toronto. They consist of eight hundred acres, thirty-three of which are residential. The six hundred twenty-three residents live in two hundred fifty houses on two of the islands, Ward's and Algonquin. The other main islands are Hanlan's Point, occupied principally by a small airport, and Centre Island, a recreation area and amusement park.

The land is owned by the Municipality of Metropolitan Toronto. In 1968 the property leases on the residential properties expired, resulting in a protracted, widely publicized controversy, in which the islanders refused evictions from their cottages, which serve most of them as permanent, year-round homes. The islanders are by no means a community of transients; the average islander has lived in his or her home twelve years, in contrast to the national average of four. But transient traffic to the islands is heavy, especially in the summer—most of it picnickers, bicyclists, and tourists. A lengthy provincial commission report recommending a twenty-five year extension of the islanders' leases was published shortly before the arrival of Welfare State International.

The residents are variously regarded as covertly wealthy and creatively shabby, squatters and legitimate heirs of residential parkland, unfriendly and exceedingly cordial. The public has strongly held, half-informed views of the islanders. The weight of popular opinion on the mainland seems to favor the continued tenancy of the islanders despite, or because of, their marginality.

Snake Island is a twenty-minute walk, and one bridge-crossing away, from the Ward's Island dock. It is roughly circular, approximately five hundred yards in diameter, and is uninhabited bush. Since it is ordinarily a lovers' nest and is said to have been a native shaman's healing site, it is liminal, sacred, or ambivalent to some island residents. It is an anomolous place. Snake Island's spatial-symbolic position is to Ward's and Algonquin what the latter are to the Toronto mainland.

The first public summation of the theme of Welfare State's project was "shamanism and technology." WSI does not normally do Shakespeare, but chose "The Tempest" as a source of images because its characters, themes, actions, and settings are so closely connected with those of the Toronto Islands. The combination of island magic and political intrigue seemed both to islanders and Welfare State people a clear match. The celebration involved roughly a hundred islanders, along with the WSI company, in organizing, making, animating, and performing.

Lasting effects of "Tempest" were experienced not by the spectators, I suspect, but by the islanders. Much of the value of the project lay in the collaborative process itself. Even though WSI arrived with a scenario several days before the celebration, the script was continually modified, as the interests and abilities of islanders became obvious. The community, already adept at quick, effective mobilization of its resources, responded immediately to the need for talent and energy. The collaboration was exceptional, since both groups were experienced in group processes and interested in what might be called "alternative culture." The Graffiti Sisters, a "loose-knit association of likeminded island women," were crucial to the liason between Welfare State people and residents. Also, WSI was assisted by three members of Artworks, a group well known for its theater in the streets of Glasgow and in rural areas of Scotland./2/ Two weeks were spent creating the environment and building the structures. Five performances were done on successive evenings for a sold-out crowd of two hundred each night.

No way of recounting "Tempest on Snake Island" can evoke what the celebration itself did. Straight descriptive accounts of rituals, especially celebrative ones, are flat and boring. Treating the celebration as a story, when the event was really a collage of collectively enacted images, would make it falsely fictional. A film was made about the event—a film of it being impossible, as I was reminded by the film crew's cameraman. The problem of viewpoint is a drastic one in such events. To illustrate, no single performer ever saw the entire celebration. The most involved islanders saw it from a perspective which combined being in character with doing management functions like ushering. The directors, who first conceived the event, also performed in it and so could not watch it. Typical audience people saw it only once and therefore could scarcely get beyond "What happens next?" "atmosphere," or some intuited grasp of its sense. So my perspective is not representative; rather, it is informed by interviews and participant-observation. The very act of asking questions meant that I did not see the event as most others did. I read the scenario and script, saw the rehearsals, participated in production meetings, helped build some of the properties and sets, read previous documentation, interviewed performers and audience, and attended the events twice as a participant-spectator, once as a field observer (taping, taking notes, photographing), and once as an assistant stage-manager (lighting fires, looking after security matters and safety, and running errands).

Any effort to find an authoritative or typical interpretation of the celebation was bound to fail. Welfare State people clearly provided skill and know-how, but with few exceptions they found interpreting the symbols of "Tempest" as unnecessary or difficult as spectators did. Although they sometimes spoke privately about the meanings of symbols, doing so was generally uncalled for. Revisions of the scenario and decisions about changes in the wording, sets, or properties were usually made on the basis of what felt right or what the pragmatics of the situation demanded. Seldom did anyone justify a revision on the basis of what something meant. Trust in each other, previous ways of doing things, or felt intuition, rather than verbal or intellectual rationale, were the criteria most often invoked.

Interpretation of the celebration, then, must be seen as a scholarly construction, a fiction, not a kind of secret lore known to Welfare State people and discovered by me. The fiction consists of inventing a conceptual structure which creates unity, but maintains the tensions among the viewpoints of Welfare State people, islanders, spectators, and me. "Tempest" itself can be treated as an interpretation of Toronto Island culture, Shakespeare's play, or universal themes such as power, life, and death, but full interpretations of the whole event did not occur even in the writings of drama critics, whose responses were generally laudatory or about their private likes and dislikes.

GREETINGS AND THE GARDEN PARTY

People purchased eight-to-ten-dollar tickets to "Tempest at Snake Island" and gathered at the foot of Bay Street on the Toronto mainland at eight o'clock to be ferried to the site. The performance was advertised by the Toronto Theatre Festival as "onstage," that is, not "fringe" or "open stage."

These few facts—the ticket, time, prestige of "onstage" status, and glossy publicity—meant the audience came with theatrical, rather than celebratory, expectations. The upper middle class, theater buffs, and the adventurous were most likely to attend. Only a few older people and children were present. Limiting the audience to two hundred, because of the size of Snake Island, probably prevented late deciders and the less organized from attending. That many were turned away left those with tickets feeling they held something special.

As one might guess from their name, the ethos of WSI is at considerable odds with that of "North America's Largest Theatre Festival." The festival program, in glossy magazine format, contained not only schedules and advertisements, but letters, seals, and signatures from seven government officials, including those of the Prime Minister of Canada and the Premier of Ontario. The festival was a new, complex bureaucracy replete with titles, relatively clear divisions of labor, and considerable economic power. Welfare State, on the other hand, is anything but glossy. Its tone is that of the street, carnival, mumming, or Punch and Judy. Around its activities is an air of ragtag humor and disdain for roles and offices taken too seriously.

The first meeting of the public occurs as spectators proceed past a ticket booth through sliding steel gates. Boris, the only character whose name they will hear during the entire celebration, greets them. He is a dimwitted hunchback, full of friendly excitability, who is subservient to the Master of Ceremonies awaiting the crowd on the ferry. Hopper, the MC, is dressed in a white suit, straw hat, bright red vest, and matching bow tie. Boris, his head and hunched back covered in dirty, shapeless white and his face touched with white, red, and black, is a medieval buffoon. He lopes around the mainland dock greeting the audience and making outlandish comments. The MC greets people as they step aboard to the accordian music of a bushy-haired islander. Hopper chats, improvises witticisms, inquires whether Boris is bothering them, and endears himself to people with his Scottish accent. Meanwhile, Flo, a third character, is washing windows on the boat and joshing with the audience. A washerwoman whose wishes to be a lady of the night surely go unfulfilled, she is full of tough humor, and practical know-how; she sports wildly patterned clothing bedecked with loads of cheap jewelery and mismatched accessories.

A film crew of three is conspicuously at work; its camera and microphone are omnipresent. Welfare State's business manager guards the flowers and umbrellas. I am milling about openly taking notes. Hopper mounts the top deck and jokes about the film-making, recording, and note-taking. The camera has transformed the audience into momentary performers; so Hopper has closed the circle by making us into performers as well. Our documenting is not part of the show, but it is not excluded from it either. The celebration will include whatever is noticed in the selected space and time--whether a real tempest, the city skyline, the ship's captain, or a note-taker. A post-modern, Western celebration, its level of reflexivity is extremely high. At one point I am taking notes on a cameraman who is filming two women, one of whom is taking a picture of her friend who is photographing Flo! Some reporters, critics, actors, and festival personnel wear buttons or tags. A few in the crowd notice, and momentarily the limelight shifts: the critic must strike the attitude appropriate to her role.

As the Ongiara pulls away from the dock, the MC climbs to a level above us where he can be seen clearly. The captain is in the corresponding position on the ship's port side. We are confirmed in our suspicion that Hopper is our "captain." As our speed increases, several large grey flags unfurl. They are not part of the boat's usual emblems, the Canadian flag and the Metro Toronto flag. On the former are stars, the moon, a unicorn, a caricature of Punch.

By now, participants are calling Boris by name; for them he is becoming a mascot. They are fond of him and show it by teasing. He has bestowed on everyone a brightly speckled cloth flower. Ten minutes later the boat docks at Ward's Island. As we disembark, we are greeted by flute music and a group of island children clad in white tunics. Most people see the large red and white sign on the Ward's Island Association Clubhouse: "Save the Toronto Island Community." Few notice the floppy straw basket which has been riding near the bow of the ferry. It is decorated with feathers and evergreen and contains two puppets, one of the Girl, the other of the drummer Boy. Hopper removes the basket to the lead cart, where he desposits it at the front of the bails of hay on which those unable to walk may ride. Those in love may also ride, he quips. The children, along with the Girl, drummer Boy, and flute band, lead the crowd on a twenty-minute stroll toward Snake Island, a place few mainlanders have heard of. Here the color-coded flowers will be required for entry so gate-crashing will not push attendance beyond two hundred. Gulls, soaring overhead, have followed us down the asphalt road past expensive sailboats, picnic tables, a frisbee course, and decaying, homemade watercraft in the yards of Algonquin Island homes.

The initial interface of the largely mainland audience with Welfare State and collaborating islanders is disarming but basically reassuring. However bizzare Boris and Flo seem, Hopper will guide and take care of us. Since mainlanders often use these ferries for going to the amusement park at Centre Island, they are willing to trust they will not be hurt or led astray. Hopper is in charge, and so far we have been serenaded as guests. Who can be suspicious when led by children, one of them a drummer Boy, the other an innocent Girl? And who can be afraid of a moronic hunchback if he knows how to obey orders and proves his kindness by distributing flowers? Thus far the event has elements of an outing, school play, and theater performance, all relatively safe.

People are chatting pleasantly as they arrive at a white, arched bridge; the heavy railway flatcars and flutes stop. Across the water is Snake Island, and most of us have already picked up the brassy music which floats from it on the smoke of several grass fires. The bridge bottlenecks the flow of human traffic, and our MC take this moment to offer final reminders of two ordinary realities--the "conveniences" and the flower-check.

Most are gabbing too much to listen. In single file we cross the bridge, which is covered with feathered kites and immense parasols constructed of willow branches, binder twine, and bits of colored

cloth. As we enter a delightfully confusing garden, some recall
scenes from ALICE IN WONDERLAND. There is a unicorn watching shyly
from the edge of the clearing. Here is one of the hostesses, known as
Graffiti Sisters, in a pink crinoline, with a necklace of bone and hat
of gull's wings. There is old Boris, snatching bites from one of the
oranges he is juggling. Windchimes rest idly over a fountain.
Banners barely flutter in the pink and orange of sunset. On them are
fish, moon, rocketships, and other symbols. The Sisters, also called
"Aunties" by our MC, are profusely greeting the long stream of guests,
as if this were a royal garden party of some decaying monarch. But
who is in charge of this island? Where is the center of action? The
audience mills about in clusters. The Boy and Girl, along with Flo,
are playing in the band. But Flo is in a different costume, so who
is she now? Puppets are being hung from the trees; others already
hide in the bushes. One of them is a silver astronaut. A few
spectators venture closer and discover a frog, an old man, and some
gaudy papier-maché ladies like these who are now playing croquet and
badminton with the guests. So much is transpiring that no one dwells
on details. All is atmosphere, friendly but topsy-turvy. The rules
for participating and spectating are not quite clear. Is it proper to
dance? Does the unicorn talk? A few strike out for the far side of
the island, but are turned back by "stage" managers posted by the
festival producers from the mainland. They display a stereotype of
mainland-style authority by flashing walkie-talkies, sporting festival
badges, and wearing white-billed sun visors, though the sun has gone
down.

Four times now we have been greeted—once at the gate, once on
the boat, once as we docked, and now this garden reception. The rites
of decorum are profuse; yet they do not reinforce the conventions of
polite social gatherings, as do cocktail parties. Instead, they make
mockery of elevated sociability and disorient our sense of propriety.
Why don't they get on with the show?

MUMMER'S "TEMPEST"

A whistle blows. We turn toward a circle of stumps and split-log
benches where Prospero, whose identity only a few will ever infer, is
lighting torches. The crowd, amused but restless for a more defined
center of attention, moves quickly. Then, recognizing the shift of
convention from garden party to theater in the round, some scurry for
front seats. Welfare State musicians and actors find their places.
They are in costume but not yet in character.

Our master of ceremonies has not changed costume. He beats a
drum and addresses us in a way that defines us as characaters in a
royal ceremony,

Lords and ladies,
I'm your life,
I am everyman's destiny.
My hand is on your shoulder
tomorrow, today & yesterday;
I am the joker up your sleeve &
    the flea in your ear.

Already we have sensed that he leads us, but his hand has comforted, not tricked or irritated, us. He does not tell the audience that the ensuing performace is "The Tempest Inspired by William Shakespeare refashioned by Welfare State International." Instead, he introduces the characters, who stare madly at us as they lumber, dart, whistle, and buffoon. Prospero is a king who studies "too much magic: the recipes of stars & songs of nuclear fission." Sebastian, his brother and prime minister, turns out to be our Boris. Miranda wears a tower on her head and tends the puppets. Ariel is a "roaming angel from heaven." Caliban appears as "a wild mermaid from the ocean deep, the fecund mother that everyman seeks." And finally, we are introduced to the men who cast Prospero and Miranda adrift.

Perhaps our MC's joke is that, despite his introductions, he never gives us names, only hints, of characters who will not remain themselves the rest of the night. Our joke on him is that most Canadians do not remember Sheakespeare, despite Stratford and high school English courses. And even the few who do cannot decide which of these characters is Caliban. Eventually, most give up trying to discern either character or plot, because they are presented with allusions to a plot and only fragments of characters. The raucous action is done with such vigor and gestural hyperbole that the audience attends to the cadences of actions and minimizes attention to words. The mummers, with bugged eyes and deeply bent knees, fight, plot downfalls, get lost at sea, send spirits to wreak havoc, circumambulate an imaginary island, court, and finally perform a marriage ceremony—all in fifteen minutes. And the audience laughs, even the children, because these outlandishly garbed characters sound so pompous as they fall over each other. Prospero has warts on his face and knobby knees under his kilt.   Ariel wear luminous, crossing-guard orange and has handlebars for wings. Ferdinand's bare chest is slickly oiled; he struts like a banty rooster. Alonso and Stephano wear pieces of the Union Jack and King George's flag. The whiteface and make-up tell us this is clowning, but not of the circus variety.

The oratorical style is motley: a patch of poetry, a strip of song, a bit of incantation, a thread of romance and intrigue. The script matches the costumes. Literary analysis of it would only reduce it to remnants of meaning, because the words function just as one more gesture or one more musical instrument. This is not literary theater; it contains no lines from Shakespeare. The script plays with images, clichés, and political rhetoric: "Fruit, wave & radio yearning for thunder" is jocularly dissociated imagery. "I saw a salmon in a garden / Sing like gold / That I never heard" is a mixed metaphor parading as a paradox. And "What right kicks a king off his stool?" is declaimed with sheer political pomposity.

So the mummer's play, on the one hand, caters to the audience by allowing it to spectate on a play, but on the other, inverts expectations by refusing the obligations to provide plot, character, or finely worked acting and poetry. And it works. We laugh at the non-fulfillment of our expectations. We do not know what to expect next.

AVIARY

As the actors finish and hurry ahead into the woods, Destiny, as we now know our MC, bids us to follow. Darkness is just descending. We pass through an aviary of bird puppets, most of them owl-like creatures made from plastic milk jugs with candles glowing inside. Far in the background we barely see Boris/Sebastian by a fire. He is yelling for his master. We do not know why. Only a few people pause. Most hurry on, because they hear an amplified synthesizer and sense something more significant.

The aviary is one of two transition spaces designed as images for brief, peripheral sighting. We either shrug "So what?" or we feel a suspicion that there is more to this than one can grasp. We are unsure whether the scene is a problem or a mystery. Are these birds, which any school child could make, more than they seem, or are they less? Is this art or the parody of it? Is this a rite of passage or a mockery of it? Is anxiety or excitement the appropriate response? Are we expected to think about these images or can we only respond without reflection?

SPACE STATION

The music pulls the crowd, and the crowd drags away the few stragglers who are trying to sense what connection the aviary has with the mummer's play. Suddenly, the scale shifts toward immensity. We are confronted with a series of spindly, white verticals that support mock electronic structures high above our heads. They could be radar screens or tv antennae. The electronic sounds force us to associate them with outer space. And now, far from being invited in close, we are kept back by a yellow rope staked across the hundred yards of frontage. We are in for a spectacle.

Prospero is walking, running, sneaking, then posing stock still with a spewing red flare. He darts in and out of abstract white shapes that suggest icebergs or perhaps futuristic wreckage. They are decorated with tiny emblems the audience cannot quite see (light houses, a wedding cake, airplanes, ships, satelites, spiders, a bomb, a moon, a skull-bearing kite, runic writings). Above him hangs a six-foot moon sliver, whose big nose, eyes, and mouth are lit from inside. To our right a new Caliban figure, a filthy, unshaven male in a hardhat, hides behind a shabby little ark with dirty broken windows. He is utterly destroying (or is he making?) something with a screeching circular saw.   The human figures are shadowy, unhighlighted, and dwarfed by their environment.

From deep in the woods, something huge stirs. The audience barely sees it. "Is it a spider?" "Oh, my God. George, look at that." "I see it, honey. It's a beetle or a lobster of some sort." "Oh, it's creepy. How did they make that?" "I could make one of those--just bamboo, plastic, wire, and tape." Momentarily, people become unguarded.

A green follow-spot illuminates the giant puppet. Its half-dozen puppeteers roll it from side to side, as its lower jaw and feelers find their way into the open near the space station, where we wait in a torrent of synthesizer music based on Holland's "Creation." Prospero's magic island has become a mad scientist's laboratory. The scale of experimenting has become so vast that it is out of control.

A humanoid creature, illuminated from inside and followed by a white spot from without, floats out of the bush on the backs of black-faced, darkly clad puppeteers. We forget Prospero and Caliban, as we look far above their heads toward the action in front of silhouetted by tree tops. The figures clash again and again. The beast's claws and beak almost rip off the head and arms of the rotund spaceman. The final battle, amid the death cries of puppeteers, leaves the beast dead. Finally, the spaceman lumbers off. Are these two creatures fragments of Prospero's imagination? Or are Prospero and Caliban puppet-servants of these two creatures? If this is a cosmic morality play, what is the moral?

Without warning, a rocket-puppet soars from the ground, hits the moon, and falls. In response, the moon slides out of the sky, lands gently on its back, and tips on its side facing us. A wave of silence and sadness ripples over the spectators. Two toothy monsters dance slowly out of the woods. Are they dragons or crocodiles? They approach the moon curiously and begin to shed tears--tears of ribbon studded with pieces of broken mirror. With their mouths, they gently lift the c-shaped moon by its tips and bear it funerarily into the grove, as the Boy and Girl walk past us through the forest of antennae playing a sad, flawed version of "Startune" on their brass instruments.

For a few moments we stand still, as the music fades. A twelve-year old points through the trees at the CN Tower, "the world's tallest free-standing structure," and remarks, "That looks like part of the play, eh?" Some in the crowd are excited, hungry to be fed more spectacles. Others are pondering. The structure of the event is reorienting our various maps of reality. How did we get from old-fashioned crinolines and English mumming to twenty-first century technocracy? Where are we? This is not England nor a space station. This is Snake Island, near metropolitan Toronto. But who ever heard of Snake Island, and which way is Toronto from here? Disoriented on an uncultivated island, we depend on the great tower for orientation. Is this how Babel was used?

The flow of the celebration is segmented, yet simple; complex, yet connected. We go from discrete space to discreet space. We witness this; it ends; we go on to that. We are surrounded by isolated arenas of action and paradoxically juxtaposed symbols, but not provided with connective tissue. We must make our own, but those who would use Shakespeare to do it only arrive at remnants of meaning. Some find their imaginations to be drudges of entertainment or advertising industries.

A spectator says, "The big human-looking creature must be the Michelin Man."

His friend remarks, "Yeah, it's just escapist entertainment to trick you into forgetting what's back in Toronto, in the real world."

In Shakespeare's "The Tempest" Caliban says to those recently shipwrecked on Prospero's island, ". . . The isle is full of noises, / Sounds, and sweet airs, that give delight, and hurt not" (Act III, Scene 1). As a result, they follow Ariel's music, not knowing they do so in service of Prospero's magic. By analogy, mainlanders, lured by the craft of Welfare State and islanders, are at once relatives, rivals, and now shipwrecked "trickees." Of course, "Tempest on Snake Island" is entertainment, but in service of what, of whom?

The images at the space station are simple and emblematic, like illustrations from MOTHER GOOSE, ALLIGATOR PIE (Dennis Lee), or WHERE THE WILD THINGS ARE (Maurice Sendak), but their meanings are enigmatic and complex. They are easy to feel but hard to think. We are not given a story line to connect them. Our only connection so far is perambulatory. We walk together from site to site. But does this action constitute celebration any more than carnival hopping or shopping center strolls? In a culture ritually undernourished, but inundated with a surplus of fat, disconnected symbols, how is a celebration on Snake Island any different from a visit to Canada's Wonderland (cf. the Disneyland and Six Flags amuzement complexes)? In short, what separates the trickstering of the "civic shamans" of

Welfare State International from the huckstering of image marketeers?
I see two crucial differences.   One is the demystification of
technique. When people first spy the creatures, they often react with
wonder ("Wow, it's scary"), mystification ("Gee, how could they make
such things?"), puzzlement ("What is it?"), and finally,
demystification ("I could make one of those myself"). The celebration
undermines an ideology of mastery (of either the technological or the
fine arts variety). Islanders regularly felt this in the preparation
process, and mainlanders sensed it in the performances. A second
factor is self-critical iconoclasm, illustrated by the next scene.

SHIPWRECK BEACH

Destiny, our guide, is now high on stilts, as if he has grown to
match the size of the creatures and dwarf the children. People are
relieved when they spot him again. He and the Aunties crowd us onto
platforms, stumps, old tires, and logs on a bit of beach hidden behind
Caliban's ark. We sit facing the brilliantly lit Toronto skyline,
which is punctuated, as always, by the phallic-needle shape of the CN
Tower.

The male version of Caliban is combing the rubbish on the beach.
Old reflectors, a greenish-blue rubber ball, dead fish, straw,
feathers, driftwood, and scum have washed up underfoot. His grimy
face peers at us from beneath the visor of a dull silver hardhat. He
wears a dirty karate outfit and moth-eaten longjohn underwear, and he
has built a model tower of junk. He has constructed something else
and hidden it with a black plastic sheet. The smoke of his hobo's
fire burns our eyes.

Far to our left the Hunchback, perched on a fat tree fallen into
the lake, barks:

Roll up, roll up, your skinny carcass.
Roll up, you bag of bone.
. . . .
Step this way to the wheel of fortune.
. . . .
The wheel spins upside down.
. . . .
The world's on fire in the iceman's kingdom.
The world spins upside down.

Caliban milks the audience for applause and laughter as he
improvises. He mocks us by sitting in his found chair as if joining

us to watch the city-as-set. He baptizes us with droplets of dirty water from his ball, which he stuffs in his shirt—a breast. He swordfights an invisible assailant, swinging his sword-tower over our heads and finally smashing it to bits. He tends his fire and with trampy pomp eventually reveals his cardboard City of Toronto, precariously balanced atop a spool once used for telephone cable. We hear a woman's voice singing across the water, "God be praised it all will soon be over. . . . Where are the tears of Friday evening? / Where are the snows of yesteryear?" Caliban is walking into Lake Ontario, floating a model of the city toward the real one. In this moment we wonder which is "real"?

Suddenly a dinghy is rowed from round the fallen trees. Death and three Madmen approach the model city. A bamboo bomber sways atop their little mast, so we easily guess what they will do with their torches. The crowd cheers enthusiastically as their city goes up in flames.

The images seem stereotypically clear; yet what is done with them contravenes the way they would be handled by Shakespeare, circuses, or McDonald's. We recognize the gestures; yet as we reflect on them, we are not sure what values we are affirming. Should we cheer? Who is hero and who, villain? Unlike stereotypes, the images seldom preach. Instead they precipitate questions, not during, but after the celebration.

Caliban slides back to shore through the filthy waters. He retrieves his punctured ball. It is a world—with a hole in it. He finds a cradle—with the bottom out of it. As he exits, his mime has transformed the ball-world into a baby lying in a cradle. Is this the basket we brought with us on the ferry? Caliban exits to the singing of "Grey Flags":

> Grey flags tear in the west wind.
> Red crabs die in the rock pools.
> Old moons fall to the seabed.
> An eagle soars from the ashes.
> An eagle soars from the sea.

Caliban's gestures alternate among various styles—allegory, clowning routine, and improvisation. He recycles garbage and yet destroys what he builds with it. He is both ecologist and technocrat. At the space station the humanoid won, but the moon was lost. At the shipwreck beach Caliban, another humanoid, wins, but the city is lost. The world-baby is saved, but the cradle has no bottom. So easy optimism and cheap resurrections are not indulged. By winning, one has not necessarily won. The audience has just been tricked by the use of clowning conventions to cheer the destruction of its own cultural achievements. Yet, Toronto still sits across the harbor, dwarfed by distance into serving as a fool's backdrop. What control

we have been given over the city's image! But what will we do with
it? Have we become a pack rather than a group? How could we dissent
from the crowd? How can we control this bombardment with images?
Does it really matter that most people neither interpret nor
criticize, but just respond by cheering or walking? How does one know
which images are major ones and which, minor?

ORACLE

We carry these questions from the littered beach, down a runway
of black and white, candlelit lanterns, past a tree-house separated
from us by a bramble thicket (and known only to its makers as
"Oracle"). This is the second transition space, but this time some
people pause longer, unwilling to be drawn on too rapidly by the
audience. Others walk past it as they would a carnival sideshow,
thinking the real action is in the big top. And others are searching
for breathing room, hoping to re-possess themselves after being
tightly bunched together with strangers. As we were climbing up from
the beach, we heard, what we now discover to be, the Boy's trombone,
playing strains of "Grey Flags." Now he is astride a low branch of
The Tree. Above him sits the Girl in a cozy bower of driftwood and
remnants of persian rug; she is dropping cardboard animals into an
egg-carton ark. She is strongly lit to radiate. A child madonna? If
the scene is Edenic, or if this is the outcome of Caliban's world
in-a-cradle, the presence of the ark and the sound of the music remind
us of the destruction of the flood. Did the Flood precede her, or
will it follow her? Is this the ark from the space station? There
are no children in Shakespeare, why here? Are these the children of
characters from the Tempest? Or are they the characters as children?
    Shakespeare's "The Tempest" and the Biblical story of the flood
have now become cross-tabulated. Having watched this scene several
times, I can hardly resist interpreting the Girl as an Eve figure or a
Marian resonance, especially if I recall Caliban's baptism of us a few
moments ago--first by water, then by fire.

SHADOW "TEMPEST"

The crowd enters a semi-circular corral opening toward the city
and constructed of split timber. Hefty emblematic lanterns gradually
brighten above our heads. We notice a lighting technician hut, tent,
microphones, and raised platform. We suspect we are near the brain of
things—the back room of the Wizard of Oz. We are being handed punch
by the Aunties and shown to rows of chairs in front of an elevated

shadow puppet screen, which blots out part of the Toronto nightlights. All the characters we have seen are gathering, some as musicians, others as puppet animators.

The shadow puppet "Tempest" is our second formal play, and again we are seated. People are noticeably more comfortable this time. Performers are behind a screen. Musicians gather at the side of it and begin playing gamelan-style music. A flickering torch behind the screen creates a mysterious aura. The scale and color of the event are greatly reduced in comparison to previous ones, and the idiom is foreign, Javanese.

The scenario which follows is punctuated by haunting musical sounds and utterances that hover on the threshold between chant and the language of trance:

> The king rocks a cradle and mucks about with rockets, producing a plague of spiders, a tempest.   Final rocket hits the moon.   It falls.   King sends it back on another rocket. Sleeps under the moon by the cradle.   Wild woman & boy steal crown & put King & cradle into a boat.   Cloud over moon.   Tempest.   Boat wrecked on an island.   King dances with native spider & chains it to palm.   Passing cloud reads "20 years later."   King grows beard.   Baby becomes girl.   Boat arrives with wild woman & young man.   King fires rocket at cloud to make tempest.   Boat founders & woman & man spill.   Man awakens & finds girl.   King puts spider as hump on man's back.   King stalks Wild Woman & holds rocket to her throat.   Girl & man with hump dance clumsily. King uses rocket to knock off spider.   Spider flies off on rocket.   All dance & sail away. Moon from behind cloud.

The shadow "Tempest" does not repeat the mummer's "Tempest" any more than the latter repeats Shakespeare's "The Tempest." Despite our being given no title and no names, we feel the play is vaguely familiar. It possesses a strong archetypal quality. We begin to sense the resonance of motifs which, one might say, recur without being repeated. Some examples will illustrate this prinicple.

In the mummer's play, Miranda carries Ferdinand on her back. He, in turn, is laden with garbage bags. She sings, "I saw a spider thru a mist / Soft as skin / that I never touched." The untouched island girl longs for experience, which Ferdinand, the city boy from the mainland, provides. In the shadow play the spider of experience is native to the island and is enslaved like Shakespeare's Caliban. This spider becomes the hump on Boy's back.

In the mummer's play Caliban is a wild mermaid on the island, while in the shadow play, Wild Woman comes from beyond the island. In fact, her role parallels that of Prospero's conspirators: she and the Boy steal his crown.

In the space station a rocket shoots down the moon. In the shadow play the moon is shot down, then put back up, where it serves as guardian-overseer of the action.

On the shipwreck beach Caliban, a maker, discoverer, and recycler of garbage, finds a cradle. In the shadow play the King brings the cradle with him to the island (as we have done with our basket of two puppets).

These ways of allowing symbols to shift shape, context, and thus meaning, prevent their reduction to intellectual allegory. A rocket, for instance, is in one action a symbol for technology; in another, it is a substitute for Ariel. A ball means in one moment "world," then in the next, "breast." A spider means "Ferdinand," then "killer," then "burden." These are resonances, not codes (either conventional or esoteric), though participants may, in the face of a given gesture, feel they are seeing a familiar convention or suspect they are not being given some secret key. "The Shadow Tempest" is not a "reflection" of "The Tempest." Rather, it is an evocative shadowing of other parts of the celebration, concentrating almost entirely on the dance of opposites (King/Wildwoman; Boy/Girl; Rocket/Moon) and the web of connections and obstructions in which the pairs are entangled.

By the end of the second "Tempest" all the major associations of the celebration have been made: masculine/King/mainland/rocket/tower, on the one hand, and feminine/Girl/islands/cradle/moon, on the other. Participants, of course, are not thinking about these connections, rather they are seeing them made and even helping effect the wedding of opposites.

WEDDING DANCE

As we begin shifting chairs to the periphery of the corral, our Destiny announces to us that the moment of the wedding has arrived. Caliban and Prospero set fire to two life-size skeletons, one male, the other female, raised high on the beach; we can see Toronto through their rib cages and pelvic bones. At the same time the Boy and Girl approach us slowly from the feet of the flames. He is a silvery astronaut, his countenance hidden behind the smokey face-shield of his helmet, his back aflame, as if he has just climbed out of a burning spaceship wreck. She is a flower child, carrying a garland in stark contrast to his anachronistic hatchet. As they lay their implements on the ground, flutes stop playing "Anna Marie," and the band begins "Swedish Masquerade." At first we watch the wedding dance of the children, but, imperceptibly, islanders and Welfare State people are inviting guests to dance. Spectators cease huddling around the blazing fire-barrels and venture toward the center of the corral. Circle dances, polkas, and reels, accompanied by resounding brass and percussion, have soon surprised most people into participating despite their self-consciousness.

The bridge from performance into celebration has been made, and the tone of the evening changes radically. We no longer need Hopper as the focus of our trust, and he remains out of character from now on, as do virtually all the others. He has turned over to us the charge promised at the beginning of the mummer's "Tempest": "For yours is the Kingdom, the power, the judgment / For this day alone: the account's in your hands." The slippage of dramatic roles and increase in the level of audience participation are tentative first steps toward ritual, away from theater.

Relations beween Metro Toronto Government and the islands are highly politicized. During the week of the celebrations, for example, islanders blocked the erection of a bike-rental shed, insisting that Metro had no building permit. Each regularly obstructs the other, to signal continuation of the tenancy feud. But "Tempest on Snake Island" was a gesture of another sort, possible only through the mediation of outsiders, the Welfare State celebration-makers. The islands are the toys of Metro Toronto. They are for recreation, relief from the city. One goes to them to be entertained. What is risked in "Tempest" is the perpetuation of the slave-as-entertainer syndrome, familiar from Roman circuses and all-black reviews for white audiences at the turn of the century. When performers forget their place and intermarriage, symbolic or otherwise, occurs, solidarities are weakened. Mainlanders may lose their commerical-technological superiority and islanders, their moral superiority. The circle dance, for instance, realigns the vengeful circumambulations of Prospero in the mummer's play ("Twice round the island to settle the score") into a momentary reunion. No celebration, much less one event in it, such as the wedding dance, actually constructs a bridge, but it at least illustrates the gestures around which reconciliation might begin.

As the wedding dance ends, Ariel does a bit of magic to conclude this part of his "insubstantial pageant." Amid his scurrying and whirly whistle, he raises a bike wheel on a pole (a resonance of the wheel of fortune on the shipwreck beach). Out of a cardboard skyscraper (cf. Caliban's flaming city) he fishes a tin can and out of the can, a moon, which a Graffiti Sister, mounting a tall ladder, hangs from the wheel. Then, out of a barrel he pulls long skinny arms, spindly white hands dangling from them. He coaxes viewers to hold them. I expect an octopus, but he hoists out the attached body: a grinning globe of Earth. From its grinning mouth he pulls a paper bird.

LAUNCH AND FINAL PROCESSION

Quickly, Miranda gives the Boy and Girl the two puppets of themselves, as they and Ariel lead us out of the corral down to a clean, sandy beach, where a glowing ship—at once a wedding cake and tower—is moored. The bird and two puppets are put on the boat, and to the wail of bagpipes it is launched from the island toward the mainland. What will come of the fledgling marriages of Miranda and Ferdinand, Girl and Boy, Girl puppet and drummer Boy puppet? Is this tower-cake a beautiful wedding of images or a grotesque grafting job like the "oriental" catuses one sees in dime stores? The puppets are in need of animation, and our hope is a mere paper bird on this foolish ship.

We are not left to see how far the boat goes. Our moment's meditation is past; the bagpipe is calling us to follow it beneath a bower of shimmering white cut-outs of boats, flying frogs, and other island symbols. We continue down a path strewn with bright, batik-covered lanterns. Without ceremony the crowd re-crosses the white bridge. We gather around a brass band and catafalque bearing a green papier-maché island. Around it coils a fat snake, eating its own tail. We, like the snake, have come full circle. What are we to make of such a circle? Does it suggest self-sufficiency, self-consumption, self-nourishment? By recycling, do we merely eat our own waste? Or do we become whole?

We are handed torches and white silhouettes lashed to poles; on them are eagles, frogs, moons, boats, snakes. And to the sambalike rhythm of "Magic Island Meringue," people dance, skip, and walk in procession back to the ferry dock. Participants take turns shouldering the canopy-covered bier. Some think of carnival in Rio; others, of the shadows in Plato's cave. Most let their feet think.

At the dock we are greeted by the stench of diesel and the drone of engines. As the guests board, the celebration makers sing "Now Is the Hour," a South Pacific bon voyage song. Meanwhile, a flying frog, symbol of the Toronto Island Community, is set afire. And Caliban lifts the Girl above his head so she can release a unicorn that soars aloft on a balloon. Mainlanders hesitate to leave, swallow lumps in their throats, and cheer. Finally, the engines rev and the water churns. The celebration of Snake Island is over.

POST-MODERN CELEBRATION

"Tempest on Snake Island" was a celebration. The more successful a celebration, the more resistant it is to analysis. Since celebrations cultivate collective spontaneity, along with attendant feelings of togetherness, wonder, chaos, laughter, and amazement, reflection is intrusive to them. Celebrations must simultaneously display symbols and prevent their overexposure to critical analysis. Protecting the celebrated moment requires vast outlays of behind-the-scenes, as well as before- and after-the-event, work. And all of it must be hidden if celebrators are to be elevated into festive spirit. In contemporary Western societies celebrations may require fund raisers, organizers, technicians, managers, directors, builders, performers, errand-runners, reporters, critics, and documentation teams, as well as participant-observers. All these people must be kept in low profile, or they inhibit festivity. Yet, they signify what is unique about most modern rituals: a high degree of reflexivity.

Festivity is not a strength of North American culture partly because of this self-consciousness. Although masses continue to be said, synagogue services held, and sermons preached, our ritual sensibility is underdeveloped. Civil ceremonies are mounted with considerable disproportion between the money spent and worth perceived. Birthdays, showers, christenings, and other domestic rituals are usually devoid of imagination and force. We lack both ritual traditions of convincing weight and repositories of festive imagination. We are not short on abilities to produce the necessities of ritual festivity: music, performance, dance, costume, masks, banners, lanterns, huts, arbors, symbolic objects, and the like. We do not have, however, the imagination and social environment for synthesizing these into meaningful and effective celebration rites. Celebration generates what we might call "formalized feeling," and our culture is too enamored with spontaneity and too suspicious of formalization for celebration to occur without considerable struggle.

"Tempest" is a good example of celebration-making, because it so thoroughly succeeded in generating spontaneous community, and, at the same time, provided for critical reflection on its own processes. In modern societies few activities can be as dangerous as unexamined public rites such as rallies, demonstrations, or festivals. If our head is lost, we risk being duped into complicity with commercial or political values we do not really hold. Yet if our head is not lost, celebration does not transpire. The dilemma of celebration in our time is how, in a segmented, individualistic, self-conscious culture, to integrate critical reflection and festive communality. Celebrative rites so regularly fail for us because the technical and imaginative skills of theater, the values of religious traditions, and our capacities for critical reflection are compartmentalized. "Tempest" was a fruitful case study, because it was one of the few such occasions in North America that achieved celebration without naïveté.

We are always driven to ask of celebrations and other kinds of rituals whether they work and what they mean. But such questions are no less tricks than magic is. "Tempest on Snake Island" worked. It galvanized a group of islanders, momentarily bridged islanders and mainlanders, entertained and educated spectators, salvaged a lot of thrown-away junk, taught numerous skills, generated several thousand dollars of income, facilitated important contacts, initiated ritual processes with ongoing possibilities, and so on. All this and more comprise the effects, though not the meaning, of the celebration. Its most significant social intention is articulated by Ariel in the last line of the mummer's play: "Once round the island for Destiny / And never again for spite." But surely spite is not forever gone between the islanders and Metro. Like the mummers, they have already gone several times round the island for vengeance. And they will go round again: "The wheel spins and turns again / and another trick's learned in the mirror-black night."

At the end of the shadow play, the spider again flies off on a rocket to the moon. Then, "all dance and sail away," and the moon comes from behind a cloud. Like the moon's phases, the cycle will go on, but it has produced a new symbolic form. At least there is now a paper bird's worth of hope that spite will not return. Welfare State has not provided an answer to the social-political problem, but has transposed it to a more sensual medium, that of a nursery rhyme celebration rite in which people are more free to imagine alternatives.

Even if the entire event was "all in fun, all in fun," as Sebastian protests, a knife, nevertheless, remains in hand. Pretend, play, drama, and ritual are modes of action that do not operate in the same way non-symbolic work does. Fun, like faith, "works" in a special way—by realignment rather than accomplishment. For example, the "fun" of ritually destroying Toronto and the CN Tower or ceremonially marrying the Boy astronaut and the flower Girl realigns their meanings. As people make the return trip, perhaps they remember the puppets that were launched on a tower-cake toward the mainland. Maybe they ask, "What is more real, the puppetry of power-politics or the puppetry of celebrations?" or "Who is a puppet to whom?" Or they mull over the meaning of a throw-away culture that spawns ragtag, pop-up celebration on such a scale.

Much ritually preoccupied, post-modern art scavenges its material from what Margaret Laurence calls "the nuisance grounds," the local dump. Welfare State's genius is like that of Christie who tells Morag, "You know how some have the gift of the second sight . . . ? Well it's the gift of the garbage-telling which I have myself, now . . . . By their christly bloody garbage ye shall know them in their glory" (1974:74-75). Like Caliban, Christie the garbage-diviner finds a baby in the dump, and Morag wonders how this thing wrapped in newspaper can be newborn and dead at the same time.

Welfare State literally and symbolically searches cultural refuse, scavenging symbols reduced to cliché by political, economic, counterculture repetition. By recontexting, they recycle them into numinous archetypes, with no attempt to preserve them or pass off motley bricolage as whole cloth. For a moment, by reorganizing rubbish—a rusty stovepipe, some tin cans, twigs, and a garbage bag—a nameless bird rises from stereotype to archetype. Its life is like that of a firework. So in tomorrow's daylight it is just rusty junk again, awaiting the magic of celebrants.

NOTES

/1/ Members of the group were: John Fox and Boris Howarth (artistic directors), Howard Steel (Business Manager), Andy Burton, David Clough, Daniel Fox, Hannah Fox, Sue Fox, Maggie Howarth, Lois Lambert, and Tony Lewery.

/2/ Neil Cameron (director), John Bolton, and Paul Yeoman.

CHAPTER 15

PARASHAMANISM

An interesting religious phenomenon is crystalizing. I call it "parashamanism." Like shamanism proper, parashamanism is not a sect, movement, or ecclesiastical institution. Rather, it is an individualistic, ritualistic practice which is presently taking shape in the margins of culture. I know over a dozen people for whom the composite figure, shaman-trickster-fool is a paradigm; I have worked closely with five of them, two for periods exceeding a year. They, in turn, have identified others who regard themselves as shamans of sorts. My concern is to say what sort of shamanism this is. Parashamanism is characteristic of the Polish Lab, Actor's Lab, and Welfare State International, as well as a number of individuals such as Ken Feit (a well know storyteller and fool), and institutes such as the Center for Shamanic Studies and Human Dimensions West. Many people who do the things that I label "parashamanic" do not like the term, but I persist in the use of it, since it indicates their common source of inspiration (shamanism) and their relation to it (para-).

The social locus of parashamanism is in the interstices among university, church/synagogue, theater, and therapy groups.

Parashamans seek healing, reflection, performance, and mystery on the borders of institutions which regard these activities as their purvue. Although parashamans are highly individualistic, they have already created temporary institutions such as teaching-training workshops, ritual events, storytelling conferences, festivals, and dream-sharings. Parashamanism is more than a fantasy aspiration; it is for some a way of living and being religious.

Parashamanism in North America is in part a response to the decline of political protest after the late 60's, the tight job market of the early 70's, the rise of popular therapy, and the separation of university religion departments from churches.

A composite sketch of the parashaman includes at least the following factors: (1) Post-Christian or liberal Jew, educated in late 60's or early 70's, with special interest in religion, anthropology, psychology, and drama. (2) Holds at least a B.A., often an M.A. (3) Treats the writings of Jung, Castaneda, and Eliade as paradigmatic texts—of religious, rather than merely scholarly, significance. (4) Reads PARABOLA and ALCHERINGA; strongly influenced by the writings of Victor Turner, Jerzy Grotowski, Jerzy Grotowski, and Richard Schechner. (5) Is performance oriented; extremely interested in ritual, storytelling, and small group processes. (6) Has strong interest in themes of death, birth, violence, and sexuality. (7) Prefers "relationships," e.g., having a "soulmate," to marriage. Has difficulties with sexual boundaries, and questions traditional gender roles. (8) Is politically leftist. (9) Resists separating the functions of teacher, healer, performer, and priest. (10) Prefers wandering or traveling to settling; fond of pilgrimage, hunting, and journey as metaphors. (11) Is relatively poor, though of middle-class background; has periodic, undependable employment. (12) Is in his or her thirties and preoccupied with rites of passage into middle age.

FICTIVE RELIGION

Parashamanism has a distinctly "fictive" (Kliever, 1979) quality, as did courtly love in the Middle Ages. In courtly love life imitated fiction, not the other way around. Parashamanism is not a "living" tradition in the sense that shamanism was in hunting cultures; it is not passed from master to student, nor is it part of a tradition of spontaneous vision. It is a textually dependent tradition. Each cycle of learning and teaching is mediated through the book, and the book is the teacher, not merely a supplement to teaching. As courtly love was "lived ballad," so parashamanism is "lived religious studies." Parashamans are not taught by shamans but by books about shamans. The irony of parashamanism is that its practitioners often teach, heal, or perform in order to know, not because they already know.

Richard Schechner (1979) and Victor Turner (1974) have identified "restored," or "liminoid," behavior which occurs "betwixt and between" anthropology and theater. They also actively contribute to its formation. Turner observes the Ndembu and writes a monograph recounting his observations. Then Schechner and Turner, along with their students, turn the ethnography into a script for enactment. Or, to cite another example, Frits Stagl and Robert Gardner buy a performance of the Yaaga, a Vedic sacrifice, for filming in India, thereby restoring it and transforming it into art (Schechner 1979:7ff). Such occurences are religio-scholarly events.

Parashamanism is part of this reflexive phenomenon, the self-consciousness of which is attributable to reflection in universities, self-examination in therapy groups, and enactment in theater. Jung and Eliade, and probably even Castaneda, did not intend that their writings become script. They claimed to be engaged in study and scholarship. But the sacralization of their writings among parashamans is not accidental. All three have in different ways been concerned with the fictional and imaginative transformation of scholarship; so what parashamanism has added is not the fictional element so much as the ritual and moral performance of scholarly fiction. Jung's ANSWER TO JOB, for example, seems on first reading to be a scholarly analysis, but a deeper reading shows that it is an implicit story. Eliade "discovers" in his scholarly writings what he created in his early fictional ones. And Castaneda, I think, writes fictional scholarship. Parashamanism goes one step further. It becomes fictional religion. Its fictionality does not prevent its actually being practiced, in fact, fictionality facilitates the practice.

As Schechner says of restoration behavior, "thus it offers the chance to re-become what one never was but might now wish to have been" (1979:3). Parashamanic performance, as I see it, is ludic ritual removed from the center of our culture to the edges of things where it is possible to be serious, religiously serious, about play, and where one can play with the sacrally serious. So distance is always implied in parashamanism. Parashamanic commitment is real, but it is also ironic and subjunctive. The parashaman's life is committed to the power of the as-if, the fictional, the playful; it is a religion of illusion. Following Robert Neale (1969:145), I would say that parashamanic faith is more like make-belief than belief.

Ricoeur (1967:11) teaches us that myth gives rise to thought, and thought re-appropriates myth critically. In an analogous way, the ritual work of gaining an education or training for a helping profession has given rise to performance, or ritual play. Ritual, when it is performative, implies an increase of self-awareness and critical consciousness. Parashamanism, then, is constituted by the ritual behavior of the religiously hyper-aware. I know that what I am doing is pretend, nevertheless, it effects changes and constellates power and so is real. Therefore, I come to believe in my play. So the implied myth of the fall among parashamans is something like this: Originally, we played our belief; then we fell into belief; and now we re-cover our make-belief—we believe that our play is holy.

The difference between original playfulness and <u>sacer</u> <u>ludus</u> (holy play) is that the latter depends on metaphoric identification, while the former depended on primal non-differentiation. In the beginning I did not know I was not a bear. Then I knew I was not a bear. Now, I am "not not" a bear, that is, I am a virtual bear, a subjunctive bear. Parashamanism is post-critical, not a-critical. I must first know that I am not Eliade's primitive, or Jung's primordial, person before I can become such metaphorically.

Parashamans are liminoid (Turner) make-believers (Neale) who are specialists in directing restorations of behavior (Schechner). Restored shamanism is neither more nor less shamanism than restored Williamsburg is the Williamsburg of the Pilgrims. Anachronisms abound, but far from discrediting parashamanism, these anachronisms, which do not fit the original model, constitute its most interesting and most adaptive features. It is important to note, then, ways in which parashamanism differs from shamanism, because the parashaman is "alongside" (para-) shamanism just as he or she is alongside therapy, religion, theater, and scholarship.

THE PARASHAMANIC HUNT

Scholarship in religious studies has not been unaware of the growing importance of shamanism, but it has insufficiently distinguished shamanism from its post-modern manifestation, parashamanism. Furthermore, it has ignored what anthropologists take to be primary, namely, the differences in social context that obtain between hunting cultures and industrial-urban-electronic cultures like ours. Parashamanism is, after all, not rooted in circumpolar, nomadic, hunting society.

Shamanism in its tribal form is rooted in hunting culture. Parashamanism is not (at least, in any literal way), but it does depend on a symbolic hunt, namely, "the search." The object of the search is not a literal animal but the self, or put more accurately, the most elusive of animals, the human one. Hunting for a job, a mate, and the self, all so important to the period 1969-1979, are, I think, the basic social factors which make animal hunting an attractive metaphor which parashamans borrow from shamans.

Wisdom begins with self-knowledge, but to know oneself requires self-objectification (reflexivity) and self-coincidence (having identity, being oneself).   Objectified, we know ourselves as introjections of other selves. I am my mother-self, my child-self, and so on. The parashamans learn this from Jung. The parashaman asks, "Who am I?" only to get plural answers: you are your heritage, your father, your shadow, your society, your animal side. Everything outside you is also inside you. Parashamanism begins with the discovery of the "society" of beings which I am. Parashamanism is the discovery that anyone or anything can become one's teacher.

The animal in parashamanism is one's teacher, as was the case in shamanism. But the animal is not, for example, a bear in the woods. Rather it is the animal-as-symbol, the teddy bear, for example. To be human, we must talk with the animals, say the parashamans. Better still, we must talk as animals, hence their interest in sound poetry and animal exercises.

Schechner maintains that hunting "is inherently, not metaphorically, theatrical/dramatic" (1977:56). It is dramatic because it demands co-operation, extended periods of stealth followed by sudden expenditures of energy, practice, and a plan or script. The agonistic quality of Western theater, which necessitates crises and climaxes, reflects its original shamanic-hunting basis.

> My thesis, says Schechner , is that the play behavior of cultures with extensive hunting activity is of a special kind that is adapted from hunting; it also influences hunting. This kind of playing is strategic, futuristic, crisis oriented, violent and/or combative; it has winners and losers, leaders and followers; it employs costumes and/or disguises (often as animals); it has a beginning, middle and end; and its underlying themes are fertility, prowess, and animism/totemism (1977:59).

The very processes which we call "dramatic" are social- artistic descendents of shamanic-hunting societies. So the current recourse to performance as a way of being religious is itself shamanic and would be such even if no one offered the shaman-trickster-fool as a symbolic self-interpretation of one's way of being in the world.

Schechner maintains that performance (the whole constellation of events, including spectators) and theater (the event enacted by a group of performers) develop in agricultural societies, whereas drama (the scenario, plan, or text) is characteristic in a unique way of hunting cultures (1977:39).

Drama, understood in this way, develops along with the need for strategizing, stalking, identifying, and attacking. Parashamanism is as strategic as shamanism ever was; and it is quite climax oriented. Since parashamans are typically of Jewish or Christian background, I should point out that the dramatic-climactic orientation of shamanism provides an avenue for the eschatology and teleological orientation of these two religions. However, there is a tension at the heart of parashamanism, perhaps even a contradiction. Parashamanism is a ludic hunt. The hunt aspect is quite goal-oriented, but the ludic aspect is quite formalistic and pragmatically "useless." I hunt because I must do so to survive, but I also hunt "just because. . . . " So parashamanism is a way of symbolically bridging our culture's dichotomy between work and play.

Parashamanism is ambivalent about storytelling, and I think the reason is that storytelling, insofar as it involves narrative continuity and forward movement, is goal-oriented. Hunting behavior evolves into Western theatrical behavior, which in turn translates futuristic hunting strategy into storytelling. To treat story moralistically (as is usually the case in the West, even in most contemporary theologies of story) is to treat it as a "hunting strategy." If a story is used as a plan or paradigm, its playful, "useless" qualities are diminished. So parashamans differ among themselves in their attitude toward story theater. Most, for example, John Fox of Welfare State, prefer more poetic-associative modes; others, for instance, Ken Feit, use narrative modes of presentation.

The moral dilemma of modern parashamanism, which arises out of the tension between work-hunt vs. play, is connected with a moral dilemma of the late 60's. The parashaman is a hunter, but one who violently detests violence. Such people are attracted to the playfulness, eclecticism, and self-consciousness of shamanism, but have moral difficulties with the climax-kill-end. They use the language and symbolism of shamanism to hunt for the nonviolent animal self or for "good violence" (Girard, 1977:37). The question, of course, is whether there is any such animal except the teddy bear. So I am being quite serious when I suggest that the teddy bear is an appropriate totem animal for parashamans. We should not forget that the teddy is named after Teddy Roosevelt, who spoke softly and carried a big stick. Ritualization and celebration, the ritual processes most connected with play, are more valued in parashamanic circles than are decorous, liturgical, or civil-ceremonial actions.

Schechner (1973:94) describes an exercise he had performers doing on their hands and knees in which they explored the world, including each other, with their muzzles. The result was that most encountered one another with heads lowered and rears raised. Sight was diminished; smell, taste, and touch were augmented.

Such "animalizing" processes are important in the renewal of theatrical and religious performances. This is one reason why the

trickster has become so important. Tricksters are humans on all
fours. They are wrongly understood as animals aspiring to peoplehood.
They are humans aspiring to animalhood. The parashamanic rationale
seems to be that we cannot be human until we integrate our Animal.
Our animal selves are projected onto our pets, hence our ambivalent
behavior toward them. We abuse and sentimentalize them at the same
time. Parashamans would remind us that our toys point to our pets,
and our pets refer us to real animals, which in turn are symbols of
our gods.

FETISHES IN PARASHAMANISM

So far I have sketched how parashamans reinterpret the hunt and
the totemic animal. Another important feature of shamanism is the
fetish or sacred object. Because ours is no animistic worldview, the
parashaman has to search for another mode of accessibility to the
"animate" object. Consistent with the religious individualism of the
parashaman, his or her gifts, finds, keepsakes, and "dumb things"
serve the function of objectifying sacredness into manipulable forms.
Such objects are hidden in suitcases, hung from shirts and hats,
stuffed in boxes, employed in ritual events, and played with. I know
of three parashamanic performances which involve unpacking suitcases
full of such objects, and of another which involves making a junk pile
of things that eventually are sacrally handled. Since there is not
yet a parashamanic society or fully blown tradition in our culture,
power objects are seldom conferred by teachers. Most of the objects,
then, are acquired undeliberately. They are junk before they become
treasure.
Treasuring is not the same as communing with the spirit of a
thing, but it is close. Jung's little manikin in a box is, I suspect,
a model for this kind of behavior. The materialism of our culture
might seem to support parashamanic treasuring of things, but the
values of disposability and consumability counter the impulse to
treasure, though not the desire to use, such objects.
Treasured objects, unlike "goods," are not for using up; and,
unlike the fetishes of shamans, they are not powers so much as they
symbolize the aspiration to power. Parashamanic treasures are
potential meanings, not yet actualized powers. They are
aesthetic-personal before they are metaphysical-social; this is a
fundamental difference between shamanism and parashamanism. The power
of treasured objects is real, but grounded in fictionality. By
employing such objects, say, mirrors, drums, medals, and hats, as if
they had power, or as if their meanings were power, parashamans allow
objects their autonomy. The things may eventually become connected
with the parashaman's life and soul.

Parashamans do not think that the spirit of their pots, stone, or pipes called them. Rather, they feel that they, or the gift-giver, project meaning onto the object; only subsequently does the meaning reflexively take hold of the owner in the guise of a power to be reckoned with. So the parashamanic object is more an amplifier, than an originator, of power. An illustrative situation is this: a parashaman cathects a black shawl with associations regarding his mother. He puts her there, as it were. Later, by working with it, it becomes The Mother. She, once his projection, becomes bigger than he.

PARASHAMANIC FLIGHT

Whereas flight in shamanism refers to an ecstatic trance or journey out of the body, it refers in parashamanism to one's own discovered bodily rhythm or some very simple dance, for example, a circle dance. Flight is not viewed as magical trance so much as unintellectualized, unformalized, spontaneous, or minimally structured movement. The flight to "other" worlds is a rhythmic visit to what is other than the merely academic, commercial, medical, theatrical, or decorous. To fly is to be in one's body with soul. It is not to leave the body but to fill it. This is why drums and flutes are as important to parashamanism as they were to shamanism. As Rodney Needham (1967) has shown, drumming is directly connected with times of rapid social transition. And flutes, the other accompaniment of parashamanic flight, are, I suggest, more prevalent and important in times of great individual isolation. The "flight" of parashamanism, then, can be characterized as the lonely, transitory search to become fully embodied in one's own biorhythms and those of the cosmos, despite one's not feeling much at home in it.

Flight has a second meaning for the parashaman. It is an ascent above social structures in order to attain a perspective on the various collectives (families, nations, etc.). Despite its deep roots in religious individualism, parashamanism has a distinct political and communal overtone more characteristic of the Jewish and Christian backgrounds than the shamanic sources of its practitioners. The moral concerns and social denunciations of parashamanism owe more to the prophets than to shamans.

Since flight symbolizes immersion in one's own bodily rhythms, as well as critical ascent above one's own socialization process, the parashaman usually feels torn between mystical withdrawal and prophetic, political involvement in society. Parashamans generate by their performances an impulse toward community, but typically they leave it just as it begins to form into an institution. Parashamanism, more than Eastern and Western mysticisms, allows the prophetic radicalism of the 60's to continue without losing its critical edge, as the collectivism of the 60's gives way to the mystical individualism of the 70's. The very playfulness and eclecticism of parashamans is as socio-critical as it is mystical or performative. In this respect, it is a child of guerilla theater. "Guerilla religion" would not be a bad term for it.

ILLNESS AND HEALING AMONG PARASHAMANS

In traditional shamanism initiates often begin their careers after an illness and gain their powers by a visionary or ritual experience of dismemberment. There are no such deliberate rituals for parashamans, though I have heard several describe their experiences with education and the church as extended terms of mental illness, and their experiences of being forced into academic or professional specialization as a dismemberment. So parashamanic performances tend to reflect these experiences not so much as themes in performances, but as a segmented structure for them.   Often they do short works-in-progress in which the connective devices are associative, subliminal, or even absent.

Some have noted that their education was a rite of passage in which the classical third stage, reintegration, was impossible. This, combined with the experience of religion as a "department" (rather than a way of integration), suggests that parashamanism is the implicit religion of religion departments. This "religion" only became explicit when universities could no longer absorb, or fully initiate, their own graduates back into the academic priesthood. Parashamans are intellectually anti-intellectual; this attitude is true of every parashaman I know. Parashamanism is what occurs when religious people who cannot be absorbed by churches or synagogues turn to universities for initiation only to find the reintegration phase of their rite of passage inoperative. The literature about religion, consequently, provides a grammar for religious restoration, much in the same way that anthropologists' films sometimes renew or destroy tribal ritual practices. The religious studies classroom, like the rehearsal space, has become, despite intentions to the contrary, an incubator of parashamanic behavior. Whereas teaching religion sometimes is a religious substitute, parashamanism is a religious substitute for an academic substitute--hence its strange dynamics.

Parashamanic rhetoric is less pentecostal than didactic and rhetorical. Considering the fascination with shamanism as part of the pietistic revival of glossolalia and spiritualism among traditional Christians and Jews obscures more than it clarifies. Parashamanism is not pietistic; it is ironic, playful, passionate, and often angry. Its sense of the book is not that of fundamentalist Christianity. Parashamans love books, not The Book. Neither the Bible nor the academic tome is central. The children's story or fantasy is, and polemical, as well as playful, motives inspire the choice.

Parashamans facilitate other people's spontaneity and healing, but may themselves be director-spectators who, even when participating or performing, are meta-participants. Their "visions" are not a set of trancelike actions. Rather, they are critical, reflective perspectives on the spontaneous, playful possibilities of human interaction. Parashamans are over-seers. Such a position as overseer is one source of power, as well as a source of others' ambivalence toward them. Like their tribal counterparts, they are always suspect. They become extremely vulnerable, precisely because their personae are not vulnerable. Parashamans are seers-of-others who seldom allow themselves to be seen, because they are still in the process of hunting the self, elusive animal that it is. Their vulnerability is toward what they hunt and toward those they would heal; they identify with both. But to all others they display a mask, because they risk losing their balance and power.

The parashaman's way of healing is not medical or herbal nor dependent upon incantations, dramatic suckings, or the consulting of oracles. The basic strategy is to create a nest of symbols and a small, supportive but temporary, group to enact those symbols. In this way parashamanism differs considerably from shamanism. This way of approaching healing draws from therapy groups, university seminars, and political caucuses, more than shamanic séances. But the "séance" in parashamanism is less a way of communing with the spirits of animals or the departed than it is a way of communing with symbols themselves. Healing occurs, in this view, by the resurrection of symbols, the first step of which is playing with them.

Parashamans would heal by teaching others to practice ritual creativity. They cure by leading the ill to "confront their blocks," while shamanism healed by exorcising foreign objects or spirits and consulting familiars. Parashamans conceive disease in organic or mechanistic metaphors rather than animistic or anthropomorphic ones. The view of disease held by most, not all, parashamans is quite static and somewhat paranoid. Disease is seen as something to be attacked and broken through. The breaking through takes differing forms depending on the parashaman; some attack intellectually or badger emotionally; others morally and didactically criticize by telling the "right" stories to do the trick. In my estimation, the healing capacities of modern parashamans are weak in comparison with their performative, religious, or intellectual abilities. Parashamans tend, like shamans, to project their own illnesses. They vascillate between identifying with illness and dissociating themselves from it. The parashamanic attack on illness often lays blame at the feet of "society," "your own laziness," or "your own fear of revealing yourself." Wound-licking, laying on of hands, begging the disease, and other such gestures of reaffirmation are rejected in favor of invective or paternal moralism aimed at the "cause" or "victim" of disease.

The parashamans, trained unwittingly in our universities and politically initiated in the 60's, would heal by telling us that we ought to be healed. For all their sophistication about symbols and the unconscious, and for all their bitterness about the compartmentalization of contemporary cultures and the coerciveness of modern institutions, they nevertheless would engender wholeness rhetorically, as well as symbolically. Not having spirits to coerce verbally, they are left only with the ill person and a sick society, and they attack both in the same way they attack their work. Since their work is play, since the ill person is probably a friend, and since the society is their own matrix of symbols, the results are mixed and the feelings ambivalent.

PARASHAMAN AS CULTURE-BRINGER

Parashamanism is an attempt to synthesize and create a traditionn; hence, the trickster-as-culture-bringer is an important symbol. The attempt to create culture, for instance, by creating rituals, making symbol charts, and inventing myths is, of course, difficult—some would say, impossible. Who can create what must be received, given, or revealed? But this is precisely what parashamans would do. Such a goal generates a glorious clumsiness typical of tricksters and fools. Only a fool would try consciously to create culture or consciously consult the unconscious.

Parashamans are inveterate travellers, permanent tourist-pilgrims. Parashamans are culture consumers who bring stolen culture and health. They are omnivorous cross-culturalists performatively and, I suspect, a-culturalists psycho-theologically, reared as they were on Jung and Eliade. Theirs is a para-religion whose vision includes the comprehensibility and communicability (at least, in principle) of all other cultural symbols. They borrow symbolic forms to transform their own. Their paraculture, which is singular in its vision of the world, depends on cultures, always plural in actuality. What parashamans do is multicultural and eclectic; the reasons they do it are monocultural and quite specific to Western, liberal Jewish and post-Christian society.

Parashamanic symbols, myths, and rituals are polytheistic. One parashamanic performance invoked Allah, a Bodhisattva, Jesus, and Buffalo Cow Woman, then concluded with a brown bagger's communion, but the aim was to "make us all one in spirit." The simultaneous practice of monotheism and polytheism of the Renaissance, to which James Hillman (1975:171) calls us, is already present in parashamanism. So far, most parashamans are resisting the theological for the sake of the mythological and ritualistic; so choosing between the one and the many gods has not become necessary. Synthesis is allowed to occur, or made to happen, at a post-reflective level. On the surface the seams and sutures are allowed to show.

The very nature of performative religion, which is what parashamanism is, allows audiences and co-participants to bracket the question of belief. Whereas the theologial mind must raise this as a crucial, or even the central, question, storytelling and ritual performance concentrate more on the doing than on the state of mind or worldview of the doer. So people can be led to perform cross-cultural polytheism long before they can be convinced to confess it verbally. Parashamanism, therefore, has a heavy investment in the nonverbal, and when dealing with verbal materials, to emphasize narrative, poetic, and oral dimensions rather than systematic or analytical ones. The discovery made by parashamans is ironic. It is that ritual can work whether one believes in it or not. When something no longer works as a cause, it may nevertheless act effectively as communication. Any rite--pilfered, syncretistic, or invented--can entertain, teach, or communicate, even if divorced from its original social context. Occasionally, such an invention or transplant can even heal.

AFTERWORD

I have deliberately avoided saying much about theology. However, these essays are intended to be pre-theological, not anti-theological. So I conclude with a beginning of sorts—one aimed at initiating theological discussions after my detour through symbolic anthropology.

A student once asked me if I was a ritologist. I could only laugh—just as well to ask if I am a parashaman. Then we both laughed. There are no ritologists in the way that there are theologians and anthropologists. To use the term "ritology" is still a bit of rhetorical magic. The word, I trust, is not premature, but one cannot suppose that calling for such a field will actually produce it.

Ritual studies has no home. Or its home is anywhere—which amounts to the same thing. I have suggested that the field be housed in religious studies. But I am less convinced than some that theology and religious studies should, or can, divide the labor tetween them—theology claiming normative methods, and religious studies, descriptive or explanatory ones. If ritual studies finds a fellow traveler in hermeneutics, as I have suggested, it will regard this dualism as untenable. Description presupposes prescription and vice-versa.

Briefly, my view is that theology consists of reflection on the symbolic utterances and practices of those who search, by one who also searches. The theologian also does research, which is search repeated in a critical, verbal mode. I mean something special by "search." Those who do it are to be found both outside and inside churches and other religious institutions. The community of those who search, and consequently, those who practice theology, has no static boundary; it is not identifiable with either a specific denomination or religious tradition. Religious community is also a series of events, not just a succession of institutions. It is the event which transpires as people embody the attitude of search and know the difference between searching and merely looking at or looking for.

Theology is secondarily reflection on doctrines, creeds, and the writings of other theologians. It is primarily reflection on religious practice, that is, on the process of concrete, repeated, symbolic search. The object of theology is this search. As for naming the object of the search, the theologian ought to be multilingual and pluralistic. "God," "Christ," and "Spirit" are the proper names in one language. We may also speak others. Theology is what we do when we reflect on these various tongues for naming what can only be apprehended by movement and silence. Theologians are those who care how the silence is broken; they break the silences and, like archeologists, label the pieces.

Conceiving of theology in this manner, I find two books especially helpful in discussing ritual studies and theology. Tom Driver's PATTERNS OF GRACE and John Dixon's THE PHYSIOLOGY OF FAITH are provocative bridges between ritual studies and theology. The volumes could hardly be more different. Driver's is conversational, anecdotal, and autobiographical. Its first chapter, "Tub Water and Holy Ground" has become infamous because of its reflective sensuality:

> He (Driver himself) had learned somewhere along the way that voice production begins in the region of the pubic bone. Such was his hermetic isolation from the ground that knowledge of the pubic origin of one's voice had not caused him to think downward. Instead, he thought only of the voice rising through the body cavity, over the vocal cords, out the mouth and into the air. He did not even ponder the physical principle that an energy moving in one direction requires an equal and opposite force in the other. The furthest down he had ever thought about voice was when he had discovered, maybe three years before, that to hit and sustain a high note while singing hymns in church, it helped if he relaxed his anus. He felt a bit dirty, perhaps subversive of worship, to have made this discovery. But church was the only place he ever sang much, and he rationalized the matter by thinking that if it made the hymns sound better to the ears of almighty God then it was justified. Even so, he was troubled by his lingering impression that people in church had no business having anuses, much less allowing them to open. What if this became public knowledge? What if the minister should invite the congregation to open their anuses and sing (24-25)?

Dixon's book is more restrained, meditative, and structured. It too is developing a reputation, but for pungent aphorisms:

Sacrality is inseparable from a common rhythm (45).

There are no privileged modes of thinking. Thought is an act of the whole organism (9).

Acts have style and style is a form of metaphor (127).

. . . The self is its rhythm of act, relation, transition, figure (137).

The natural state of all organisms is unity. The inalienable state of being human is duality (33).

Ritual is the somatic embodiment of the experience of the holy. Much of the contemporary return to ritual is falsified because it emerges from argument (188).

Driver and Dixon, despite fundamental differences in style and tone, have much in common. Both consider the form of theological writing to be as determinative as its content. And both regard art as essentially theological. Driver (xvii) tells us that the arrangement of PATTERNS OF GRACE is musical. And THE PHYSIOLOGY OF FAITH, says Dixon (xviii), is on the model of painting, rather than argument. Driver was able to include only one of his photographs (as cover and frontispiece). And Dixon's publisher was unable to accomodate the format of his original manuscript, which included different styles on opposing pages, as well as much more nonpropositional material. But the direction is clear: these two theological volumes are less linear, less systematic, and less archetectonic than has been the tradition in theological writing. They are not so much systematic or homiletical as ritualized. This renewed attention to form is but one of several signs of a rise in ritual consciousness among theologians.

The themes of the two books are almost identical: physicality and the body, time and process, pattern and structure, selfhood, action, rhythm. Neither theologian merely writes about the concrete; both write on the basis of it. Dixon moves from the physics of relativity to "the physiology of faith," while Driver moves from personal reminiscence in a bathtub to breathing, "a human experience as the Word of God."

Theologies of ritual (which are not the same as liturgical theologies) cannot be written until ritual thinking is possible. I, of course, do not mean routinized thinking, but that which is in the skin, of the bones and breath. It is not sufficient to make actions, objects, and spaces our subject matter. We must actually, tangibly, imbue our thinking with the concreteness of ritual.   I find such reflection in the works of Dixon and Driver.

Theology, like theater, is now in a deeply reflexive phase. "Theology," says Dixon (148), "is not religion, or the definition of religion or the authority of religion. It is one of the embodiments of religion. It is the self-consciousness of religion. When its concern becomes its own techniques, it is exhausted."

Theological self-consciousness is deadly if we abide in it. But self-awareness has been necessary to enable us to perceive the idolatry of language, rationality, systematization, objectivity, and permanency (see Driver, 33-38). If contemporary theologians ever succeed in doing this and then are then able to give up hyper-reflexivity before it fixates into narcissism, we will have something of value to share with anthropologists and liturgists.

REFERENCES

Angeloglou, Maggie
    1970   A History of Make-Up.
               New York: Macmillan.

Anonymous
    1972   Image and Identity:
               The Role of Masks in Various Cultures.
               Los Angeles:
               Museum of Cultural History
               Galleries, U.C.L.A.

Artaud, Antonin
    1958   The Theater and Its Double.
               Trans. Mary C. Richards.
               New York: Grove

Austin, J.L.
    1965   How to Do Things with Words.
               Ed. J.O. Urmson.
               New York: Oxford.

Babcock, Barbara A., ed.
    1978   The Reversible World:
               Symbolic Inversion in Art and Society.
               Ithaca: Cornell University Press.

Bachelard, Gaston
    1969   The Poetics of Space.
               Trans. Maria Jolas.
               Boston: Beacon.

Bateson, Gregory
    1972   Steps to an Ecology of Mind.
               New York: Chandler.

Bauman, Richard
    1975   "Verbal Art as Performance."
               American Anthropologist 77/2:290-311.

Bellah, Robert
    1974   "Civil Religion in America."
               American Civil Religion.
               Ed. Russell E. Richey and Jones, Donald G.
               New York: Harper & Row.

Benkard, Ernest
   1929   Undying Faces: A Collection of Death Masks.
               Trans. Margaret M. Greer.
               London: Hogarth.

Berger, Peter
   1969   The Sacred Canopy:
               Elements of a Sociological Theory of Religion.
               Garden City: Doubleday.

Birdwhistell, Ray L.
   1970   Kinesics and Context:
               Essays on Body Motion Communication.
               Philadelphia: University of Pennsylvania Press.

Booth, Gotthard
   1957a   "Basic Concepts of Psychosomatic   Medicine."
               Cross Currents 7:14-20.

Booth, Gotthard
   1957b   "Science and Spiritual Healing."
               Healing: Human and Divine.
               Ed. Simon Doniger.
               New York: Association.

Booth, Gotthard
   1962a   "Healing the Sick."
               Pastoral Psychology 13/125:11-24.

Booth, Gotthard
   1962b   "Disease as a Message."
               Journal of Religion and Health 1/4:309-318.

Booth, Gotthard
   1963a   "Values in Nature and in Psychotherapy."
               Archives   of General Psychiatry 8:22-32.

Booth, Gotthard
   1963b   "Biological Types and Forms of Religion."
               Unpublished address presented at the 23rd Annual
               Memorial Meeting of the Schilder Society.

Booth, Gotthard
1966   "The Cancer Patient and the Minister."
           Pastoral Psychology 17/161:15-24.

Booth, Gotthard
1967   "The Voice of the Body."
           Religion and Medicine.
           Ed. D. Belgum
           Ames, IA: Iowa University Press.

Booth, Gotthard
1974   "The Biological Roots of the Generation Gap."
           Psychiatria Fennica n.v.:111-118.

Booth, Gotthard
1975   "Three Psychobiological Paths Toward Death:
           Cardiovascular Disease, Tuberculosis, and Cancer."
           Bulletin of the New York Academy of Medicine
           51/3:415-431.

Booth, Gotthard
1979   The Cancer Epidemic:
           Shadow of the Conquest of Nature.
           New York: Edwin Mellen.

Bordieu, P.
1973   "The Berber House."
           Rules and Meanings.
           Ed. Mary Douglas.
           Harmondsworth, England: Penguin.

Bouyer, Louis
1955   Liturgical Piety.
           Notre Dame, Ind.:
           University of Notre Dame Press.

Brook, Peter
1968   The Empty Space.
           New York: Avon.

Burke, Kenneth
1969   A Grammar of Motives.
           Berkeley: University of California Press.

Burns, Elizabeth
1972   Theatricality:
          A Study of Convention in Theater
          and in Social Life.
          New York: Harper & Row.

Burzynski, Tadeusz and Osinski, Zbigniew
1979   Grotowski's Laboratory.
          Warsaw: Interpress.

Campbell, Joseph
1979   The Masks of God: Primitive Mythology.
          New York: Viking.

Capra, Fritjof
1975   The Tao of Physics.
          Boulder: Shambala.

Cassirer, Ernst
1955   The Philosophy of Symbolic Forms,
          Volume 2: Mythical Thought.
          Trans. Ralph Manheim.
          New Haven: Yale Universsity Press.

Castile, Rand
1971   The Way of Tea.
          Tokyo: Weatherhill.

Christian, William A., Jr.
1972   Person and God in a Spanish Valley.
          New York: Seminar.

Cole, David
1975   The Theatrical Event:
          A Mythos, a Vocabulary, a Perspective.
          Middletown, CT: Wesleyan University Press.

Conze, Edward, Trans., ed.
1958   Buddhist Wisdom Books:
          The Diamond Sutra, The Heart Sutra.
          New York: Harper & Row.

D'Aquili, Eugene D., et al.
1979   The Spectrum of Ritual:
          A Biogenetic Structural Analysis.
          New York: Columbia University Press.

Delattre, Roland
　　1978　　"Ritual Resourcefulness and Cultural
　　　　　　Pluralism."
　　　　　　Soundings 61/3:281-301.

Dixon, John W., Jr.
　　1976　　"The Physiology of Faith."
　　　　　　Anglican Theological Review 58/4:407-431.

Dixon, John W., Jr.
　　1979　　The Physiology of Faith:
　　　　　　A Theory of Theological Relativity.
　　　　　　San Francisco: Harper & Row.

Douglas, Mary
　　1973a　　Natural Symbols:
　　　　　　Explorations in Cosmology.
　　　　　　New York: Vintage.

Douglas, Mary, ed.
　　1973b　　Rules and Meanings:
　　　　　　The Anthropology of Everyday Knowledge.
　　　　　　Harmondsworth, England: Penguin.

Driver, Tom F.
　　1978　　"Concerning Methods for Studying Rituals:
　　　　　　Less is More."
　　　　　　Paper presented to the Ritual Studies
　　　　　　Consultation of the American Academy of
　　　　　　Religion. New Orleans.

Durkheim, Emile
　　1965　　The Elementary Forms of the
　　　　　　Religious Life.
　　　　　　Trans. Joseph W. Swain.
　　　　　　New York: Free Press.

Eliade, Mircea
　　1959　　Cosmos and History:
　　　　　　The Myth of the Eternal Return.
　　　　　　Trans. Willard Trask.
　　　　　　New York: Harper & Row.

Eliade, Mircea
   1961   The Sacred and the Profane:
           The Nature of Religion.
           New York: Harper & Row.

Eliade, Mircea
   1963   Myth and Reality.
           Trans. Willard Trask.
           New York: Harper & Row.

Erikson, Erik
   1968   "The Development of Ritualization."
           The Religious Situation, 1968.
           Ed. Donald R. Cutler.
           Boston: Beacon.

Evans-Pritchard, E.E.
   1956   Nuer Religion.
           Oxford: Clarendon.

Evans-Pritchard, E.E.
   1973   "Time is Not a Continuum."
           Rules and Meanings.
           Ed. Mary Douglas.
           Harmondsworth, England: Penguin.

Fernandez, James W.
   1971   "Persuasions and Performances."
           Myth, Symbol and Culture.
           Ed. Clifford Geertz.
           New York: Norton.

Ferro-Luzzi, Gabriella E.
   1977   "Ritual as Language:
           The Case of South Indian Food Offerings."
           Current Anthropology 18/3:507-514.

Finnegan, Ruth
   1969   "How to Do Things with Words:
           Performative Utterances Among the Limba of
           Sierra Leone."
           Man (N.S.) 4:537-552.

Firth, Raymond
    1973   Symbols: Public and Private.
            Ithaca: Cornell University Press.

Fletcher, Angus
    1964   Allegory: The Theory of a Symbolic Mode.
            Ithaca: Cornell University Press.

Freud, Sigmund
    1953-196The Standard Edition of the Complete
            Psychological Works. 24 vols.
            Ed., trans. James Strachey.
            London: Hogarth.

Gadamer, Hans-Georg
    1976   Philosophical Hermeneutics.
            Berkeley: University of California Press.

Gaster, Theodor H.
    1951   "Errors of Method in the Study of Religion."
            Freedom and Reason:
            Studies in Memory of Morris Raphael Cohen.
            Ed. Salo Baron, et al.
            New York: Conference on Jewish Relations.

Gaster, Theodor H.
    1953   Festivals of the Jewish Year:
            A Modern Interpretation and Guide.
            New York: William Sloane.

Gaster, Theodor H.
    1954   "Myth and Story."
            Numen 2:1-40.

Gaster, Theodor H.
    1955   "Mythic Thought in the Ancient Near East."
            Journal of the History of Ideas 16:422-426.

Gaster, Theodor H.
    1958   The Oldest Stories in the World.
            Boston: Beacon.

Gaster, Theodor H.
    1961   Thespis: Ritual, Myth and Drama in the
            Ancient Near East.
            Rev. ed.
            New York: Harper & Row.

Gaster, Theodor H.
    1962   "Myth, Mythology."
            The Interpreter's Dictionary of the Bible.
            Ed. George Buttrick.
            New York: Abingdon.

Gaster, Theodor H.
    1964   The Dead Sea Scriptures in English Translation
            with Introduction and Notes.
            New York: Doubleday.

Gaster, Theodor H.
    1969   Myth, Legend, and Custom in the Old Testament.
            New York: Harper & Row.

Gaster, Theodor H.
    1974   "Jewish Myth and Legend."
            Encyclopaedia Britannica: Macropedia 10:191-196.
            Chicago: Encyclopaedia Britannica.

Gay, Volney P.
    1979   Freud on Ritual:
            Reconstruction and Critique.
            A.A.R. Dissertation Series, No. 16.
            Missoula, MT: Scholar's Press.

Geertz, Clifford
    1966   "Religion as a Cultural System."
            Anthropological Approaches
            to the Study of Religion.
            Ed. Michael Banton.
            A.S.A. Monographs, No.3.
            London: Tavistock.

Geertz, Clifford
    1971   "The Balinese Cockfight."
            Myth, Symbol and Culture.
            Ed. Clifford Geertz.
            New York: Norton.

Gerhart, Mary
1977   "Generic Studies:
        Their Renewed Importance in Religious and
        Literary Interpretation."
        Journal of the American Academy of
        Religion 45/3:309-325.

Girard, Rene
1977   Violence and the Sacred.
        Trans. Patrick Gregory.
        Baltimore: Johns Hopkins University Press.

Gluckman, Max
1963   Order and Rebellion in Tribal Africa.
        London: Cohen and West.

Goffman, Erving
1959   The Presentation of Self in Everyday LIfe.
        Garden City: Doubleday.

Goffman, Erving
1967   Interaction Ritual:
        Essays on Face-to-Face Behavior.
        Garden City: Doubleday.

Goffman, Erving
1971   Relation in Public:
        Microstudies of the Public Order.
        New York: Harper & Row.

Goffman, Erving
1974   Frame Analysis:
        An Essay on the Organization of Experience.
        New York: Harper & Row.

Grainger, Roger
1974   The Language of the Rite.
        London: Darton, Longman and Todd.

Gray, Bennison
1972   "Repetition in Oral Literature."
        Journal of American Folklore 84/331-334:289-303.

Grimes, Ronald L.
   1976   Symbol and Conquest:
            Public Ritual and Drama in Santa Fe, New Mexico.
            Ithaca: Cornell University Press.

Grimes, Ronald L.
   1978   "The Rituals of Walking and Flying:
            Public Participatory Events at Actor's Lab."
            The Drama Review 22/4:77-82.

Grimes, Ronald L.
   1979a   "The Actor's Lab:
            The Ritual Roots of Human Action."
            Canadian Theatre Review 22:9-19.

Grimes, Ronald L.
   1979b   "Modes of Ritual Necessity."
            Worship 53/2:126-141.

Grotowski, Jerzy
   1968   Towards a Poor Theater.
            New York: Simon and Schuster.

Grotowski, Jerzy
   1973   "Holiday: The Day That Is Holy."
            The Drama Review 17/2:113-119.

Grotowski, Jerzy
   1978   "The Art of the Beginner."
            International Theater Information,
            Spring-Summer, 7-11.
            Paris: International Theater Institute.

Grotowski, Jerzy
   1980   "The Theater of Sources."
            Unpublished address.
            York University, Ontario.

Hall, Edward T.
   1973   The Silent Language.
            Garden City: Doubleday.

Hall, Edward T.
  1976   Beyond Culture.
           Garden City: Doubleday.

Hardison, O.B., Jr.
  1965   Christian Rite and Christian Drama in the Middle
           Ages: Essays in the Origin and Early History of
           Modern Drama.
           Baltimore: Johns Hopkins University Press.

Harner, Michael
  1980   The Way of the Shaman:
           A Guide to Power and Healing.
           New York: Harper & Row.

Heilman, Samuel C.
  1976   Synagogue Life:
           A Study in Symbolic Interaction.
           Chicago: University of Chicago Press.

Herold, Erich
  1967   The Art of Africa:
           Tribal Masks.
           Photos by Jindrich Marco.
           London: Hamlyn.

Hillman, James
  1975   Re-Visioning Psychology.
           New York: Harper & Row.

Huizinga, Johann
  1955   Homo Ludens:
           The Play Element in Culture.
           Boston: Beacon.

Huxley, Sir Julian.
  1966   "A Discussion on Ritualization
           of Behaviour in Animals and Man."
           Philosophical Transactions of the Royal Society
           of London (Series B) 251:247-526.

Jackson, Anthony
  1968   "Sound and Ritual."
           Man (N.S.) 3:293-299.

Jennings, Theodore W.
    1978   "On Ritual Knowledge."
            Paper presented to the Ritual Studies
            Consultation of the American Academy of Religion.
            New Orleans.

Jung, C.G.
    1958   "Transformation Symbolism in the Mass."
            Psyche and Symbol:
            A Selection from the Writings of C.G. Jung.
            Ed. Violet De Laszlo.
            Garden City: Doubleday.

Jungmann, Josef A.
    1955   The Mass of the Roman Rite:
            Its Origins and Development, vol. 2.
            New York: Benziger.

Kane, Cornelius T.
    1978   Habit: A Theological and Psychological Analysis.
            Washington, D.C.: University Press of America.

Kiev, Ari
    1964   Magic, Faith and Healing:
            Studies in Primitive Psychiatry Today.
            New York: Free Press.

Kliever, Lonnie D.
    1979   "Fictive Religion: Rhetoric and Play."
            Paper presented to the American Academy of
            Religion. New York City.

Kolankiewicz, Leszek
    1978   On the Road to Active Culture.
            Wroclaw, Poland: n.p.

Kuhn, Thomas S.
    1962   The Structure of Scientific Revolutions.
            Chicago: University of Chicago Press.

La Fontaine, J.S., ed.
　　1972　　The Interpretation of Ritual:
　　　　　　Essays in Honour of A.I. Richards.
　　　　　　London: Tavistock.

Langer, Susanne
　　1953　　Feeling and Form.
　　　　　　New York: Scribners.

Laurence, Margaret
　　1974　　The Diviners.
　　　　　　Toronto: McClelland and Stewart.

Lawson, Thomas E.
　　1976　　"Ritual as Language."
　　　　　　Religion 6:123-139.

Leach, Edmund
　　1968　　"Ritual."
　　　　　　International Encyclopedia of Social
　　　　　　Sciences 13:520-526.
　　　　　　Ed. D.L. Sills.
　　　　　　New York: Macmillan.

Leach, Edmund
　　1970　　Claude Levi-Strauss.
　　　　　　New York: Viking.

Leggett, Trevor
　　1978　　Zen and the Ways.
　　　　　　London: Routledge and Kegan Paul.

Lévi-Strauss, Claude
　　1966　　The Savage Mind.
　　　　　　Chicago: University of Chicago Press.

Lévi-Strauss, Claude
　　1967　　Structural Anthropology.
　　　　　　Trans. Claire Jacobson
　　　　　　and Brooke Grundfest Schoepf.
　　　　　　Garden City: Doubleday.

Lincoln, Bruce
1977   "Two Notes on Modern Rituals."
        Journal of the American   Academy of Religion
        45/2:147-160.

Lommel, Andreas
1972a   Masks: Their Meaning and Function.
        New York: McGraw-Hill.

Lorenz, Konrad
1966   On Aggression.
        Trans. Marjorie Latzke.
        London: Methuen.

Malinowski, Bronislaw
1954   Magic, Science and Religion and Other Essays.
        Garden City: Doubleday.

Marshal, L.
1973   "Each Side of the Fire."
        Rules and Meanings.
        Ed. Mary Douglas.
        Harmondsworth, England: Penguin.

Mennen, Richard
1976   "Jerzy Grotowski's Paratheatrical Projects."
        The Drama Review 19/4:58-69.

Mitchell, Leonel L.
1977   The Meaning of Ritual.
        New York: Paulist.

Mol, Hans
1976
        Identity and the Sacred.
        New York: Free Press.

Moore, Sally F. and Myerhoff, Barbara G., eds.
1977   Secular Ritual.
        Amsterdam: Van Gorcum.

Moore, Sally Falk and Myerhoff, Barbara, eds.
1975   Symbol and Politics in Communal Ideology:
        Cases and Questions.
        Ithaca: Cornell University Press.

Morgan, John H., ed.
1979   Understanding Religion and Culture:
        Anthropological and Theological Prespectives.
        Washington, D.C.: University Press of America.

Morris, Charles
1938   Foundations of the Theory of Signs.
        Chicago: University of Chicago Press.

Munro, Thomas
1930   "Appendix II: A Questionaire
        for Picture Analysis."
        Great Pictures of Europe.
        New York: Coward-McCann.

Murray, Joan
1980   "New Rites: Irland and Mordowanec."
        Artsmagazine 12/50:31-34.

Myerhoff, Barbara
1978   Number Our Days.
        New York: Simon and Schuster.

Neale, Robert E.
1969   In Praise of Play:
        Toward a Psychology of Religion.
        New York: Harper & Row.

Needham, Rodney
1967   "Percussion and Transition."
        Man (N.S.) 2:606-614.

Neumann, Erich
1976   "The Psychological Meaning of Ritual."
        Quadrant 9/2:5-34.

Nicoll, Allardyce
1963   The World of Harlequin:
        A Critical Study of
        Commedia Dell' Arte.
        Cambridge: Cambridge University Press.

Nieoczym, Richard
1974   "Theatre as a Pedestrian Concern."
          Toronto: Actor's Lab.

Nieoczym, Richard
1977   "Blood Wedding: Working Script."
          Unpublished manuscript.

Nordstrom, Lou
n.d.   "Mysticism and Transcendence:
          Reflections on Liberation and Emptiness."
          Unpublished manuscript.

Okakura, Kakuzo
1964   The Way of Tea.
          New York: Dover.

Ong, Walter J.
1967   The Presence of the Word:
          Some Prolegomena for Cultural and
          Religious History.
          New Haven: Yale.

Ong, Walter J.
1977   "Maranatha: Death and Life in the Text of
          the Book."
          Journal of the American Academy of Religion
          45/4:419-449.

Ortiz, Alfonso
1969   The Tewa World:
          Space, Time and Becoming in a Pueblo Society.
          Chicago: University of Chicago Press.

Otto, Rudolph
1958   The Idea of the Holy.
          Trans. John W. Harvey.
          New York: Oxford University Press.

Palmer, Richard E.
    1969   Hermeneutics: Interpretation Theory
            in Schleiermacher, Dilthey,
            Heidegger and Gadamer.
            Evanston: Northwestern University Press.

Polhemus, Ted, ed.
    1978   Social Aspects of the Human Body.
            Harmondsworth, England: Penguin.

Rappaport, Roy A.
    1971   "Ritual, Sanctity, and Cybernetics."
            American Anthropologist 73:59-76.

Reik, Theodor
    1976   Ritual: Psychoanalytic Studies.
            Trans. Douglas Bryan.
            New York: International Universities.

Ricoeur, Paul
    1967   The Symbolism of Evil.
            Trans. Emerson Buchanan.
            New York: Harper & Row.

Ricoeur, Paul
    1973   "The Hermeneutical Function of Distanciation."
            Philosophy Today 17:129-141.

Ricoeur, Paul
    1976   Freud and Philosophy:
            An Essay on Interpretation.
            Trans. Denis Savage.
            New Haven: Yale University Press.

Ricoeur, Paul
    1976b   Interpretation Theory.
            Fort Worth: Texas Christian University
            Press.

Schechner, Richard
    1973   Environmental Theater.
            New York: Hawthorn.

Schechner, Richard and Schuman, Mady, eds.
    1976   Ritual, Play and Performance:
            Readings in the Social Sciences / Theater.
            New York: Seabury.

Schechner, Richard
   1977   Essays on Performance Theory, 1970-1976.
           New York: Drama Book.

Schechner, Richard
   1979   "Restoration Behavior."
           Unpublished paper.

Schieffelin, Edward L.
   1976   The Sorrow of the Lonely and the Burning of
           the Dancers.
           New York: St. Martin's.

Sekida, Katsuki
   1975   Zen Training: Methods and Philosophy.
           Ed., intro. A.V. Grimstone.
           New York: Weatherhill.

Shalleck, Jamie
   1973   Masks.
           New York: Viking.

Siirala, Aarne
   1981   The Voice of Illness:
           A Study in Therapy and Prophecy.
           New York: Edwin Mellen.

Simonton, Carl
   1975   "Belief Systems and Management of the
           Emotional Aspects of Malignancy."
           The Journal of Transpersonal Psychology 7/1:29-47.

Slater, Philip
   1966   Microcosm: Structural, Psychological,
           and Religious Evolution in Groups.
           New York: John Wiley.

Sommer, Robert
   1969   Personal Space:
           The Behavioral Basis of Design.
           Englewood Cliffs: Prentice-Hall.

Sperber, Dan
　　1975　　Rethinking Symbolism.
　　　　　　Trans. Alice L. Morton.
　　　　　　Cambridge: Cambridge University Press.

Strenkovsky, Serge
　　1937　　The Art of Make-Up.
　　　　　　Ed. Elizabeth S. Teber.
　　　　　　New York: Dutton.

Stryk, Lucien, ed.
　　1968　　World of the Buddha: A Reader.
　　　　　　Garden City: Doubleday.

Suzuki, Shunryu
　　1970　　Zen Mind, Beginner's Mind.
　　　　　　New York: Weatherhill.

Swantz, Marja-Liisa
　　1970　　Ritual and Symbol in Transitional Zaramo Society.
　　　　　　Uppsala: Gleerup.

Tambiah, S.J.
　　1968　　"The Magical Power of Words."
　　　　　　Man (N.S.) 3:175-208.

Tillich, Paul
　　1958　　The Dynamics of Faith.
　　　　　　New York: Harper & Row.

Tillich, Paul
　　1960　　"The Religious Symbol."
　　　　　　Symbolism in Religion and Literature.
　　　　　　Ed. Rollo May.
　　　　　　New York: Braziller.

Turner, Victor W.
　　1957　　Schism and Continuity in an African Society:
　　　　　　A Study of Ndembu Village LIfe.
　　　　　　Manchester: Manchester University.

Turner, Victor W.
    1961   Ndembu Divination: Its Symbolism and Techniques.
            Rhodes-Livingstone Papers, No. 31.
            Manchester: Manchester University.

Turner, Victor W.
    1962   Chihamba the White Spirit:
            A Ritual Drama of the Ndembu.
            Rhodes-Livingstone Papers, No. 33.
            Manchester: Manchester University.

Turner, Victor W.
    1966   "Color Classification in Ndembu Ritual."
            Anthropological Approaches to the Study
            of Religion.
            Ed. Michael Banton.
            A.S.A. Monographs, No. 3.
            London: Tavistock.

Turner, Victor W.
    1967   The Forest of Symbols:
            Aspects of Ndembu Ritual.
            Ithaca: Cornell University Press.

Turner, Victor W.
    1968a   The Drums of Affliction:
            A Study of Religious Processes Among the
            Ndembu of Zambia.
            Oxford: Clarendon for the International
            African Institute.

Turner, Victor W.
    1968b   "Myth and Symbol."
            International Encyclopedia of Social Sciences
            10:576.
            Ed. David L. Sills.
            London: Macmillan, Free Press.

Turner, Victor W.
    1969a   The Ritual Process:
            Structure and Anti-Structure.
            Chicago: Aldine.

Turner, Victor W.
   1969b   "Forms of Symbolic Action: Introduction."
               Ed. Robert F. Spencer.
               Proceedings of the 1969 Annual Spring Meeting
               of the American Ethnological Society.
               Seattle: University of Washington.

Turner, Victor W.
   1974a   Dramas, Fields and Metaphors:
               Symbolic Action in Human Society.
               Ithaca: Cornell University Press.

Turner, Victor W.
   1974b   "Liminal to Liminoid, in Play, Flow
               and Ritual: An Essay in Comparative Symbology."
               Rice University Studies 60:53-92.

Turner, Victor W.
   1977   "Liminality and the Performative Genres."
               Paper presented to the Burg Wartenstein Symposium
               No. 76, "Cultural Frames and Reflections: Ritual,
               Drama, and Spectacle."
               New York: Werner-Gren Foundation for
               Anthropological Research.

Turner, Victor W.
   1978   Images and Pilgrimage in Christian Culture:
               Anthropological Perspectives.
               Written with Edith Turner.
               New York: Columbia University Press.

Turner, Victor W.
   1979   "Dramatic Ritual / Ritual Drama:
               Performance and Reflexive Anthropology."
               The Kenyon Review (N.S.) 1/3:80-93.

Tyson, Ruel W.
   1975   "Program Notes on the Practical Criticism of
               Religious Action."
               Working paper presented to the Consultation on
               the Systematic Study of Meaningful Forms,
               American Academy of Religion. Chicago.

Van Gennep, Arnold
    1960   The Rites of Passage.
              Trans. Monika B. Vizedom and Gabrielle L.
              Caffee.
              Chicago: University of Chicago Press.

Wallace, Anthony
    1970   Culture and Personality.
              2nd ed.
              New York: Random House.

Warren, Henry Clarke, trans.
    1963   Buddhism in Translations.
              New York: Atheneum.

Winquist, Charles E.
    1981   "The Epistemology of Darkness."
              Journal of the American Academy of
              Religion 49/1:23-34.

ABOUT THE AUTHOR

Ron Grimes is currently Associate Professor of Religion and Culture at Wilfrid Laurier University, Waterloo, Ontario, Canada, N2L 3C5. He holds a B.A. from Kentucky Wesleyan College, an M.Div. from Emory University, and a Ph.D. from Columbia University and Union Theological Seminary. Presently, he is working on a book about ritual, fiction, and theatre.